# The Law of Mental Health

**Fourmat Publishing**

# The Law of Mental Health

by John Williams, LL.B (Wales), LL.B (Cantab), Barrister,
Lecturer in Law at the University College of Wales,
Aberystwyth

London
**Fourmat Publishing**
1990

ISBN 1 85190 083 7

First published 1990

*All rights reserved*

© 1990 Fourmat Publishing
133 Upper Street, London N1 1QP
Printed and bound in Great Britain by
Billing & Sons Ltd, Worcester

# Preface

This book seeks to provide a guide to the law relating to mental health. Although it is quite clearly a legal textbook, it is intended to be used not only by lawyers but also by other professionals whose work involves caring for people who are mentally ill or have mental handicaps. I have avoided the temptation to compromise this legal approach as I believe that a comprehensive understanding of law is essential for those who are given the responsibility for making decisions affecting people with mental handicaps or who have a mental illness. The author appreciates his own limitations when addressing non-lawyers who work in this area. His intention is not to instruct approved social workers and others on the exercise of their professional judgement, but rather to provide the legal framework within which that judgement may be exercised. It is hoped that good practice can be developed through a greater awareness of the legal implications of mental health care and that the law will become more of a "tool" than a "tyrant" for the practitioner.

I have resisted the opportunity to examine critically the current legal provisions. This should not be taken as meaning that I am in any way satisfied with the status quo. My own feelings are that this is an area where the rights of people can quite easily be forgotten and assumptions all too readily made about the inability of people to control their own lives. However, such issues are best explored elsewhere as this book's main value will be as a reference work for those called upon to operate the existing system. It is hoped that the case for reform will be sympathetically heard by those able to effect change.

In writing this book I am indebted to a number of people. To my mother and my late father I am grateful for the many sacrifices which they made to ensure that my education continued way beyond the school leaving age. My brother and sister and their families have also provided me with much support and encouragement. Particular thanks go to Penny Hogan for her patience, support and for the more mundane task of helping to prepare the manuscript. Mona Gilbey, Bill Hines and Meirion Derrick of the UCW Law Library have, as always, been invaluable in the help and assistance which they have so readily given. I would also express my gratitude to Fred Warne, the Electoral Officer of Shrewsbury and Atcham Borough Council, and to Dr. John Hughes from Aberystwyth. Both provided me with a much-needed insight into some of the practical implications of this subject. Finally, my special thanks go to Frank Hall, the Principal Training Officer for Dyfed Social Services. I have learnt much from my discussions with him and appreciate not only his willingness to challenge my assumptions, but also his healthy intolerance of me in my opinionated mode.

The effect of the Children Act 1989 has been incorporated into the text. It is envisaged that the legislative changes will be brought into force in early 1991. A number of proposals for change have been introduced since this book reached final proof stage. The Government has recently published its White Paper *Caring for People* which makes radical changes in the way in which community care is provided. These changes will be implemented by the National Health Service and Community Care Bill which has just commenced its Parliamentary passage.

December 1989,  Rhagfyr 1989,
Department of Law,  Adran y Gyfraith,
University College of Wales,  Coleg Prifysgol Cymru,
Aberystwyth.  Aberystwyth.

# Contents

|  |  | Page |
|---|---|---|
| Chapter 1: | **Hospital admission, guardianship and other civil procedures** | 1 |
| | 1. The definition of mental disorder | 1 |
| | 2. Approved social workers | 3 |
| | 3. The nearest relative | 8 |
| | 4. General powers of access, examination, conveyance and detention | 13 |
| | 5. Compulsory measures of admission and detention | 17 |
| | 6. Guardianship | 30 |
| | 7. The reclassification of patients | 33 |
| | 8. Transfer of patients | 34 |
| | 9. Discharge of patients | 38 |
| | 10. Absence from hospital | 40 |
| | 11. Other powers which are available | 44 |
| | 12. Provisions relating to children | 46 |
| Chapter 2: | **Admission through the criminal process** | 52 |
| | 1. Remand to hospital under the Mental Health Act 1983 | 52 |
| | 2. Hospital orders and guardianship orders | 56 |
| | 3. Interim hospital orders | 60 |
| | 4. Restriction orders | 62 |
| | 5. Magistrates' power to commit for restriction order | 65 |
| | 6. Transfer of prisoners to hospital | 66 |
| Chapter 3: | **Institutional care and treatment** | 72 |
| | 1. Introduction | 72 |
| | 2. Hospitals, special hospitals and managers | 72 |
| | 3. Nursing homes and mental nursing homes | 74 |

vii

## THE LAW OF MENTAL HEALTH

|  |  |  |
|---|---|---|
| 4. Protection of detained patients | | 84 |
| 5. Duty of managers to provide information | | 86 |
| 6. Correspondence of patients | | 87 |
| 7. Consent to treatment | | 91 |
| 8. Residential care homes | | 101 |

**Chapter 4: Mental Health Review Tribunals** — 111
1. Introduction — 111
2. Applications and references in respect of Part II patients — 112
3. Applications and references in respect of Part III patients — 115
4. The powers of a Mental Health Review Tribunal — 118
5. Procedure before a tribunal — 125
6. Disclosure and representation — 133
7. The conduct of the hearing — 135

**Chapter 5: Community care** — 138
1. Introduction — 138
2. Guardianship — 138
3. After-care upon leaving hospital — 140
4. National Health Service Act 1977 — 141
5. Provision of accommodation by local authorities — 143
6. Section 29 National Assistance Act 1948 — 146
7. Provision for children — 149
8. The Social Fund — 165

**Chapter 6: Mental capacity and the criminal law** — 175
1. The defence of insanity — 175
2. Diminished responsibility — 182
3. Fitness to plead — 186

**Chapter 7: Protecting the property and financial affairs of patients** — 190
1. The Court of Protection — 190
2. Enduring powers of attorney — 206
3. Miscellaneous methods of protecting property and income — 218

**Chapter 8: Mental health and legal capacity** — 220
1. Family law — 220
2. Contract — 230
3. Wills — 231

| | |
|---|---:|
| 4. Tort | 232 |
| 5. The electoral process | 233 |
| 6. Driving licences | 236 |
| **Index** | **239** |

# Table of cases

*page*

Ash v Ash [1972] Fam 135, [1972] 1 All ER 582,
    [1972] 2 WLR 347 ................................. 223
Attorney-General v Associated Newspaper Group plc and
    others [1988] The Times 21 October ................. 111
Attorney-General for Northern Ireland v Gallagher [1963]
    AC 349, [1961] 3 All ER 299, [1961] 3 WLR 619 ....... 177
Attorney-General for South Australia v Brown [1960]
    AC 432, [1960] 1 All ER 734, [1960] 2 WLR 588
    (PC) ........................................ 178, 179

B (A Minor) (Wardship: Sterilisation), Re [1988] 1 AC 199,
    [1987] 2 All ER 206, [1987] 2 WLR 1213 ........... 98, 99
Banks v Goodfellow (1870) LR 5 QB 549 ................ 231
Bennett v Bennett [1969] 1 All ER 539, [1969] 1 WLR 430 . 221
Bird v Luckie (1850) 8 Hare 301 ....................... 231
Birkin v Wing (1890) 63 LT 80 ........................ 230
Bolam v Friern Hospital Management Committee [1957]
    2 All ER 118, [1957] 1 WLR 582 .................... 101
Bratty v Attorney-General for Northern Ireland [1963] AC
    386, [1961] 3 All ER 523, [1961] 3 WLR 965 (HL) . 177, 179
Burgess Case [1785] 2 Lud EC 381 ..................... 233

Chatterton v Gerson [1981] QB 432, [1981] 1 All ER 257,
    [1980] 3 WLR 1003 ................................ 97

D (J), Re [1982] Ch 237, [1982] 2 All ER 37,
    [1982] 2 WLR 373 ............................ 195–196
D (A Minor) (Wardship: Sterilisation), Re [1976] Fam 185,
    [1976] 1 All ER 326, [1976] 2 WLR 279 ............ 98–99
DML, Re [1965] Ch 1133, [1965] 2 All ER 129,
    [1965] 3 WLR 740 ................................ 194
Dorrell v Dorrell [1972] 3 All ER 343, [1972] 1 WLR 1087  226
DPP v Beard [1920] AC 479 (HL) ..................... 177

E (Mental Health Patient), Re [1985] 1 All ER 609, [1985]
  1 WLR 245 (CA) ................................... 192
East Sussex County Council v Lyons [1988]
  The Times 2 January ......................... 106–107

F v West Berkshire Health Authority [1989] 2 All ER
  545 ........................................... 100–101

Gillick v West Norfolk and Wisbech Area Health Authority
  and the DHSS [1986] AC 112, [1985] 3 All ER 402, [1985]
  3 WLR 830 ...................................... 97–98
Greenslade v Dare (1855) 20 Beav 284 ................. 230

Harrod v Harrod [1854] 1 K & J 4 ..................... 221

Imperial Loan Co v Stone [1892] 1 QB 592 ............. 230

Julian v Julian (1972) 116 SJ 763 .................... 226

Kaczmarz v Kaczmarz [1967] 1 All ER 416,
  [1967] 1 WLR 317 ............................... 225
Katz v Katz [1972] 3 All ER 219, [1972] 1 WLR 955 . 223–224

L (WJG), Re [1966] Ch 135, [1965] 3 All ER 865,
  [1966] 2 WLR 233 ............................... 196
Lee v Lee (1973) 117 SJ 616, (1973) 4 Fam Law 114 ..... 226

Mason v Mason [1972] Fam 302, [1972] 3 All ER 315,
  [1972] 3 WLR 405 ........................... 225–226
Matthews v Baxter (1873) LR 8 Ex 132 ................ 230
Morriss v Marsden [1952] 1 All ER 925,
  [1952] 1 TLR 947 ........................... 232, 233

N, dec'd., Re [1977] 2 All ER 687, [1977]
  1 WLR 676 (CA) ................................. 205

Park, In the Estate of [1954] P 112, [1953] 2 All ER 1411,
  [1953] 3 WLR 1012 ..................... 221, 223, 226
Parker v Parker [1972] Fam 116, [1972] 1 All ER 410,
  [1972] 2 WLR 21 ................................ 226
Perry v Perry [1963] 3 All ER 766, [1964] 1 WLR 91 ..... 225
Powell v Guest (1864) 18 CBNS 72 .................... 234

R v Abramovitch (1912) 7 Cr App R 145 ............... 179
R v Atkinson [1985] Crim LR 314 (CA) ................ 184
R v Birch [1989] The Guardian 5 May .................. 63

*Table of cases*

R v Burles [1970] 2 QB 191, [1970] 1 All ER 642,
  [1970] 2 WLR 597 ................................. 187
R v Burns (1973) 58 Cr App R 364 (CA) ................ 179
R v Byrne [1960] 2 QB 396, [1960] 3 All ER 1,
  [1960] 3 WLR 440 (CCA) ....................... 183, 184
R v Charlson [1955] 1 All ER 859, [1955] 1 WLR 317 ..... 177
R v Codere (1916) 12 Cr App R 21 ..................... 178
R v Davis (1881) 14 Cox 563 .......................... 177
R v Di Duca (1959) 43 Cr App R 167 (CCA) ............. 185
R v Dickie [1984] 3 All ER 173, [1984] 1 WLR 1031,
  [1984] Crim LR 497 (CA) ...................... 179, 180
R v Eaton [1976] Crim LR 390, (1975) 119 SJ 793 (CA) .... 63
R v Fenton (1975) 61 Cr App R 261, [1975]
  Crim LR 712 (CA) ................................ 184
R v Gittens [1984] QB 698, [1984] 3 All ER 252,
  [1984] 3 WLR 327 (CA) ........................... 184
R v Gomez (1964) 48 Cr App R 310 (CCA) ............. 183
R v Hallstrom, ex parte W; R v Gardner, ex parte L
  [1986] QB 1090, [1986] 2 All ER 306, [1986]
  2 WLR 883 .................................... 41, 118
R v Haynes (1859) 1 F & F 666 ........................ 178
R v Howell (1985) 7 Cr App R(S) 360 ................... 63
R v Kemp [1957] 1 QB 399, [1956] 3 All ER 249,
  [1956] 3 WLR 724 ................................ 176
R v Lincoln (Kesteven) Magistrates' Court, ex parte
  O'Connor [1983] 1 All ER 901, [1983] 1 WLR 335 ...... 58
R v McBride [1972] Crim LR 322 (CA) .................. 57
R v McCarthy [1967] 1 QB 68, [1966] 1 All ER 447,
  [1966] 2 WLR 555 (CCA) ......................... 187
R v M'Naughten (1843) 10 Cl & F 200 ............. 175–176
R v Matheson [1958] 2 All ER 87, [1958] 1 WLR 474 ..... 179
R v Mbatha (1985) 7 Cr App R(S) 373 (CA) .............. 63
R v Mental Health Act Commission, ex parte W
  [1988] The Times 27 May .......................... 92
R v Mental Health Review Tribunal, ex parte
  Clatworthy [1985] 3 All ER 699 ...................... 2
R v Mental Health Tribunal, ex parte Pickering
  [1986] 1 All ER 99 ........................... 119–120
R v Mersey Mental Health Review Tribunal, ex parte D
  [1987] The Times 13 April ........................ 119
R v Merseyside Mental Health Review Tribunal, ex parte
  Kay [1989] The Independent 8 June ................ 122
R v Oxford Regional Mental Health Tribunal, ex parte
  Secretary of State for the Home Department [1987]
  3 All ER 8, [1987] 3 WLR 522 (HL) ............ 122, 123

R v Podola [1960] 1 QB 325, [1959] 3 All ER 418,
   [1959] 3 WLR 718 (CCA) .................... 186, 187, 189
R v Pritchard (1836) 7 C & P 303 ..................... 186
R v Ramsgate Justices, ex parte Kazmarek (1984)
   80 Cr App R 366 ...................................... 59
R v Rivett (1950) 34 Cr App R 87 (CCA) ........... 175, 179
R v Robertson [1968] 3 All ER 557, [1968]
   1 WLR 1767 .......................................... 186
R v Sullivan [1984] AC 156, [1983] 2 All ER 673,
   [1983] 3 WLR 123 (HL) .............................. 177
R v Tandy [1988] Crim LR 308 .................... 184–185
R v Toland (1973) 58 Cr App R 453, [1974]
   Crim LR 196 (CA) .................................... 63
R v Webb [1969] 2 QB 278, [1969] 2 All ER 626,
   [1969] 2 WLR 1088 .................................. 187
R v Windle [1952] 2 QB 826, [1952] 2 All ER 1 (CA) ..... 178
Rhodes, Re (1890) 44 Ch D 94 ....................... 230
Robins Case [1791] 1 Fras 69 ........................ 233

S v S [1962] P 133, [1961] 3 All ER 133, [1961] 3 WLR 742 223
Sabatini, Re (1969) 114 SJ 35 ........................ 232
Secretary of State for Home Department v Mental Health
   Review Tribunal for the Mersey Regional Health Authority;
   Same v Mental Health Review Tribunal for Wales
   [1986] 3 All ER 233, [1986] 1 WLR 1170 ..... 118, 122–123
Smith v Smith [1973] 4 Fam Law 24 ............... 224, 226
Sodeman v The King [1936] 2 All ER 1138 .............. 178

T v T [1988] 1 All ER 613 ............................ 192
TB, Re [1967] Ch 247, [1966] 3 All ER 509,
   [1967] 2 WLR 15 .................................... 192
Talbot v Talbot (1971) 115 SJ 870 ..................... 226
Thurlow v Thurlow [1976] Fam 32, [1975] 2 All ER 979,
   [1975] 3 WLR 161 ............................. 224, 225

W, Re [1970] 2 All ER 502 ...................... 191–192
W v L [1974] QB 711, [1973] 3 All ER 884, [1973]
   3 WLR 859 (CA) ...................................... 2
Walker, Re [1905] 1 Ch 160 ......................... 231
Wellesley v Duke of Beaufort (1827) 2 Russ 1,
   5 LJOS Ch 85 ........................................ 98
Williams v Williams [1964] AC 698, [1963] 2 All ER 994,
   [1963] 3 WLR 215 .................................. 223
Winkle, Re [1894] 2 Ch 519 ......................... 192

# List of abbreviations

| | |
|---|---|
| ASW | Approved social worker |
| CA 1989 | Children Act 1989 |
| CAA 1968 | Criminal Appeal Act 1968 |
| CCETSW | Central Council for Education and Training in Social Work |
| CSDPA 1970 | Chronically Sick and Disabled Persons Act 1970 |
| COPR 1984 | Court of Protection Rules 1984 – SI No 2035 |
| CP(I)A 1964 | Criminal Procedure (Insanity) Act 1964 |
| DP(SCR)A 1986 | Disabled Persons (Services, Consultation and Representation) Act 1986 |
| EA 1981 | Education Act 1981 |
| EPA 1985 | Enduring Powers of Attorney Act 1985 |
| E(SEN)R 1983 | Education (Special Educational Needs) Regulations 1983 – SI No 29 |
| MCA 1973 | Matrimonial Causes Act 1973 |
| MCR 1977 | Matrimonial Causes Rules 1977 |
| MHA 1983 | Mental Health Act 1983 |
| MHR 1983 | Mental Health (Hospital, Guardianship and Consent to Treatment) Regulations 1983 – SI No 893 |
| MHRT | Mental Health Review Tribunal |
| MHRTR 1983 | Mental Health Review Tribunal Rules 1983 – SI No 942 |
| NAA 1948 | National Assistance Act 1948 |
| NA(A)A 1951 | National Assistance (Amendment) Act 1951 |
| NHSA 1977 | National Health Service Act 1977 |
| NH&MNHR 1984 | Nursing Homes and Mental Nursing Homes Regulations 1984 – SI No 1578 |
| RCHR 1984 | Residential Care Homes Regulations 1984 – SI No 1345 |

RHA 1984    Registered Homes Act 1984
RPA 1983    Representation of the People Act 1983
RTA 1988    Road Traffic Act 1988
SFM         Social Fund Manual – DHSS

# Chapter 1

# Hospital admission, guardianship and other civil procedures

## 1. The definition of mental disorder

*(a) Mental disorder*

Part II of the Mental Health Act 1983 ("MHA1983") gives considerable powers to approved social workers ("ASWs"), doctors and relatives over people suffering from a mental disorder. For the purposes of the MHA 1983 (other than Part VII – see page 191) a "patient" is defined as "a person suffering or appearing to be suffering from mental disorder" (s 145 (1) MHA 1983). It is desirable that the definition of mental disorder should be precise and leave as little as possible to discretion. Unfortunately the definition in s 1(2) MHA 1983 does not provide the degree of certainty which one would have hoped for in this area of law. Mental disorder is defined as:

> "mental illness, arrested or incomplete development of mind, psychopathic disorder and other disorder or disability of mind and 'mentally disordered' shall be construed accordingly."
>
> (s 1(2)MHA 1983.)

This broad-based definition is for many purposes of the MHA 1983 insufficient – some statutory provisions only apply where the patient is shown to be within one of four specific categories of mental disorder rather than within the general definition in s 1 (2) MHA 1983 (for example, admission under s 3 MHA 1983 – see page 21). The four specific categories are mental illness, mental impairment, severe mental impairment and psychopathic disorder. These are considered in greater detail below.

Section 1(3) MHA 1983 makes it clear that promiscuity or other immoral conduct, sexual deviancy or dependence on alcohol or drugs must not be construed as implying that a person has a mental disorder. Any one of these conditions does not in itself bring a person within s 1(2) MHA 1983; however, if there is other evidence of mental disorder s 1(3) does not prevent a classification being made in respect of such a person (see *R* v *Mental Health Review Tribunal, ex parte Clatworthy* (1985)).

### (b) Mental illness

A definition of mental illness is nowhere to be found in the MHA 1983. Case law does, however, provide a rather crude definition. Lawton LJ in *W* v *L* (1974) said that the words "mental illness" had no special legal or medical meaning; they were ordinary words of the English language and should be construed in an ordinary way. He proposed a lay person's definition: would an ordinary and sensible person have said of the patient, "Well, the fellow is obviously mentally ill"?

In practice the decision as to whether a person is mentally ill is a clinical one and the expression invariably has to be defined by reference to what the doctor says it means in a particular case rather than to any precise legal criteria.

### (c) Mental impairment and severe mental impairment

Mental impairment means a state of arrested or incomplete development of mind which includes *significant* impairment of intelligence and social functioning and is associated with abnormally aggressive or seriously irresponsible conduct. Severe mental impairment also requires a state of arrested or incomplete development of mind, but includes *severe* impairment of intelligence and social functioning and is associated with abnormally aggressive conduct. (See s 1(2) MHA 1983.)

The distinction between the two is important as certain provisions of the MHA 1983 do not apply to mentally impaired persons, or apply in a modified form (for example s 3(2)(b) MHA 1983 – see page 21). However, in practice the distinction may at times be difficult to recognise, and categorisation of a person will ultimately depend upon a clinical judgement.

During the Parliamentary debates on this definition, much concern was expressed regarding people with a mental handicap, and the extent to which the MHA 1983 should apply to them. Is compulsory detention in hospital appropriate? The definition represents a compromise and was intended by the Government to

## Hospital admission, guardianship and other civil procedures

include only those people with a mental handicap who are in need of hospital detention, usually for their own safety or that of others. Whether or not it is so exclusive depends upon how the requirements as to social functioning and aggressive or seriously irresponsible conduct are interpreted. It should be borne in mind that although severe mental impairment and mental impairment restrict the number of mentally handicapped persons subject to long term detention, the general definition may include some people with a mental handicap by its use of the words "any other disorder or disability of mind". However, as will be seen below, the powers of detention available in such cases are restricted to admission for assessment and emergency assessment (see pages 17 and 24).

*(d) Psychopathic disorder*

Section 1(2) MHA 1983 defines psychopathic disorder as a persistent disorder or disability (whether or not including significant impairment of intelligence) which results in abnormally aggressive or seriously irresponsible conduct. The disorder or disability must be persistent so the patient must have been suffering from it for a period of time. Unlike impairment, the disorder or disability must *result* in abnormally aggressive or seriously irresponsible conduct rather than be merely *associated* with it.

It is thought that some psychopaths will not benefit from treatment in hospital. Although treatability is no longer included as part of the definition, the effect of ss 3, 37 and 47 is that compulsory admission is not possible unless the treatment is likely to alleviate or prevent deterioration of the patient's condition (for treatability see page 22). As with impairment, there is no legal guidance as to what is meant by abnormally aggressive or seriously irresponsible conduct.

## 2. Approved social workers

*(a) Appointment and approval*

Section 114(1) MHA 1983 imposes upon each local social services authority a duty to appoint "sufficient numbers of approved social workers for the purpose of discharging the functions conferred upon them" by the Act. The number of ASWs to be appointed is to be determined by the local authority; it will be influenced by, amongst other matters, geographical factors and the need for out-of-hours provision. One of the roles of the ASW is to prevent the need for compulsory admission to hospital. It is, therefore, necessary for a local authority, when deciding upon the number of ASWs for its area, to recognise the time involved in such preventive community-based work. An ASW must be an officer of the local social services authority and is appointed to act as such for the purposes of the Act (s 145(1) MHA 1983). Before a social worker can be appointed as an ASW, he/she must be approved by the authority as having appropriate competence in dealing with persons suffering from mental disorder (for mental disorder see page 1).

Arrangements for the approval of ASWs are found in the directions given by the Secretary of State in DHSS Circular LAC (86)15. These arrangements are designed to ensure that all ASWs have received appropriate and adequate training for the statutory duties they are required to perform. An authority must have regard to the concern of Parliament that high standards should be set and maintained in this important work. Particular regard should be had to the following matters:

(i) approval should only be given to those who hold the Certificate of Qualification in Social Work; *or* a qualification recognised by the Central Council for Education and Training in Social Work ("CCETSW"); *or* were warranted Mental Health Officers in post on 28 October 1982; *or* gained substantial experience as a warranted Mental Health Officer between 1 January 1975 and 27 October 1982;

(ii) the authority needs to ensure that he/she has completed training at a course approved by CCETSW; *or* has succeeded in an assessment organised by CCETSW in accordance with its rules up to 1 April 1987; *or* has received appropriate training (which began before 1 April 1987) in carrying out the duties of an ASW under the Act;

(iii) no approval should be made for longer than five years, after which there may be a re-approval (note that re-approval, or lack of it, should not be used as a disciplinary measure).

(s 114(3) MHA 1983 and DHSS Circular LAC (86) 15 paras 6 and 7.)

If an ASW moves from one authority to another, the latter should enquire of the former whether he/she satisfactorily carried out the duties before it approves him/her. Approval may be withdrawn from an ASW who is no longer required to carry out the duties. Before this is done, there should be due consultation; if there is no mutual agreement the authority's own internal procedures for dealing with such matters should be used.

## (b) Duty of ASW to make an application

Central to the MHA 1983 is the personal duty imposed upon ASWs to make applications for admission or guardianship (see pages 17 and 30). The policy of the legislation is that the powers of compulsion in the Act should not be used on the basis of medical evidence alone, but rather on broader statutory criteria. The decision to make an application is taken by the ASW and not the local social services authority; it requires a professional and personal assessment of all the relevant evidence rather than total reliance on the opinion of a relative or doctor. This personal responsibility is emphasised by the wording of s 13(1) MHA 1983 which refers to cases where "he is satisfied" and where "it is necessary or proper for the application to be made by him". Although this does entail personal responsibility, s 139(1) MHA 1983 provides that no civil or criminal proceedings may be brought unless the act was done in bad faith or without reasonable care.

A duty to make an application arises only in respect of patients within the area of the local social services authority which appointed the ASW. This includes patients who are actually present in the area but ordinarily resident in the area of another authority (for example a patient who is an informal patient in a hospital outside his/her own area or a traveller who is temporarily within an authority's area). It follows that the duty is removed if a patient is temporarily absent from the ASW's area (for example on holiday); the duty is then imposed upon some other area's ASWs. However, such a situation requires a degree of co-operation between ASWs in each area, and an application should be made by the more appropriate person (see below for applications outside an ASW's area).

The duty to make an application only arises if the ASW is satisfied that one ought to be made (s 13(1) MHA 1983). This involves the ASW in assessing all the information, including the medical reports, and deciding whether the statutory criteria for admission have been met. The ASW must also be of the opinion that it is necessary or proper for the application to be made by him/her rather than by the nearest relative or an ASW in another area (for example, the area of permanent residence). In deciding whether it is necessary or proper, he/she must have regard to any wishes expressed by the relatives, or any other relevant circumstances (s 13(1) MHA 1983).

Where the ASW is considering an application for admission to hospital, he/she must interview the patient in a suitable manner. One purpose behind such an interview is to enable the ASW to satisfy himself/herself that detention in hospital is, in all the circumstances of the case, the most appropriate way of providing the care and medical treatment which the patient needs (s 13(2) MHA 1983). This is particularly important because the ASW should always seek the least restrictive alternative available to him/her, and in this context should address his/her thoughts to the necessity of admission, which is the most extreme form of compulsion available under Part II MHA 1983. The requirement that the interview should be conducted in a suitable manner is designed to meet those cases where there may be some difficulty in communication. For example, if the patient is deaf it will be necessary to use the expertise of a person able to communicate with him/her. Similarly, the ASW should take account of difficulties the patient may have in communicating in English; interpreters should be used or ASWs who can communicate in the patient's own language. Problems occur if the patient is unwilling to communicate with the ASW. Ultimately the only legal power the ASW can rely upon is that found in s 135(1)(b) MHA 1983 which empowers a justice of the peace to issue a warrant empowering a constable to enter premises and remove a person to a place of safety. However, this only applies in limited circumstances (see pages 15–17) and may merely defer the problem since detention in hospital is intended to be preliminary to making an application under Part II MHA 1983. In these circumstances the ASW is effectively prevented from fulfilling his/her duty to interview the patient and making an application where appropriate. It is hoped the courts would not be too strict in their interpretation of the word "interview" and would be satisfied with something less than a formal dialogue provided there had been a genuine attempt to engage the patient in a discussion of his/her future. Furthermore, the ASW is protected by s 139(1) MHA 1983 provided that his/her action was not in bad faith or done without reasonable care. However, it should not be assumed that detention in hospital is appropriate because a patient has refused to be interviewed by an ASW, or has not been co-operative.

The nearest relative of a patient has the power to require the local social services authority to direct an ASW to take the patient's case into consideration under s 13(1) MHA 1983 with a view to making an application for admission to hospital (s 13(4) MHA 1983). If such a direction is given, the ASW must consider the

## Hospital admission, guardianship and other civil procedures

case as soon as it is practicable; unreasonable delay is not acceptable. When considering a case in response to a direction, the ASW must act in accordance with s 13(1) and (2) MHA 1983. Should the ASW decide not to make an application, he/she must inform the nearest relative of the reasons for his/her decision in writing. This will enable the nearest relative to make an application himself/herself if he/she wishes (see pages 8 – 12). The duty to inform the nearest relative is a personal obligation imposed upon the ASW. A direction under s 13(4) MHA 1983 may only be given in respect of a patient within the local social services authority's area; it applies only where consideration of the case is with a view to admission to hospital and not to an application for guardianship.

An ASW may also make an application in respect of a patient outside the area of his/her own local social services authority, although there is no legal duty to do so (s 13(3) MHA 1983). As noted above, there may be situations where a patient is temporarily outside his/her own local authority area (for example in hospital or on holiday) and in these circumstances a measure of agreement between the two authorities is required. The duty under s 13(1) MHA 1983 is upon the ASW in the area where the patient is actually present at the relevant time. However, an ASW in the area of the patient's permanent residence may have a better understanding of the case and be the more appropriate person to make the application. In this situation the first ASW may consider that the application should be made by the second ASW. The duty under s 13(1) MHA 1983 would be satisfied if the first ASW concludes that it is not necessary or proper for the application to be made *"by him"* as specified in the subsection. The second ASW could then exercise his/her power under s 13(3). It should be noted that in these circumstances a direction under s 13(4) MHA 1983 could only be given to the first ASW.

Section 13 should not be construed as restricting the power of an ASW to make an application. Nor should it be construed as authorising or requiring an application to be made which contravenes s 11(4) MHA 1983. This subsection prevents an application being made if the nearest relative objects; it also requires the ASW to consult the person appearing to be the nearest relative (s 13(5) MHA 1983; for s 11(4) MHA 1983 see page 22).

## 3. The nearest relative

### (a) Who is the nearest relative?

The nearest relative of a patient may play an important part in the admission, guardianship, care and discharge of a patient under the MHA 1983. It is, therefore, important to identify the nearest relative, and this is done in s 26 MHA 1983. There are two parts to the definition: firstly, who is a "relative", and secondly which of those persons is the "nearest" relative?

(i) A "relative" of a patient for the purposes of the MHA 1983 means any of the following persons:
- husband or wife;
- son or daughter;
- father or mother;
- brother or sister;
- grandparent;
- grandchild;
- uncle or aunt;
- nephew or niece.

(s 26(1) MHA 1983.)

"Husband or wife" includes a person who is living with the patient as his/her wife/husband and has been doing so for a period of not less than six months. This extended definition of spouse also applies to a person who was so living immediately before the patient's admission to hospital as an in-patient. However, a person falling within this category cannot be the nearest relative if the patient is married and his/her husband or wife cannot be excluded under s 26(5) MHA 1983 (s 26(6) MHA 1983; see (ii) and (iii) below). Relationships of the half blood are to be treated as those of the whole blood and an illegitimate person as the legitimate child of his/her mother. (See s 26(2) MHA 1983.)

(ii) Although s 26(1) MHA 1983 provides a list of relatives, it may eventually transpire that the "nearest relative" is not actually a relative at all. However, the MHA 1983 provides that normally the nearest relative is the highest surviving person in the above list. If, within one category of relative, there are relatives of the whole blood and of the half blood, preference will be given to the former. Furthermore, within a category of relative, preference will be given to the elder or eldest. No regard is had to the sex of the relative for the purpose of determining the nearest relative (see s 26(3) MHA 1983).

## Hospital admission, guardianship and other civil procedures

The patient may be receiving care from, or ordinarily reside with, a relative or may have done so immediately before admission to hospital as an in-patient. In these circumstances the nearest relative is determined by giving preference to that relative over any others. Where there are two or more such relatives, the nearest relative is determined according to s 26(3) MHA 1983 (s 26(4) MHA 1983).

Certain relatives are prevented from being the nearest relative even though they are identified as such by the rules outlined above. These relatives are as follows:

(i) a relative who is not ordinarily resident in the United Kingdom, the Channel Islands or the Isle of Man, and the patient is so resident;

(ii) a husband/wife of the patient who is permanently separated from the patient either by agreement or by order of the court;

(iii) a husband/wife who has been deserted by the patient for a period which has not yet come to an end;

(iv) a person under the age of eighteen years, other than the spouse or a parent of the patient.

(s 26(5)(a) – (c) MHA 1983.)

The nearest relative is to be ascertained as if a relative who comes within one of the above categories were dead.

If the patient ordinarily resides with a person other than a relative and has done so for a period of not less than five years, then that person is to be treated as if he/she were a relative of the patient. However, when identifying the nearest relative, that person will be treated as being last in the s 26(1) MHA 1983 list. Furthermore, he/she cannot be treated as the nearest relative if the patient is married unless the husband or wife can be disregarded under (ii) or (iii) of the above list of proscribed persons under s 26(5) MHA 1983.

Once the nearest relative has been ascertained, he/she may, in writing, authorise another person to perform the functions of nearest relative. However, he/she may not appoint the patient or a person who is disqualified under s 26(5) MHA 1983. (See Mental Health (Hospital, Guardianship and Consent to Treatment) Regulations 1983 r 14.)

*(b) Court-appointed nearest relative*

The county court has the power to order that the functions of nearest relative are to be performed by some person other than the one identified under s 26 MHA 1983. An application for an order may be made by *any* relative of the patient, any other person with whom the patient is residing (or resided prior to admission to hospital as an in-patient) or any ASW (s 29(2)(a) – (c) MHA 1983). The court may appoint the applicant as acting nearest relative except where the application is made by an ASW in which situation the local social services authority is appointed. Alternatively it may appoint any other person named in the application who is a proper person to act as such and is willing to do so. (See s 29(1) and (2) MHA 1983.)

An application under the section may be made on one of the following grounds:

(i) the patient has no nearest relative within the meaning of the MHA 1983, or it is not reasonably practicable to ascertain whether he/she has such a relative or who that relative is;

(ii) the nearest relative is incapable of acting as such by reason of mental disorder or some other illness;

(iii) the nearest relative unreasonably objects to the making of an application for admission for treatment or a guardianship application in respect of the patient (see pages 22 and 31);

(iv) the nearest relative has exercised without due regard to the welfare of the patient or the interests of the public his/her power to discharge the patient from hospital or guardianship (see page 38).

(s 29(3) MHA 1983.)

An application to a county court is made by originating application filed in the court for the district in which the patient's place of residence is situated. "Place of residence" means, in relation to a patient receiving treatment as an in-patient at a hospital or other institution, that hospital or institution. Normally the application will be heard in chambers, although the judge can order otherwise. It is possible for the judge to interview the patient either in the presence of, or separately from, the other parties either at the court or elsewhere. Alternatively the judge may direct the registrar to interview the patient and make a report in writing. The nearest relative must be made a respondent to the proceedings unless the application is based on (i) above or the court orders otherwise. There is also a general discretion on the part of the court to order that any other person, not being the patient, shall be made a respondent. At the hearing the court may

## Hospital admission, guardianship and other civil procedures

accept as evidence of facts stated any report made by a medical practitioner or a report made, in the course of his/her official duties, by any of the following persons:

- a probation officer;
- an officer of a local authority or voluntary organisation exercising statutory functions on behalf of a local authority;
- an officer of a hospital authority.

Such reports are subject to the proviso that the respondent shall be told the substance of any part of it which the judge considers to be material for the fair determination of the application. (See County Court Rules 1981 O 49 r 12(1)−(6).)

Where the application is made under (i) or (ii) above, the court may specify a period for which the order is to continue in force unless the order is discharged under s 30 MHA 1983 (see below). This may be useful where the nearest relative is ill and an acting nearest relative is appointed by the court to act during his/her indisposition. If no period is specified in the order, and the order is not discharged under s 30 MHA 1983 (see below), it will cease to have effect at the following times:

- where the patient was liable to be detained or subject to guardianship, or where he/she becomes so liable or subject within three months of the order, the date upon which he/she ceases to be so liable (note that this does not include being transferred under s 19 MHA 1983 − see page 34);
- where the patient was not liable to detention or subject to guardianship at the time of the order, and does not become so liable or subject within a three month period, the date upon which that period expires.

(s 30(4)(a) and (b) MHA 1983.)

Applications under (iii) and (iv) above, which are pending immediately before the expiration of the period for which the patient is liable to be detained under an admission for assessment (see page 17), have the effect of extending that period of detention. The patient will remain liable to detention, in any case, until the application under s 29 MHA 1983 has been disposed of and, if an order is made under the section, detention will continue for a further period of seven days. For the purposes of this provision, an application is deemed to have been finally disposed of upon the expiry of the time allowed for appealing against a court decision or, if notice of appeal has been given, the time at which the appeal has been heard or withdrawn. (See s 29 (4)(a) and (b) MHA 1983.)

Where a county court has made an appointment under s 29 MHA 1983, any provisions of the MHA 1983 which refer to the nearest relative shall apply in relation to the patient as if they referred to a person so appointed. This still applies even if the person who was the nearest relative at the time the order was made is no longer the nearest relative, for example as a result of death (see s 29(6) MHA 1983). The subsection does not, however, apply to applications to a Mental Health Review Tribunal ("MHRT") under s 66(1)(h) MHA 1983 (see page 114).

An order under s 29 MHA 1983 may be varied or discharged under s 30. Applications for discharge may be made by the following persons:

- the court-appointed acting nearest relative;
- where the order was made under ground (i) or (ii) above, the nearest relative;
- where the person who was the nearest relative at the time of the order has ceased to be the nearest relative, the person who, under s 26 MHA 1983, is the new nearest relative.

(s 30(1)(a) and (b) MHA 1983.)

Section 29 MHA 1983 orders may also be varied by the county court on the application of the acting nearest relative or an ASW. Upon an application to vary, the court may substitute for the acting nearest relative a local social services authority provided that the authority is prepared to act as nearest relative. Alternatively, the court may vary the order by appointing some other person who is, in its opinion, a proper person to exercise the functions of nearest relative and is willing to do so. (See s 30(2) MHA 1983.)

If an acting nearest relative dies, an application for variation or discharge under s 29 MHA 1983 may be made by any relative of the patient (s 30(3)(a) MHA 1983). Until such time as the order is discharged or varied, the functions of nearest relative are not exercisable by any person (s 30(3)(b) MHA 1983). This applies to applications to an MHRT under s 66 and s 69 MHA 1983 (see pages 112 and 115).

For special provisions relating to children, see page 51.

## 4. General powers of access, examination, conveyance and detention

*(a) Access to a patient*

The statutory duties and powers of an ASW and others will be considered in this chapter. However, at this point it is worth noting the general powers that are available to an ASW and other persons authorised under the MHA 1983 who are seeking access to, or details or an examination of a person that he/she believes to be suffering from a mental disorder. Under s 115 MHA 1983, an ASW may enter and inspect premises in which a mentally disordered patient is living if he/she has reasonable cause to believe that the patient is not under proper care. This power only applies to premises within the area of the appointing authority; hospitals are specifically excluded. The power of entry may only be exercised at a reasonable time. Thus, unless it is necessary for the safety and welfare of the patient, the power should normally be exercised during the daytime rather than at night. The ASW may be required to produce a duly authenticated document showing that he/she is an ASW.

Section 115 MHA 1983 gives a power only to enter and inspect. If entry is refused, there is no power to enter by force. It is, however, a criminal offence to refuse to allow the inspection of premises, or to refuse to allow visiting, interviewing or examination of any person by somebody who is authorised under the MHA 1983. There is also a general criminal offence of obstructing an authorised person in the exercise of his/her functions. This covers situations where a relative or friend makes it impossible or extremely difficult for the ASW to interview the patient or for a medical practitioner to conduct an examination (s 129(1)(a), (b) and (d) MHA 1983).

Section 129(2) MHA 1983 makes it an offence to refuse to withdraw when requested to do so by a person authorised under the MHA 1983 to conduct an interview or examination *in private*. There is no general right to interview a person in private, and in the absence of any express power it is questionable whether an ASW has the right to insist on a private interview with the patient. However, before an ASW makes an application for admission, s 13(2) MHA 1983 requires him/her to interview the patient in a "suitable manner" (see page 6). This provision was inserted to cover cases where patients might find it difficult to communicate because of disability or linguistic reasons. "Suitable manner" could be interpreted to include interviewing in private if appropriate in the circumstances. Nevertheless, when faced with a hostile and unreasonably obstructive friend or relative, an ASW is better advised to rely, if all else fails, on the general offence of obstructing an authorised person in the exercise of his/her functions under s 129(1)(d) MHA 1983 rather than s 129(2).

Section 24 MHA 1983 specifies that certain interviews and examinations are to be in private. The nearest relative may authorise a registered medical practitioner to examine a patient in order to advise him/her as to the exercise of his/her power of discharge. Such an examination should take place at a reasonable time and the registered medical practitioner is allowed to examine the patient in private (s 24(1) MHA 1983; for the nearest relative's power of discharge see page 38). As well as examining the patient, the registered medical practitioner may also require the production of records relating to the detention or treatment of the patient in hospital. These records may be inspected (s 24(2) MHA 1983).

Special provisions apply in respect of a patient liable to be detained in a mental nursing home (see pages 74–84). An application for that person's discharge may be made by the Secretary of State, a regional health authority, district health authority or special health authority (see s 23(3) MHA 1983 – page 39). When an application is made, any registered medical practitioner authorised by the Secretary of State or the authority, or any person authorised under Part II Registered Homes Act 1984, may at any reasonable time visit the patient and interview him/her in private (s 24(3)(a) and (b) MHA 1983; for Registered Homes Act 1984 see pages 74–84). If that person is a registered medical practitioner, he/she may examine the patient in private and inspect other records which relate to the patient's treatment in the home (s 24(4) MHA 1983). Any person authorised under this provision may require the production of documents which constitute, or are alleged to constitute, the authority for the patient's detention. It is a criminal offence to refuse to produce for inspection to an authorised person any documents or records which are required under s 24(2) or (3) MHA 1983 (s 129(1)(c) MHA 1983).

A local social services authority may institute criminal proceedings for any of the above offences (s 130 MHA 1983). Upon conviction, a person is liable to a maximum of three months' imprisonment, or a fine not exceeding level 4 of the standard scale, or both (s 129(3) MHA 1983).

## Hospital admission, guardianship and other civil procedures

### (b) Police powers

In extreme cases it may be necessary for an ASW to obtain the assistance of the courts and the police. Under s 135(1) MHA 1983, an ASW may seek a warrant from a justice of the peace authorising a constable to enter premises and remove a person to a place of safety. Before issuing a warrant there must be a reasonable cause to suspect that a person believed to be suffering from a mental disorder:

(i) has been, or is being ill treated, neglected or kept otherwise than under proper control, in any place within the jurisdiction of the justice;

(ii) being unable to care for himself/herself, is living alone in any such place.

(s 135(1)(a) and (b) MHA 1983.)

It is not necessary for the ASW to provide the court with the name of the person, nor is it necessary for the justice to name him/her in the warrant. However, the warrant must identify the premises to be entered.

The warrant gives the constable authority to enter the premises using force if necessary. He/She must be accompanied by an ASW (not necessarily the one who laid the information) and by a registered medical practitioner (s 135(4) MHA 1983). This is necessary because the constable is empowered, "if thought fit", to remove the person to a place of safety with a view to making an application in respect of him/her, or other arrangements for his/her treatment or care. In forming this opinion the constable needs the assistance of other professionals. However, the MHA 1983 does not give the doctor the power to medically examine the person. Unless it is a case of emergency, the registered medical practitioner cannot conduct an intrusive examination of the person and will have to rely on observation alone if consent is not forthcoming.

Once removed to a place of safety, the person acquires the status of "patient" (see s 135(3) MHA 1983; for the definition of patient see page 1). A place of safety is defined as residential accommodation provided by a local social services authority under the National Assistance Act 1948 or National Health Service Act 1977; a hospital as defined by the 1977 Act; a police station; a mental nursing home or residential home for mentally disordered persons (see pages 74 and 101) or any other suitable place the occupier of which is willing temporarily to receive the patient. He/She may be detained there for a maximum period of seventy-two hours; it must be stressed that this is a *maximum* period and should not be regarded as being the norm. Detention in a place of safety is for a specific purpose, namely the determination of whether an application under Part II MHA 1983, or other arrangements for treatment or care should be made. Once it has been decided that an application or alternative arrangements are necessary, the decision should be implemented without any delay and definitely within the seventy-two hour period. If, however, it is decided that no action should be taken, then the *raison d'être* for the detention disappears and the patient should be released. Detention under s 135(1) MHA 1983 does not give a general holding power.

A justice of the peace may also issue a warrant in respect of a patient who is already liable to detention under the MHA 1983 (s 135(2) MHA 1983). Information may be laid before the justice by a constable or any other person authorised under the MHA 1983 to take a patient to any place, or to take or retake a patient into custody. Before issuing a warrant, there must be a reasonable cause to believe that the patient is to be found on premises within the jurisdiction of the justice and that admission has been refused, or a refusal is apprehended (s 135(2)(a) and (b) MHA 1983). Unlike s 135(1) MHA 1983, the patient must be named. The warrant authorises the constable to enter the premises, by force if necessary, and remove the patient. He/She may be accompanied by a registered medical practitioner or by any person authorised to take or retake the patient (s 135(4) MHA 1983). A patient who is removed under such a warrant should be taken to the place where he/she is required to live under the terms of the detention.

A police constable who finds, in a place to which the public have access, a person who appears to be suffering from a mental disorder may remove him/her to a place of safety within s 135 MHA 1983. The constable must be of the opinion that the person is in need of care and control and that removal is necessary in that person's interests or for the protection of others. Upon removal, the person may be detained for a period not exceeding seventy-two hours for the purpose of enabling him/her to be examined by a registered medical practitioner and interviewed by an ASW. Any necessary arrangements for admission or care should be made within that period. (See s 136(1) and (2) MHA 1983.)

A person who is to be conveyed to any place, ordered to be kept in custody or detained in a place of safety under any provision of the MHA 1983 is deemed to be in legal custody (s 137(1) MHA

## Hospital admission, guardianship and other civil procedures

1983). Anybody who is responsible for conveying or detaining a person under the terms of the MHA 1983 has all the powers, authorities, protection and privileges of a constable (s 137(2) MHA 1983). Thus the person responsible may call upon others to assist him/her in performing his/her functions; anybody obstructing such a person in the exercise of his/her duty will be liable to arrest. Anyone who escapes whilst in legal custody may be retaken by the person who had legal custody of him/her immediately before the escape, or by any constable or ASW (s 138(1)(a) MHA 1983). In the case of an escapee liable to be detained in hospital under Part II MHA 1983, or subject to guardianship, he/she may also be retaken by any person who could take him/her into custody under s 18 MHA 1983 if he/she were absent without leave (s 138(1)(b) MHA 1983; for absence without leave see pages 41–43). The time limits under s 18 MHA 1983 for taking into custody a person absent without leave apply to s 138(1)(b) MHA 1983 (see page 42).

Where a person escapes whilst being taken to, or detained in, a place of safety under ss 135 or 136 MHA 1983, he/she may not be retaken after the seventy-two hour period has expired (s 138(3) MHA 1983). For this purpose, time starts running either at the time of the escape or the time at which actual detention at the place of safety commences, whichever is the earlier.

The police also have a power under s 17(1)(e) Police and Criminal Evidence Act 1984 to enter and search premises for the purpose of saving life or limb, or preventing serious damage to property. This power can be usefully employed in extreme cases where a failure to intervene might cause injury to the patient or to some other person. A warrant is not required.

## 5. Compulsory measures of admission and detention

The MHA 1983 provides for the compulsory admission and detention in hospital of people with a mental disorder. A number of different procedures are available. These are discussed below.

### (a) Admission for assessment

An application for admission for assessment may be made in respect of a patient on the following grounds:

    (i) he/she is suffering from mental disorder of a nature or degree which warrants the detention of the patient in hospital for assessment, or for assessment followed by medical treatment, for at least a limited period; *and*

(ii) he/she ought to be detained in the interests of his/her own health or safety or with a view to the protection of other persons.

(s 2(2) MHA 1983.)

The application may be made by an ASW or by the nearest relative and must be addressed to the managers of the hospital to which admission is sought (s 11(1) and (2) MHA 1983).

No application can be made unless the applicant has personally seen the patient within the period of fourteen days ending with the date of the application (s 11(5) MHA 1983). If made by an ASW, he/she must, before or within a reasonable time after the application, take such steps as are practicable to *inform* the nearest relative of the patient that it has been made. It is an obligation to inform rather than consult (contrast s 3 MHA 1983 below). He/She should also inform the nearest relative of the right to apply for discharge under s 23(2)(a) MHA 1983 (see pages 38–40).

Section 2(3)(b) MHA 1983 requires that the patient *ought* to be admitted *in the interests* of his/her own health or safety or with a view to the protection of others. This wording is more general than the wording of s 3 MHA 1983, as s 2 involves a shorter period of detention of the patient (s 3 MHA 1983 deals with admission for treatment – see (*b*) below). Detention need not be necessary for all of the specified purposes; it is sufficient that the patient should be admitted for one of them. "Health or safety" is undefined and is broad in its application. It can include considerations of the safety of the patient in the home and of the patient's physical as well as mental health. The expression "protection of others" is also undefined. There is some uncertainty whether it is restricted to physical protection of, for example, the patient's care-giver, or whether emotional, welfare and financial protection is included. As the word "protection" is not qualified in the MHA 1983, it is submitted that the broader definition is correct. However, as with the other provisions of the MHA 1983, the least restrictive alternative should always be favoured. It is unnecessary to be specific in the application as to the form of mental disorder relied upon; the generic definition applies.

Both (i) and (ii) must be satisfied: the fact that the patient ought to be detained for his/her own safety, or to protect others, is not in itself sufficient. It must also be shown that detention in

## Hospital admission, guardianship and other civil procedures

hospital for assessment for a limited period is warranted.

Applications under s 2 MHA 1983 must be supported by written recommendations from two registered medical practitioners who have personally examined the patient either together or separately. Not more than five days must have elapsed between separate examinations (s 12(1) MHA 1983). The recommendations may be separate or they may be joint (s 12(7) MHA 1983). They must state that both doctors are satisfied that the conditions set out in the section have been met. Each practitioner must have signed the recommendations either before or on the day of the application (s 12(1) MHA 1983). One of the registered medical practitioners must be approved by the Secretary of State as having special experience in the diagnosis or treatment of mental disorder (s 12(2) MHA 1983). The act of approval has been delegated to regional health authorities acting on general advice given by the Secretary of State (see National Health Service Functions (Directions to Authorities and Administrative Arrangements) Regulations 1982, SI 287). Either the approved practitioner or, failing that and if it is practicable, the other practitioner must have previous acquaintance with the patient (s 12(2) MHA 1983).

There are also prohibitions on who may supply a medical recommendation. If admission is sought to a hospital which is not a mental nursing home (see page 75), and the patient is not a private patient, one of the recommendations may be given by a doctor on the staff of that hospital. However, both recommendations may be given by doctors on the staff of such a hospital if the following conditions are satisfied:

(i) compliance with the one-doctor rule would result in delay causing serious risk to the health or safety of the patient; *and*

(ii) one of the practitioners works at the hospital for less than half the time he/she is bound by contract to work in the health service; *and*

(iii) where one of the practitioners is a consultant, the other does not work (whether at that hospital or elsewhere) in a post where he is under the consultant's directions.
(s 12(4)(a) – (c) MHA 1983.)

A general practitioner who is employed part time in a hospital is not, for the purposes of s 12 MHA 1983, to be regarded as a practitioner on its staff (s 12(6) MHA 1983).

Medical recommendations cannot be given by any of the following persons:

(i) the applicant;
(ii) a partner of the applicant or of the practitioner who has given the other recommendation;
(iii) a person employed as an assistant by any of the persons mentioned in (i) and (ii);
(iv) a person who receives an interest in the receipt of any payments made on account of the maintenance of the patient;
(v) subject to s 12(4) as outlined above, a practitioner on the staff of the hospital to which the patient is to be admitted.

(s 12(5)(a) – (e) MHA 1983.)

Also prohibited from providing a recommendation are the parents, parents-in-law, son/daughter, son/daughter-in-law, brother/sister or brother/sister-in-law of the patient, of any person mentioned in s 12(5)(a) – (e) MHA 1983 or of a practitioner who provided the other medical recommendation (s 12(5) MHA 1983).

The maximum period of detention under s 2 MHA 1983 is twenty-eight days. Before the expiry of that period, an application for discharge can be made under s 23(2)(a) MHA 1983 (see page 38). Subject to one exception, the period cannot be extended and the patient must be released unless some other authority for detention is obtained (for example, admission under s 3 MHA 1983 – see below) or the patient becomes an informal patient. The one exception to this rule is where an application is made for the appointment of a nearest relative under s 29 (4) MHA 1983 (see page 9).

It would be contrary to the spirit of the legislation if a patient after release was readmitted under s 2 MHA 1983 within a short period of time, particularly where there were a series of such readmissions, as this would avoid the extra safeguards for the patient in s 3 MHA 1983. The relatively short period of detention is therefore an important consideration in deciding whether or not to use s 2 as opposed to s 3 MHA 1983.

Although s 2 MHA 1983 is referred to as admission for assessment, it does provide for medical treatment as well. However, the wording of the section does not allow admission for treatment alone, as it must follow an assessment made within the twenty-eight day period. Patients admitted under s 2 MHA 1983 are subject to the consent to treatment provisions of ss 56 – 64 MHA 1983 (see pages 91–101). Emergency applications may be made *admission, guardianship and other civil procedures*

MHA 1983, and these may be converted into admis-
...essment (see *(c)* below).

*...on for treatment*

...MHA 1983 provides that:

"...application for admission for treatment may be made
...pect of a patient on the grounds that –

(a) he is suffering from mental illness, severe mental impairment, psychopathic disorder or mental impairment and his mental disorder is of a nature or degree which makes it appropriate for him to receive medical treatment in hospital; and

(b) in the case of psychopathic disorder or mental impairment, such treatment is likely to alleviate or prevent a deterioration of his condition; and

(c) it is necessary for the health or safety of the patient or for the protection of other persons that he should receive such treatment and it cannot be provided unless he is detained under this section."

As with s 2 MHA 1983, an application for admission for treatment may be made by an ASW or by the patient's nearest relative and addressed to the managers of the hospital to which admission is sought (s 11(1) and (2) MHA 1983). No application can be made unless the applicant has personally seen the patient within the period of fourteen days ending with the date of application (s 11(5) MHA 1983). The person making the application must state his/her relationship to the patient (s11(1) MHA 1983). If an ASW is making the application he/she must first *consult* the person, if any, who appears to be the nearest relative (s 11(4) MHA 1983). This involves more than just informing the nearest relative as is required under s 2 MHA 1983; the ASW must take note of any comments which the nearest relative might make. However, the ASW is relieved of the duty to consult if it appears to him/her that in the circumstances such consultation is "not reasonably practicable or would involve unreasonable delay" (s 11(4) MHA 1983). It is important that this provision is not interpreted as removing, for reasons of convenience, the obligation to consult; the fact that non-consultation would make admission easier is not in itself a good enough reason. The proviso is designed to cover situations such as those where the whereabouts of the nearest relative are unknown and there is no prospect of his/her being traced without an inordinate amount of investigative work on the part of the ASW. For example, if it were known that the nearest relative had left the country for an unknown destination, it would not be reasonably practicable to expect a full-scale investigation into his/her whereabouts. It may also be impracticable if the patient is unable to recall who his/her relatives are, and neighbours and friends are unable to help. What amounts to unreasonable delay depends upon the circumstances of the case. It depends very much upon the seriousness of the patient's condition and the need for him/her to be admitted to hospital for treatment. An application under s 3 MHA 1983 cannot be made if the nearest relative informs the ASW or the local social services authority that he/she objects (s 11(4) MHA 1983). If the ASW considers that an application is necessary despite the objection, he/she may apply to the county court for an order appointing an acting nearest relative (see s 29(3) MHA 1983 and page 9).

For admission under s 3 MHA 1983 it must be shown that the patient is suffering from one of the four specific forms of mental disorder. Moreover, it must be appropriate for the patient to be treated in a hospital. If treatment in the community is more appropriate, and available, admission is not possible. This reflects the need always to keep the least restrictive alternative in mind. Section 3(2)(b) MHA 1983 introduces the "treatability test" in respect of patients suffering from psychopathic disorder or mental impairment. The test requires that the treatment envisaged is likely to alleviate or prevent a deterioration of the patient's condition; it does not require that the treatment should *cure* the patient. Finally, the ASW is required to determine whether the treatment is necessary for the health and safety of the patient or for the protection of other persons, and cannot be provided unless he/she is detained (s 3(2)(c) MHA 1983). It is important to note that s 3(2)(c) MHA 1983 refers to the *treatment* being necessary for either of those purposes and not the detention. The question of detention only arises where such treatment would not be received unless the patient was compulsorily detained. In those cases where the patient has shown himself/herself not to be unwilling to enter hospital voluntarily, compulsory admission should be avoided and the patient admitted as an informal patient. If the *treatment* is not necessary for either of the stated purposes, the patient cannot be admitted simply on the basis that *detention* is so necessary. Section 3 MHA 1983 is concerned with admission for treatment and not detention for purely social reasons.

The application must be founded upon the written recommen-

## Hospital admission, guardianship and other civil procedures

dations of two registered medical practitioners. Section 12 MHA 1983 applies to s 3 applications in the same way as it applies to those under s 2 (see page 19). Each practitioner must state that he/she is of the opinion that the conditions set out in s 3(2) MHA 1983 have been complied with. Separate or joint recommendations are acceptable (s 11(7) MHA 1983). In addition, each recommendation must include:

(i) particulars of the grounds for his/her belief that the patient is suffering from one of the specified disorders (note that each may specify more than one disorder, but there must be at least one disorder in common – s 11(6) MHA 1983);

(ii) in the case of psychopathic disorder or mental impairment, the reason why he/she thinks it is treatable;

(iii) a statement as to why he/she considers that the treatment is necessary for the health or safety of the patient or for the protection of others;

(iv) if other treatment is available, the reason why it is not appropriate.

(s 3(3)(a) and (b) MHA 1983.)

Subsections 12(1)–(6) MHA 1983 apply to admissions for treatment in the same way that they apply to admissions for assessment (see pages 19–20).

A patient admitted under s 3 MHA 1983 is initially liable to be detained in hospital for a period of six months beginning on the day of admission (s 20(1) MHA 1983). However, the period of detention may be renewed under s 20 MHA 1983. Renewal is in the first instance for an additional six month period and thereafter for periods of one year (s 20(2)(a) and (b) MHA 1983). Within a two month period ending on the day when the patient will cease to be liable to be detained (either because the original six month period, or the subsequent additional period, will expire), the responsible medical officer (see page 28) has a duty to examine the patient. If it appears to him/her that the conditions in s 20(4) MHA 1983 have been satisfied, he/she must furnish a report to the managers of the hospital in which the patient is detained (s 20(3) MHA 1983). The conditions in s 20(4) MHA 1983 are as follows:

"(a) the patient is suffering from mental illness, severe mental impairment, psychopathic disorder or mental impairment, and his mental disorder is of a nature or degree which makes it appropriate for him to receive medical treatment in a hospital; and

(b) such treatment is likely to alleviate or prevent a deterioration of his condition; and

(c) it is necessary for the health or safety of the patient or for the protection of other persons that he should receive such treatment and that it cannot be provided unless he continues to be detained."

(s 20(4) MHA 1983.)

An alternative to the treatability test in s 20(4)(b) is provided in cases of mental illness or severe mental impairment. If it appears to the responsible medical officer that the patient, if discharged, is unlikely to be able to care for himself/herself or to obtain the care necessary to guard against serious exploitation, this is acceptable in place of the treatability test. Where a report is furnished, the authority for detention is renewed for six or twelve months, depending upon whether it is the first or subsequent renewal (s 20(8) MHA 1983).

If the form of mental disorder specified in the responsible medical officer's report is different from the one in the original application, that application will have effect as though the later disorder were specified in it. In this situation it is unnecessary for the appropriate medical officer to provide a report under s 16 MHA 1983 (s 16 deals with the reclassification of patients — see page 33).

## (c) Admission for assessment in cases of emergency

An emergency procedure for admission for assessment is provided by s 4 MHA 1983. The grounds for admission under s 4 MHA 1983 are the same as for admission for assessment under s 2 MHA 1983. However, the procedure can only be used in cases of "urgent necessity", for example where it is impossible or extremely difficult to obtain the necessary second medical recommendation but it is essential that the patient be admitted without delay because he/she may do serious damage to himself/herself, some other person or property. This type of situation may arise in rural areas where there are few registered medical practitioners scattered over a large geographical area. However, inconvenience should not be a reason for using the emergency procedure. Emergency applications may be made by an ASW or by the nearest relative, and they must include a statement that it is of urgent necessity that the patient be admitted under s 2 MHA 1983 and that compliance with the provisions of that section would involve undesirable delay (s 4(2) MHA 1983).

## Hospital admission, guardianship and other civil procedures

The applicant must have seen the patient within the previous twenty-four hours rather than the fourteen days under s 2 MHA 1983 (ss 4(5) and 11(5) MHA 1983). If an application is made by an ASW, s 4 does not impose an obligation upon him/her to inform the nearest relative (because s 11(3) MHA 1983 does not refer to "emergency applications" but to s 2 admissions only — see ss 2, 11(3) and 145(1) MHA 1983). However, as a matter of good practice, the nearest relative should be informed either before or after the application has been made.

In the first instance, an emergency application need only be founded on one of the medical recommendations required under s 2 MHA 1983. If it is practicable, the recommendation should be provided by a practitioner who has had previous acquaintance with the patient. However, the practitioner need not be one who has been approved under s 12(2) MHA 1983 (see page 19). The recommendation should comply with the requirements of s 12 MHA 1983 so far as they are applicable to single recommendations (for s 12 MHA 1983 see pages 19–20). The medical recommendation should verify the statement in the application that it is of urgent necessity that the patient should be detained under s 2 MHA 1983 and that complying with that section would involve undesirable delay (s 4(3) MHA 1983).

An emergency application ceases to have effect upon the expiry of seventy-two hours from the date of admission to the hospital. Detention may be continued if a second medical recommendation is provided within that period. Both recommendations must together comply with the terms of s 12 MHA 1983 other than the requirement regarding the time of signature of the second recommendation (see page 19). The effect of a second recommendation is to convert the s 4 admission into an admission for assessment and treatment under s 2 MHA 1983. This means that the patient may be detained for a period of twenty-eight days; however, the twenty-eight day period starts running from the time that the patient was first detained under s 4 MHA 1983 and not the date of the second recommendation (s 4(4)(a) and (b) MHA 1983). For an emergency application to be converted into an admission for assessment, it is necessary only for the second medical recommendation to be "given and received" by the hospital managers. This may cause difficulties in respect of the ASW's duty under s 11(3) MHA 1983 to take steps to inform the nearest relative of the application. As the conversion can, in theory, take place without the knowledge of the ASW, he/she may not be in a position to inform the nearest relative. It is, therefore, important that where any such conversion takes place without the ASW being directly involved, the hospital managers notify him/her so that he/she can endeavour to inform the nearest relative.

### (d) Admission of patients already in hospital

The MHA 1983 makes provision for the admission of persons already in hospital. A patient who is detained subject to an admission for assessment may be the subject of an application under s 3 MHA 1983 (application for treatment) if the requirements of that section are satisfied (s 5(1) MHA 1983). Similarly, as noted in *(c)* above, an emergency application may be converted into an admission for assessment and treatment (s 4(4) MHA 1983). Applications under ss 2, 3 or 4 MHA 1983 may be made in respect of any *voluntary* in-patient regardless of whether he/she is being treated for a mental or physical disorder. The relevant requirements outlined in *(a),(b)* and *(c)* apply as if the patient were not in hospital; however, the ready accessibility of doctors makes it highly unlikely that an in-patient will be subject to an emergency application under s 4 MHA 1983 (s 5(1) MHA 1983).

In addition to these forms of in-patient admission, the MHA 1983 also enables a registered medical practitioner in charge of the treatment of a voluntary in-patient to detain him/her for a period of up to seventy-two hours (s 5(2) and (6) MHA 1983). This provision applies to in-patients who have a physical or mental disorder. Before the registered medical practitioner can exercise this limited power of detention, it must appear to him/her that an application for admission for assessment or treatment ought to be made in respect of the in-patient. In these circumstances the registered medical practitioner must furnish a report to that effect to the hospital managers and the seventy-two hours will start running from that moment. The practitioner in charge of the patient may nominate no more than one other registered medical practitioner *on the staff of that hospital* to act for him/her under s 5(2) MHA 1983 in his/her absence (s 5(3) MHA 1983). No other registered medical practitioner may exercise this power of detention. The purpose behind the seventy-two hour period of detention is to enable an ASW to assess the patient's case and decide whether a full admission under s 2 or 3 MHA 1983 should be made.

A first-level nurse trained in nursing people with a mental illness or mental handicap has the power to detain for a period of six hours without any further authority a patient who is *receiving treatment for a mental disorder* as a voluntary in-patient (s 5(4)

*Hospital admission, guardianship and other civil procedures*

MHA 1983 and Mental Health (Nurses) Order 1983). It must appear to the nurse that:

(i) the patient is suffering from mental disorder to such a degree that it is necessary for his/her health or safety or for the protection of others for him/her to be immediately restrained from leaving hospital; and

(ii) it is not practicable to secure the immediate attendance of a practitioner for the purpose of furnishing a report under s 5(2) MHA 1983.

(s 5(4)(a) and (b) MHA 1983.)

The nurse may record this in writing and, if he/she does so, the patient may be detained for six hours from the time the record is made or until such time as a registered medical practitioner is available to make a report under s 5(2) MHA 1983, whichever is the earlier (s 5(4) MHA 1983). If a registered medical practitioner makes a report in respect of such a patient, the seventy-two hour period of detention includes the time that the patient was detained under the nurse's holding power (s 5(5) MHA 1983). A record made under s 5(4) MHA 1983 must be delivered by the nurse or person authorised by him/her to the hospital managers as soon as possible after it is made (s 5(5) MHA 1983).

*(e) Rectification of applications and recommendations*

There is provision in the MHA 1983 for correcting mistakes that may have been made in an application for admission for assessment or for treatment. Section 15(1) MHA 1983 provides that if, within fourteen days of the patient's admission, an application or recommendation is found to be defective or incorrect, it may be amended within that period by its signatory. The consent of the managers must, however, be obtained before doing so. Furthermore, if within that fourteen day period it appears to the managers that one of the two recommendations is insufficient to warrant detention of the patient, they may give notice of that fact to the applicant. Where notice is given, the medical recommendation is to be disregarded unless:

(i) a fresh medical recommendation complying with the relevant provisions of the MHA 1983 (other than the provision which relates to the time of signature and the interval between each examination – see pages 19 and 20) is furnished to the managers within the fourteen day period; and

(ii) that fresh recommendation and the other recommendation together comply with the MHA 1983.

(s 15(2)(a) and (b) MHA 1983.)

This procedure can also be used where each of the medical recommendations is, when taken separately, correct but when taken together they are insufficient to justify detention (s 15(3) MHA 1983), for example, when neither of the medical practitioners has been approved as required by s 12(2) MHA 1983 (see page 19). The s 15(2) procedure may be used in respect of either of the medical recommendations. However, s 15(3) MHA 1983 may not be used where there is no form of mental disorder common to both recommendations as required by s 11(6) MHA 1983.

The s 15 MHA 1983 procedure cannot be made to extend the effect of an emergency application beyond the seventy-two hour period specified in s 4(4) MHA 1983 unless that application has been converted into an application for assessment and treatment (s 15(4) MHA 1983).

*(f) The effect of an application for admission*

Upon the admission to hospital of a patient under s 2 or s 3 MHA 1983, a registered medical practitioner will be put in charge of his/her treatment. This practitioner is known as the responsible medical officer (s 34(1) MHA 1983). Where a patient is admitted to hospital by virtue of an application made by the nearest relative under the MHA 1983 (other than an emergency application), the managers of the hospital must, as soon as is practicable, inform the local social services authority for the area in which the patient resided immediately before admission. That authority must then arrange for the patient to be interviewed by a social worker (not necessarily an approved social worker) who must provide a report for the managers on the patient's social circumstances (s 14 MHA 1983). An application for admission gives the applicant, or any suitable responsible adult authorised by the applicant (for example an ambulance person), the power to convey the patient to the hospital. However, the hospital is not under an obligation to accept a patient. Section 140 MHA 1983 imposes an obligation upon every regional health authority in England and the district health authorities in Wales to notify local social services authorities operating in its area of hospitals in which arrangements are in force for the reception, in cases of real urgency, of patients requiring treatment for a mental disorder. The DHSS Memorandum states that this obligation will be met if the social services are kept aware of psychiatric catchment areas for particular hospitals, with suitable notes explaining, for example, where the catchment area for elderly patients differs from that for younger (DHSS Memorandum – Mental Health Act 1983, para 273: see also the duty of regional health authorities to provide courts with information about hospital places if requested – s 150 MHA 1983).

For the purposes of admission under Part II MHA 1983, a "hospital" is defined as any health service hospital within the meaning of the National Health Service Act 1977, any accommodation provided by a local authority and used as a hospital by or on behalf of the Secretary of State under the 1977 Act, or a mental nursing home registered as such under the Registered Homes Act 1984 (s 145(1) and s 34(2) MHA 1983; see page 75). The patient must be conveyed to the hospital within fourteen days of his/her last medical examination for the purposes of the application, but, in the case of an emergency application, the time limit is twenty-four hours from the required medical examination or from the time the application is made, whichever is the earlier (s 6(1)(a) and (b) MHA 1983). If the patient escapes within these time limits, or after he/she has been successfully conveyed to the hospital within the authorised period of detention, he/she may be retaken as he/she will be in legal custody under s 137(1) MHA 1983. The retaking may be by the person having custody of him/her immediately before the escape, a constable, any ASW, any officer on the staff of the hospital or any person authorised by the managers of the hospital (s 138(1) MHA 1983; see also s 18 MHA 1983 pages 41–43). Note that a person required or authorised to convey or detain a patient has all the powers, authorities, protection and privileges of a constable (s 137(2) MHA 1983 – see page 17). In the case of an application in respect of a voluntary in-patient, the hospital has authority to detain the patient from the time that the application comes into effect.

Responsibility for the patient passes from the applicant to the hospital managers as soon as he/she is accepted by a member of the hospital staff authorised to do so. It is unnecessary for that person to check the signature or qualifications of the applicant or the medical practitioner, nor is it usually necessary to check matters of fact or opinion contained in the application (s 6(3) MHA 1983). However, some degree of scrutiny is required and it is incumbent upon the applicant to ensure that full documentation accompanies the patient to the hospital as proof of the power to detain. The hospital will be entitled to refuse admission if there is inadequate or clearly unreliable documentation. In the case of an admission for treatment, all previous applications under which the patient was detained will cease to have effect. Thus detention under an application for assessment will cease. Similarly, guardianship will cease once an application for admission for treatment comes into operation (s 6(4) MHA 1983).

## 6. Guardianship

### (a) Applications for guardianship

A possible alternative to compulsory detention in hospital is the provision of care and support within the community. In some cases, such care may be provided on an informal basis without the need for any legal backup, and ASWs and other professionals may provide necessary support (for care in the community see page 138). However, for some people this type of arrangement may not be sufficient and yet admission into hospital would be inappropriate. Guardianship is a less restrictive alternative to admission. It gives the guardian certain exclusive powers in respect of the patient but at the same time allows the patient to remain within the community.

Only persons who have attained the age of sixteen years can be received into guardianship (s 7(1) MHA 1983: see part 12 of this chapter (page 46) for children and young persons under that age). The application must state the exact age of the patient or, if not known, it must state that he/she is believed to have attained sixteen years (s 7(4) MHA 1983). Applications can only be made by either an ASW or by the nearest relative (s 11(1) MHA 1983). He/She must have seen the patient within the period of fourteen days ending with the date of the application (s 11(5) MHA 1983). The grounds for a guardianship application are as follows:

(i) the patient is suffering from mental disorder, being mental illness, severe mental impairment, psychopathic disorder or mental impairment; and

(ii) the mental disorder is such as warrants his/her reception into guardianship; and

(iii) it is necessary in the interests of his/her welfare or for the protection of other persons that the patient should be received into guardianship.
(s 7(2)(a) and (b) MHA 1983.)

Before an ASW makes an application, he/she must consult the

person (if any) who appears to be the nearest relative of the patient unless it appears that it is not reasonably practicable or that it would involve unreasonable delay (s 11(4) MHA 1983). Consultation should take place whenever possible; only in genuine cases of impracticability (for example, the nearest relative cannot be traced) or delay (for example, the nearest relative is known to live in Australia but the address is not known) should the ASW rely on the exception. An application cannot be made by an ASW if the nearest relative has notified that social worker that he/she objects to it being made. In these circumstances, the ASW may consider proceedings under s 29 MHA 1983 for the appointment of an acting nearest relative (see page 9).

A guardianship application may name either a local social services authority or any person to act as guardian, including the applicant himself/herself. However, if an individual is to act as guardian, the application must be accepted by the local authority social services in the area in which he/she resides. Furthermore, the application must be accompanied by a written statement that the person is willing to act as guardian. (See s 7(5) MHA 1983 and Mental Health (Hospital, Guardianship and Consent to Treatment) Regulations 1983 r 5(1)(b).)

The local authority which accepts such an application is known as the responsible local social services authority. Before it accepts an application, the authority must satisfy itself that the named person is suitable to act as guardian of the patient; guardianship does not commence until the application is accepted. In the case of an authority rather than an individual acting as guardian, it is referred to as the responsible local social services authority. (See s 34(3)(a) and (b) MHA 1983.)

A guardianship application must be founded upon the written recommendations of two registered medical practitioners, one of whom must be approved under s 12(2) MHA 1983 (see page 19). Unless it is impracticable, one of the registered medical practitioners should have a previous acquaintance with the patient.

Medical recommendations cannot be given by the applicant, a partner of the applicant, a partner of the practitioner providing the other recommendation, a person who will benefit financially from the maintenance of the patient or the person named as guardian in the application (s 12(5) and (7) MHA 1983). The prohibition also applies to the spouse, parent, parents-in-law, son/daughter-in-law, brother/sister-in-law of the patient, or of any person listed in s 12(5) above, or of the medical practitioner providing the other medical recommendation (s 12(5) MHA 1983).

The practitioners must have examined the patient either together or separately, but in the latter case no more than five days must have elapsed between each examination (s 12(1) MHA 1983). The recommendations must include a statement that in their opinions the conditions in s 7(2)(a) and (b) MHA 1983 have been complied with. The recommendations must give particulars as to the nature of the disorder, why this warrants reception into guardianship, and why it is thought that guardianship is necessary in the interests of the patient's welfare or for the protection of others (s 11(3) MHA 1983). Both recommendations must have at least one form of mental disorder in common, or the application will be invalid; however, this does not prevent individual practitioners specifying more than one form of disorder (s 11(6) MHA 1983). Either separate recommendations or a joint one signed by both practitioners will be acceptable (s 11(7) MHA 1983).

If the application appears to have been duly made and founded upon the necessary medical recommendations, no further proof is required of signature or qualifications or of any fact or opinion stated therein (s 8(3) MHA 1983). A defective or incorrect application or medical recommendation may be amended by the person signing it within the first fourteen days of the patient's reception into guardianship if the local social services authority consents. Once this has been done, the amended application or recommendation is treated as if it had been originally made in that form (s 8(4) MHA 1983).

## (b) Transfer of guardianship

In certain circumstances a private guardianship may be transferred to the local social services authority. A general power of transfer is given by s 19 MHA 1983 (see page 34). However, where the guardian dies or gives notice in writing to the "local social services authority" that he/she wishes to relinquish the office, guardianship then vests in the "local social services authority" (s 10(1) MHA 1983). The authority is obliged to accept guardianship; it has no discretion in the matter (s 10(1)(a) and (b) MHA 1983). It is unclear whether the authority twice referred to in s 10(1) MHA 1983 is the *responsible* local social services authority (ie the one in whose area the guardian lives), or the authority for the area in which the patient resides if different, or whether it refers to each of them in turn. Whereas it is sensible to expect the notice of termination to be received by the responsible local social services authority, it is arguably in the patient's interests if guardianship is transferred to his/her own local authority in those cases where it is a different one. It is submitted that this is the better interpretation, although it is only partly supported by the literal rule of interpretation (see s 145(1) for the definition of local social services authority). It should also be noted that the whole of s 10 MHA 1983 is badly drafted as it consistently refers to "local social services authority" in situations where the *responsible* local social services authority is clearly intended.

If a private guardian becomes incapacitated by illness or some other cause and prevented from performing the functions of guardian, they *may* be performed *on his/her behalf* by the local social services authority or any other person approved by that authority (s 10(2) MHA 1983). The reference here is to the *responsible* authority (see DHSS Memorandum – Mental Health Act 1983, para 89). Unlike s 10(1), the authority is not obliged to act as temporary guardian. However, if it decides to do so, it will be the agent of the private guardian and so will be bound to accept his/her views. Furthermore, the transfer under s 10(2) is not permanent; it only lasts for the duration of the private guardian's incapacity.

## 7. The reclassification of patients

### (a) Reclassification by the appropriate medical officer

Under s 16 MHA 1983, a patient's mental disorder may be reclassified by the appropriate medical officer. For a patient under private guardianship, the appropriate medical officer is the nominated medical attendant (s 16(5)(a) MHA 1983; see page 139). If a local social services authority is guardian, then the appropriate medical officer is the responsible medical officer, that is the medical officer authorised by the authority to act as such (s 16(5)(b) and s 34(1) MHA 1983; see page 38). In the case of a patient liable to be detained for assessment or treatment, the appropriate medical officer is the responsible medical officer, that is the registered medical practitioner in charge of the patient's treatment (s 16(5)(b) and s 34(1)(a) MHA 1983).

If it appears to the appropriate medical officer that a patient subject to detention or guardianship is suffering from a mental disorder other than the form or forms specified in the application, he/she *may* (not must) furnish a report to that effect to the managers of the hospital or to the guardian. However, before furnishing the report, he/she *must* consult with one or more persons who have been professionally concerned with the patient's medical treatment (s 16(3) MHA 1983). That person need not be medically qualified; he/she may, for example, be a social worker involved in the patient's case. When such a form is furnished, the original application will have effect as though the new form of mental disorder were specified in it. The managers of the hospital or the guardian must ensure that the patient and the nearest relative are informed that a report has been made (s 16(4) MHA 1983). An application to the Mental Health Review Tribunal ("MHRT") may be made by the patient or the nearest relative within twenty-eight days of receipt of the notice (s 66(1)(d) and (2)(d) MHA 1983; for MHRT see pages 111–137).

If the responsible medical officer in his/her report concludes that a patient detained in hospital is suffering from psychopathic disorder or mental impairment, he/she must include in the report a statement that further medical treatment in hospital is likely to alleviate or prevent deterioration of the patient's condition (for the treatability test see page 22). Where he/she reports that treatment is not likely to have that effect, the authority of the managers to detain the patient in hospital ceases (s 16(2) MHA 1983).

### (b) Reclassification by a Mental Health Review Tribunal

A Mental Health Review Tribunal has the jurisdiction under s 72(5) MHA 1983 to reclassify a patient's disorder when, upon any application under the MHA 1983, it does not direct that the patient be discharged. An MHRT may reclassify the disorder if it is satisfied that the patient is suffering from a form of disorder different from the form specified in the application, order or direction. It may direct that the application, order or direction be amended by substituting the new form of disorder. See Chapter 4 for MHRTs.

## 8. Transfer of patients

### (a) Introduction

A patient liable to be detained in a hospital may be transferred to another hospital, or into the guardianship of a local social services authority or a person approved by such an authority (s 19(1)(a) MHA 1983); a patient subject to the guardianship may be transferred to another guardian or transferred to a hospital (s 19(1)(b) MHA 1983). Additional provisions are found in s 10 MHA 1983 for the transfer of guardianship upon the death etc of the guardian, and in s 123 MHA for transfer to and from special hospitals (see pages 32 and 36). A patient may also be *de facto* transferred to another hospital through the leave of absence provisions (see page 40).

*(b) Transfer from hospital to hospital*

If it is necessary to transfer a patient to another hospital under the control of the same managers as the one in which he/she is currently detained, no special provisions apply. This is also the situation where the patient is detained in a mental nursing home and it is sought to transfer him/her to another one under the management of the same managers. The patient may be detained in the second hospital or mental nursing home and he/she will be treated as if he/she had been admitted to that hospital at the time of the original application (s 19(3) MHA 1983).

Rule 7(2) Mental Health (Hospital, Guardianship and Consent to Treatment) Regulations 1983 ("MHR 1983") provides that authority for a transfer of a patient to a hospital under different managers must be given by the managers of the hospital in which he/she is currently liable to be detained (Part 1 of Form 24 must be used). Those managers must be satisfied that arrangements have been made for the admission of the patient to the hospital to which he/she is being transferred within a period of twenty-eight days from the date of the authority for transfer. Part 2 of Form 24 must be used by the managers of the receiving hospital to record the patient's admission. Under s 19(2)(a) MHA 1983, the patient is to be treated as if he/she had been admitted to the receiving hospital on the date that he/she was originally admitted to the transferring one. Where the patient is detained in a mental nursing home and is maintained under a contract with a regional health authority, district health authority or a special health authority, the authority for transfer may be given by an officer of that health authority instead of by the managers (r 8(4)(b) MHR 1983).

Without prejudice to the above provisions, any patient who is for the time being liable to be detained in a special hospital (see page 72) other than under ss 35, 36 or 38 MHA 1983 (see pages 52, 54 and 60) may, upon the directions of the Secretary of State, be removed into any other special hospital. The Secretary of

State may also direct that a patient be transferred from a special hospital into an ordinary hospital; this power is without prejudice to the general powers of transfer. Section 19(2) and s 19(4) apply to both types of transfer. (See s 123(1)–(3) MHA 1983.)

### (c) Transfer from hospital to guardianship

A patient may be transferred from hospital to the guardianship of a local social services authority or any person approved by that authority. The managers of the hospital in which the patient is liable to be detained must provide authority for transfer in the form set out in Part 1 of Form 25. The local social services authority which will be responsible for the patient upon transfer must indicate on Part 2 of Form 25 that it has agreed to the transfer and must specify the date upon which it is to take place. Where the person named in the authority for transfer is other than a local social services authority, his/her agreement must be obtained and recorded on Part 3 of Form 25. (See r 7(3) MHR 1983.)

If the patient is being detained in a mental nursing home and is maintained under a contract with a regional health authority, district health authority or a special health authority, any authorisation for transfer may be given by an officer of that health authority instead of the managers (r 7(4)(b) MHR 1983).

### (d) Transfer from guardianship to hospital

This type of transfer involves a greater loss of liberty than those outlined above. Consequently, safeguards are needed to ensure that the patient's interests are not arbitrarily overridden. Before such a transfer can be made, it must be authorised by the responsible local social services authority in the form set out in Form 27. Authority can only be given where the following conditions have been satisfied:

(i) an application for admission for treatment has been made by an ASW on Form 9 (note that an ASW has a duty to consult the nearest relative in accordance with s 11(4) MHA 1983, and is also subject to the s 13 duty to make an application, as if the application were one for admission for treatment — see pages 5 and 21);

(ii) the application must be founded upon medical

recommendations given by two registered medical practitioners in accordance with s 12 MHA 1983 (see page 19);
(iii) the application has been accepted by the managers of the hospital to which it is addressed;
(iv) the responsible local social services authority is satisfied that arrangements have been made for the admission of the patient to that hospital within the period of fourteen days, beginning with the date of the authority for transfer;
(v) the responsible local social services authority has taken such steps as are practicable to inform the person (if any) appearing to be the patient's nearest relative of the patient's transfer.
(r 8(3) MHR 1983.)

The transfer must take place within fourteen days, beginning with the date on which the patient was last examined by a medical practitioner for the purposes of (ii) above. A record of admission to hospital must be made on Form 14 and attached to the application by the managers of the hospital to which the patient has been transferred. The original guardianship application is to be treated as if it were an application for admission for treatment, and as if the patient had been admitted to the hospital at the time of that application (s 19(2)(d) MHA 1983).

*(e) Transfer from guardianship to guardianship*

A patient subject to guardianship under Part II MHA 1983 may be transferred to the guardianship of another local social services authority or another person. Authority for the transfer must be given by the guardian, and it must be agreed by the local social services authority which will be the responsible one if the transfer is effected. Parts I and II of Form 26 must be used for these purposes. The receiving local social services authority must specify a date upon which the transfer is to take place. If the proposed new guardian is not a local social services authority, his/her agreement must be obtained and recorded in the form specified in Part III of Form 26 (see r 8(2) MHR 1983). For the purposes of MHA 1983, the new guardian is to be treated as though it were the authority or person mentioned in the original application (s 19(2)(c) MHA 1983).

## (f) Conveyance to hospital on transfer

Where a patient is to be transferred under r 7(2) or r 8(3) MHR 1983, the following persons are authorised to take the patient and convey him/her to the receiving hospital:

(i) transfer from hospital to hospital under r 7(2):
- an officer of the managers of either hospital;
- any person authorised by the managers of the receiving hospital;

(ii) transfer from guardianship to hospital under r 8(3):
- an officer of the responsible local social services authority;
- any person authorised by that authority.

(r 9(1)(a) and (b) MHR 1983.)

## 9. Discharge of patients

### (a) General power of discharge

A patient's liability to detention or subjection to guardianship will cease if a written order for discharge is made under s 23 MHA 1983. An order for the discharge of a patient detained in hospital under s 2 or s 3 MHA 1983 may be made by the responsible medical officer, the managers or the nearest relative of the patient. Where the patient is subject to guardianship, the order for discharge may be made by the responsible medical officer, the responsible local social services authority or the nearest relative of the patient. Where the power of discharge is conferred upon a body or authority, it can be exercised by three or more authorised members of that body or authority, or by three or more members of a committee or sub-committee authorised to exercise the power. (See s 23(2)(a) and (b) MHA 1983.)

The MHA 1983 does not specify the circumstances in which an order for discharge may be made; it is unnecessary to show that the original grounds no longer exist. In order to assist the nearest relative in the exercise of the power of discharge from detention or guardianship, any registered medical practitioner authorised on his/her behalf may, at any reasonable time, visit the patient and examine him/her in private. The medical practitioner may require that records relating to the detention or treatment of the patient in hospital should be produced and he/she has the authority to examine them. (See s 24(1) and (2) MHA 1983.)

## Hospital admission, guardianship and other civil procedures

Any order made by the nearest relative for the discharge of guardianship must be served upon the responsible local social services authority and may be in the form set out in Form 35 (see r 15(2) MHR 1983). If the nearest relative wishes to discharge a patient who is liable to be detained in hospital, he/she must give at least seventy-two hours' notice in writing to the managers of the hospital (see r 15(1) MHR 1983). The responsible medical officer may, within seventy-two hours of such notice being given, furnish a report to the managers that in his/her opinion the patient, if discharged, would be likely to act in a manner dangerous to himself/herself or to some other person. Where the responsible medical officer makes such a report, the order for discharge made by the nearest relative will be of no effect. For the forms to be used for such reports see r 15(3) MHR 1983. Moreover, the nearest relative is prevented from making another discharge order during a six month period beginning with the date of the report. (See s 25(1)(a) and (b) MHA 1983.)

Where a report by the responsible medical officer is made in respect of a patient who is detained under an application for admission for treatment, the managers must inform the nearest relative of that fact (s 25(2) MHA 1983). This is particularly important, as the nearest relative has the right to apply to an MHRT within twenty-eight days (see s 66(1)(g) and (2)(d) MHA 1983 and page 113). The nearest relative has no such right to apply to an MHRT if the patient is admitted for assessment.

Special provisions apply when a patient is liable to be detained in a mental nursing home for assessment or for treatment (see page 74). Without prejudice to s 23(1) MHA 1983, an order for discharge may be made by the Secretary of State and, if the patient is detained under a contract with a regional health authority, district health authority, or special health authority, by that authority. Where such an application is made, the following persons may visit and interview the patient:

(i) any registered medical practitioner authorised by the Secretary of State or, in the case of an application by one of the health authorities, by the authority;

(ii) any other person (whether a registered medical practitioner or not) authorised under Part II Registered Homes Act 1984 to inspect the home (see page 86).

(s 24 (3)(a) and (b) MHA 1983.)

The visit must take place at a reasonable time. If the visit is by a registered medical practitioner, he/she may examine the patient in private and may require the production of any documents, or inspect any records, relating to the treatment of the patient in the home. Any other visitor authorised under s 24(3) MHA 1983 may require the production of, and inspect, any documents which constitute, or are alleged to constitute, the authority for the patient's detention. (See s 24(4) MHA 1983.)

## 10. Absence from hospital

### (a) Leave of absence from hospital

The responsible medical officer may grant a patient leave of absence from the hospital in which he/she is liable to be detained under ss 2–5 MHA 1983. Such leave may be for a specified occasion (for example, to visit the shops or to attend a family function), or for an indefinite or specified period. Where it is granted for a specified period, it may be extended without the patient being required to return to the hospital. If the responsible medical officer considers it necessary in the interests of the patient or for the protection of others, he/she may impose conditions on the leave of absence. The conditions may vary. They may stipulate that the patient is to live at a specific address, or to stay in another hospital for the purpose of receiving a different type of treatment. Alternatively, they may require the patient to contact a named individual at specified times. However, the conditions may not impose greater restrictions on the patient than are available by virtue of the detention. Whilst the patient is on authorised leave of absence, he/she continues to be "liable to be detained" and therefore the consent to treatment provisions apply (see pages 91–96).

The responsible medical officer may, if necessary in the interests of the patient or for the protection of other persons, direct that the patient remains in custody during his/her absence (s 17(3) MHA 1983). Custody may be given to any officer of the hospital staff or any other person authorised in writing by the managers. Where the leave of absence is subject to a condition that the patient resides in another hospital, custody may be given to any officer on the staff of that other hospital (s 17(3) MHA 1983). This is important as it means that ss 137 and 138 MHA 1983 apply (see pages 16–17 but note s 18(1) MHA 1983 below). A custody condition may be included to enable the patient to make escorted visits away from the hospital (see DHSS Memorandum – Mental Health Act 1983, para 73).

Leave of absence may be revoked and the patient recalled by the

## Hospital admission, guardianship and other civil procedures

responsible medical officer if it appears to him/her that it is necessary for the "patient's health or safety or for the protection of other persons" (s 17(4) MHA 1983). The reference in this subsection is to "health and safety" rather than the "interests" of the patient (contrast with ss 17(1)–(3) MHA 1983). Written notice of the revocation must be given to the patient or to the person who is for the time being in charge of him/her. Under s 17(5) MHA 1983, a patient having leave of absence cannot be recalled after he/she has ceased to be liable to be detained under the Act. He/She will cease to be liable when the period of detention has expired (see pages 20 and 23); liability to detention will also cease when he/she has been on leave of absence for six months unless:

(i) he/she has returned to the hospital; or
(ii) he/she is absent without leave at the end of the six month period.

(s 17(5) MHA 1983.)

There developed a practice under which the patient's leave of absence was revoked immediately before the expiry of the six month period. The patient was then detained for a short period of time and then granted further leave of absence. This enabled practitioners to place the patient in the community but at the same time exercise the control over him/her that is not available under guardianship. However, in *R* v *Hallstrom, ex parte W; R* v *Gardner, ex parte L* (1986) the court reaffirmed that the power of revocation could only be used in the interests of the patient's health or safety or for the protection of others. It is unlawful to use this power as a means of defeating the six month provision of s 17(5) MHA 1983.

### (b) Absent without leave

A patient who is liable to be detained in hospital under Part II MHA 1983 is absent without leave if:

(i) he/she absents himself/herself from the hospital without leave under s 17 MHA 1983; or
(ii) fails to return to hospital upon the expiry of the period for which s 17 MHA 1983 leave was granted; or
(iii) fails to return to hospital after a notice under s 17(4) MHA 1983 has been issued; or
(iv) absents himself/herself from any place where he/she is

required to reside under a condition imposed on his/her s 17 MHA 1983 leave of absence.
(s 18(1)(a)–(c) MHA 1983.)

Such a patient may be returned to the hospital or place by an ASW, any officer on the staff of the hospital, a constable or any person authorised in writing by the managers of the hospital. Where the patient is required under a leave of absence condition to reside at another hospital, the references to an officer on the staff of the hospital and to the hospital managers include such personnel from that other hospital (s 18(2) MHA 1983). The power to return the patient exists whether or not leave of absence under s 17 was subject to a condition of custody. Special provisions apply where a person is liable to be taken into custody in England or Wales under s 18(1) MHA 1983 but is found in some other part of the United Kingdom, the Channel Islands or the Isle of Man. Constables of the police forces for those other parts of the British Isles have the same power as is given to English and Welsh forces by s 18(1) MHA 1983, and they may take the patient into custody and return him/her to England or Wales (s 88(1) and (2) MHA 1983). Furthermore, if the patient is found in Scotland or Northern Ireland, a mental health officer within the Mental Health (Scotland) Act 1984 and an approved social worker within the Mental Health (Northern Ireland) Order 1986 may exercise the power of an ASW to take the patient into custody under s 18(1) MHA 1983 (s 88(3) MHA 1983).

A patient subject to guardianship who absents himself/herself, without leave from the guardian, from the place where he/she is required by the guardian to reside, may be taken into custody under s 18(3) MHA 1983 and returned to that place. He/She may be taken into custody by any officer on the staff of a local authority, by any constable or by any person authorised in writing by the guardian or a local social services authority. However, the provisions of s 88 MHA 1983 which relate to patients found in other parts of the British Isles (see above) do not apply to guardianship (s 88(4) MHA 1983).

Subject to s 18(5) MHA 1983 which is considered below, a patient cannot be taken into custody under ss 18(1) or (3) MHA 1983 after the expiry of a period of twenty-eight days beginning with the first day of his/her absence without leave. If the patient has not returned, or been taken into custody, within that period he/she will cease to be liable to be detained or subject to guardianship even though the s 20 MHA 1983 period of time has not expired (s 18(4) MHA 1983; for s 20 see page 23). A new application will have to be made in respect of that patient. If

## Hospital admission, guardianship and other civil procedures

he/she is returned within that period, he/she will be liable to be detained or subject to guardianship until the s 20 period of time expires. If on the day (or within a week ending on the day) when detention or guardianship would normally cease under the provisions of the MHA 1983, the patient is absent without leave, he/she will remain liable to detention/guardianship:

(i) in any case until the expiry of the twenty-eight day period mentioned in s 18 MHA 1983 or the date of his/her return, whichever is the earlier; and

(ii) if he/she returns within the twenty-eight day period, for a further period of one week beginning with the day of return. (Note this extension also applies to a patient returning within a week ending on the date that authority ceases under s 20 MHA 1983 – his/her detention/guardianship may continue for a further seven days from the date of return even though that may exceed the normal duration of the authority.)

(s 21(1)(a) and (b) MHA 1983.)

The extended times of detention or guardianship provided for in s 21 MHA 1983 are designed to allow any examination or report under s 20(3) or s 20(6) MHA 1983 to be made and furnished (s 21(2) MHA 1983; for s 20 MHA 1983 see page 23). If authority for detention or guardianship is renewed by virtue of s 21 MHA 1983, it is treated as having commenced on the day that it would otherwise have expired under s 20, rather than on the date on which s 21 authority actually ceased (s 21(3) MHA 1983).

Special provision is made for those patients detained under ss 2, 4 and 5 MHA 1983. Such a patient cannot be taken into custody, even though the period of twenty-eight days has not elapsed, if the appropriate period specified in s 2(4) (twenty-eight days' admission for assessment), s 4(4) (seventy-two hours' emergency application), s 5(2) (seventy-two hours' doctor's holding power) or s 5(4) (six hours' nurse's holding power) has expired (s 18(5) MHA 1983).

It is an offence to induce or knowingly assist another person liable to be detained or subject to guardianship under the MHA 1983 to absent himself/herself without leave (s 128(1) MHA 1983). A person who knowingly harbours a patient who is absent without leave or is otherwise liable to be retaken under the MHA 1983 also commits an offence (s 128(2) MHA 1983).

## 11. Other powers which are available

*(a) Removal to suitable premises under the National Assistance Act 1948*

Under the National Assistance Act 1948 ("NAA 1948") a magistrates' court may make an order the effect of which is to authorise the transfer of a person to suitable premises for the purpose of securing necessary care and attention. This power may be exercised in respect of persons who:

(i) are suffering from grave chronic disease, or being aged, infirm or physically incapacitated, are living in insanitary conditions; and

(ii) are unable to devote themselves, and are not receiving from other persons, proper care and attention.

(s 47(1)(a) and (b) NAA 1948.)

Some persons suffering from mental disorders which do not come within the MHA 1983, and some persons with mental handicaps, may fall within the above definition. However, it must be stressed that the legal effect of admission under each Act is different, and that detention under the NAA 1948 does not attract powers and duties under the MHA 1983. This is particularly important when considering consent to treatment; the provisions of ss 56–64 MHA 1983 do not apply to persons detained under the NAA 1948 (for consent to treatment under MHA 1983 see pages 91–96).

An application for an order under the NAA 1948 should be made by the "appropriate authority" for the area in which the person is residing. Appropriate authorities for the purposes of the NAA 1948 are district councils, London boroughs and the Common Council of the City of London (s 47(12) NAA 1948). Before an application is made, a medical officer of health must certify in writing to the authority that, after thorough inquiry, he/she is satisfied that in the interests of a person to whom the section applies who is residing in its area, or of preventing injury to the health of, or serious nuisance to, other people, it is necessary to remove the person from the premises. The application must be made to the magistrates' court having jurisdiction over the place where the premises are situated. (See s 47(1) and (2) NAA 1948.)

If the court is satisfied on the oral evidence of the allegations in the certificate it may, if it considers it expedient, order the removal of the person to whom the application relates. An officer of the appropriate authority should be specified as the

## Hospital admission, guardianship and other civil procedures

individual responsible for carrying out the order. The person must be removed to a suitable hospital or other place specified in the order which is in, or within a convenient distance of, the area of the appropriate authority. The order gives authority for detention and maintenance of the person. However, before an order can be made, the person who manages the hospital or other suitable premises must have been heard at the hearing of the application or given seven clear days' notice of the time and place at which it is proposed to be made. (See s 47(3) NAA 1948.)

Orders under s 47(3) NAA 1948 may authorise the person's detention for up to three months; the court may from time to time extend the detention for a period not exceeding three months at a time (s 47(4) NAA 1948). No application for an order under s 47(3) or (4) NAA 1948 can be made by a court unless the person in respect of whom the application has been made, or some person who is in charge of him/her, has been given seven clear days' notice of the intended application and the time and venue (s 47(7)(a) NAA 1948). The court may vary the order so as to substitute for the place of detention named in an order another suitable place which is either in, or within convenient distance of, the appropriate authority's area (s 47(5) NAA 1948). Before such a variation, the person managing the proposed new place of detention must have been heard at the hearing or given seven clear days' notice of its time and location.

An application to the court for the revocation of a s 47(3) or (4) NAA 1948 order may be made six clear weeks after the date on which the order was made. Seven clear days' notice of the application and the time and venue at which it is proposed to be made must be given to the medical officer of health (s 47(7)(b) NAA 1948). The application may be made by, or on behalf of, the person specified in the order. Upon such an application the court may, if it considers it expedient to do so, revoke the order (s 47(6) NAA 1948).

The requirement to give notice of applications under s 47 NAA 1948 may lead to unacceptable delay in removing a person from unsuitable surroundings. To meet this problem, the National Assistance (Amendment) Act 1951 ("NA(A)A 1951") provides for an emergency application for a s 47(3) NAA 1948 order. Emergency applications may be made by the appropriate authority, or by the medical officer of health if he/she is authorised to make such applications by that authority. Under s 1(1) NA(A)A 1951, the notice required under s 47(7) NAA 1948 is waived if a medical officer of health and another registered medical practitioner certify that in their opinions it is necessary

45

to remove the person without delay. It is also unnecessary to give the seven days' notice of the application to the manager of the intended place of detention if he/she agrees to accommodate the person. An application may be heard by a full magistrates' court for the area in which the person resides, or by a single justice for that area. Orders may be made *ex parte* if the court considers that it is necessary. The provisions of s 47 NAA 1948 apply to emergency orders, except that the three month duration of the order (s 47(4) NAA 1948) is replaced by a period of three weeks. An application for revocation of an emergency order cannot be made. (See s 1(4) NA(A)A 1951.)

## 12. Provisions relating to children

### (a) Care and supervision proceedings

The power of the courts to make hospital orders and guardianship orders under s 1(3)(d) and (e) Children and Young Persons Act 1969 has been repealed by the Children Act 1989 ("CA 1989"). A significant part of the CA 1989 deals with preventive action that can be taken by local authorities in partnership with parents, other professionals and voluntary organisations. These are considered in greater detail in Chapter 5. However, the CA 1989 retains the power of the court to make care or supervision orders in respect of children who have not yet reached the age of seventeen years, or sixteen years in the case of a child who is married (s 31(1)(a),(b) and (3) CA 1989).

Section 92 (7) CA 1989 provides that care proceedings may be brought in the High Court, county court or magistrates' court. The Lord Chancellor may by order specify particular courts for certain types of proceedings. Rules may also be made permitting family proceedings to be commenced in the same court as any proceedings under the CA 1989 which are already in progress. (See Sch 11 Part I para 1(1) – (3) CA 1989.)

When determining any question concerning the child's upbringing, the court must regard the child's welfare as the paramount consideration (s 1(1) CA 1989). Regard must be had to the prejudicial effect of delay; particular regard must be had to the following matters:

(i) the ascertainable wishes and feelings of the child (considered in the light of age and understanding);

(ii) his/her physical, emotional and educational needs;
(iii) the likely effect of any change in circumstances;
(iv) his/her age, sex, background and any characteristics which the court considers relevant;
(v) any harm which he/she has suffered or is at risk of suffering;
(vi) how capable each of his/her parents, and any other person in relation to whom the court considers the question to be relevant, is of meeting his/her needs;
(vii) the range of powers available to the court under the CA 1989.

(s 1(3)(a)–(g) CA 1989.)

The court shall not make an order unless it considers that to do so would be better for the child than making no order at all (s 1(5) CA 1989).

Applications for care proceedings may be made by any local authority or by an authorised person (the NSPCC or person authorised by the Secretary of State). If the application is made by an authorised person it must, if practicable to do so, consult the local authority in whose area the child is ordinarily resident (s 31(6) CA 1989). An application by an authorised person will not be entertained by the court if the child is subject to an earlier application which has not been disposed of, or is already subject to a valid care or supervision order (s 31(7) CA 1989). When hearing an application for a care or supervision order, the court must have regard to the general principle that any delay is likely to prejudice the welfare of the child. A timetable should be drawn up by the court which may give such directions as are appropriate for ensuring that it is adhered to (s 32(1) CA 1989). Rules of court may be made specifying periods within which certain steps must be taken, and ensuring that the proceedings are disposed of without delay (s 32(2) CA 1989).

The court may only make a care or supervision order if satisfied:
(a) "that the child concerned is suffering, or is likely to suffer, significant harm; and
(b) that the harm, or likelihood of harm, is attributable to –
  (i) the care given to the child, or likely to be given to him if the order were not made, not being what it would be reasonable to expect a parent to give to him; or
  (ii) the child's being beyond parental control."

The grounds upon which an order can be made are wide. They encompass the child who is sexually abused or subject to other forms of physical abuse or neglect. In addition, they may also include children whose home environment threatens their mental health in a situation where community support is inadequate. "Harm" in s 31(2) CA 1989 is defined as including "ill treatment or the impairment of health or development". "Ill treatment" includes acts which are not physical, for example mental cruelty. "Development" means physical, intellectual, emotional, social or behavioural development. "Health" means both physical and mental health. (See s 31(9) CA 1989.)

Where the question of whether the child has suffered significant harm is dependent upon his/her health or development, the court must compare his/her health or development with that "which could reasonably be expected of a similar child" (see s 31(10) CA 1989). The reference to a "similar child" must be to one of a level of health or development which the child in question would, but for treatment in the home environment, have been expected to achieve. Thus if the child has become over-anxious or neurotic as a result of mental cruelty on the part of the carers, his/her health or development will be compared with that of a child who has not been subjected to such conduct. In the case of a child with, for example, a mental handicap, the comparison must be made with a child having a similar handicap in order to see whether his/her health or development has been impaired as a consequence of the home environment. Attention can, therefore, be focused on whether the special needs that such a child may need to foster his/her health or development are being suitably catered for. This point is echoed in the wording of s 31(2) CA 1989 which refers to a standard of care below "what it would be reasonable to expect a parent to give him". Regard will be had to the standard of care expected of parents with children having special needs as a consequence of mental disorder or mental handicap.

Applications to the court for variation or discharge may be made by the person having parental responsibility for the child, or by the child himself/herself. The designated local authority may also apply for the variation or discharge of a care order, as may the supervisor in the case of a supervision order.

## (b) Care orders

Discussion in this section is focused on care orders, while in Chapter 5 the powers of a local authority to look after a child are considered. If a care order is made in respect of a child, it is the duty of the local authority designated to receive the child to keep him/her in care as long as the order remains in force (s 33(1) CA 1989). In cases where the application has been made by an authorised person and the designated authority has not been informed under s 31(6) CA 1989, the child may be kept in that person's care until received into care by the authority (s 33(2) CA 1989). The designated authority has parental responsibility over the child for as long as he/she is in care, and has the power, subject to the welfare principle, to determine the extent to which a parent/guardian may meet parental responsibility (s 33(4) and (5) CA 1989).

However, the authority may not cause the child to be brought up in a religious creed different from the one he/she would have been brought up in if the order had not been made. Nor may it give or refuse consent to the making of an application or order under ss 18 or 55 Adoption Act 1976. The authority cannot appoint a guardian for the child. (See s 33(6) CA 1989.)

The CA 1989 encourages continued contact between a child in care and his/her parents or former carers. Before making a care order, the court must consider the arrangements which have been made or are proposed by the authority regarding contact with the child. Parties to the proceedings should be invited to comment on the arrangements (s 34(11) CA 1989). Where a care order has been made, the local authority should normally allow the child reasonable contact with his/her parents, guardian, a person in whose favour a residence order was made under s 8 CA 1989, or a person given care of the child in wardship proceedings (s 34(1) CA 1989). Any of these people, or anybody else who has the leave of the court, may apply to the court for an order with respect to contact which is to be allowed between him/her and the child. The local authority or the child may also apply to the court for an order with respect to contact between a named person and the child (s 34(3) CA 1989). Upon an application under s 34(3), the court may make an order authorising the authority to refuse to allow contact between the child and any person mentioned in s 34(1) (s 34(4) CA 1989). In cases of urgency, and where necessary to safeguard the welfare of the child, the authority may refuse contact that would otherwise be required by virtue of s 34(1). This can only be done in a real emergency. Such refusal may not last more than seven days. If a longer period is thought necessary, an application under s 34(2) should be made. Any order under s 34 may impose such conditions as the court considers appropriate. These may include, for example, conditions as to time of contact and whether or not it should be supervised (s 34(10) CA 1989). Orders under s 34 may be made either at the same time as the care order itself or later (s 34(10) CA 1989).

An order authorising the authority to refuse to allow a child contact with any of the persons mentioned in s 34(1) CA 1989 may be made only if the court considers it necessary to do so to promote the child's welfare. The refusal order may be subject to such conditions as the court considers appropriate (for example, a time limit). The Secretary of State may make regulations relating to the use of s 34(6) by an authority. He/She may also make regulations regarding the circumstances in which an order under s 34 can be departed from by the authority (s 34(8) CA 1989).

Orders made under s 34 CA 1989 may be varied or discharged by the court. Applications may be made by the person in whose favour it was made, the authority or the child concerned (s 34(9) CA 1989).

The provisions of ss 23, 24 and Sch 2 Part II CA 1989 relating to the placement of a child being looked after by an authority apply when the child is subject to a care order (see page 152). However, if the child is subject to a care order, the authority has a duty to provide accommodation for him/her (s 23(1)(a) CA 1989). Furthermore, the authority may not allow such a child to live with his/her parent or a person having responsibility for him/her except in accordance with regulations made by the Secretary of State (s 23(5) CA 1989). It is envisaged that the regulations will follow closely the Charge and Control Regulations under the Children and Young Persons Act 1969.

*(c) Supervision orders*

A supervision order places the child under the supervision of a designated local authority or probation officer. Supervisors have the duty to advise, assist and befriend the supervised child. If the supervision order is not wholly complied with, or if the supervisor considers that the order may no longer be necessary, he/she may apply to the court for variation (s 35(1)(c) CA 1989). As supervision orders involve care within the community, they are considered in greater detail in Chapter 5 (see page 156).

*Hospital admission, guardianship and other civil procedures*

## (d) The nearest relative

Special provisions apply when determining the nearest relative of a child or young person in the care of a local authority by virtue of a care order under the CA 1989. Section 27 MHA 1983, as amended by the CA 1989, states that the authority is deemed to be the nearest relative in preference to any person except a spouse. Where a guardian has been appointed under the CA 1989 (not a guardian under the MHA 1983), or where a residence order under s 8 CA 1989 is in force, the nearest relative of the child will be the guardian or the person named in the residence order, whichever is appropriate. (See s 28(3) and (4) MHA 1983 as amended by CA 1989.)

# Chapter 2

# Admission through the criminal process

## 1. Remand to hospital under the Mental Health Act 1983

*(a) Remand for report*

If the Crown Court or a magistrates' court decides that bail is inappropriate it may, subject to the following conditions, remand the accused person to hospital for a report on his/her mental condition (s 35 MHA 1983). For the purposes of this provision, an accused person is:

(a) in the case of the Crown Court

– any person awaiting trial before the court for an offence punishable with imprisonment; or

– any person who has been arraigned before the court for an offence punishable with imprisonment who has not been sentenced or otherwise dealt with for that offence;

(b) in the case of the magistrates' court

– any person who has been convicted by the court for an offence punishable on summary conviction with imprisonment;

– any person charged with such an offence if the court is satisfied that he/she did the act or omission charged, but it has not convicted him/her, or he/she has consented to the exercise of the power.

(s 35(2)(a) and (b) MHA 1983.)

Any person who has been convicted by a court of an offence the sentence for which is fixed by law will not be regarded as an accused person for the purposes of s 35 MHA 1983, for example a person who has been convicted of murder by a court will be

## Admission through the criminal process

outside the section as he/she will receive the mandatory life sentence. If he/she has been charged but not yet convicted of murder, the provisions of s 35 will apply. The reference to offences punishable on summary conviction with imprisonment includes a person under twenty-one years of age even though there may be a statutory prohibition or restriction on actually imprisoning him/her (s 55(2) MHA 1983).

A hospital means any health service hospital within the meaning of the National Health Service Act 1977 and any accommodation provided by a local authority and used by it as a hospital or used on behalf of the Secretary of State (s 145(1) MHA 1983). In addition, the definition also includes a mental nursing home which stated in its application for registration that it intends to admit persons detained under the MHA 1983. That fact must be specified in the certificate of registration; in addition it will be entered in a separate part of the register by the Secretary of State. (See s 55(5) MHA 1983 and s 23(5) RHA 1984 – see page 79.)

Before it can remand an accused person to hospital, the court must receive either written or oral evidence from a registered medical practitioner approved by the Secretary of State under s 12 MHA 1983 (s 54(1) MHA 1983; for s 12 MHA 1983 see page 12). Where written evidence is presented, it may be received in evidence without proof of signature or requisite qualifications or authority. However, the court may require the practitioner to be called to give oral evidence (see s 55(2)(a) MHA 1983). On the basis of this evidence the court must be satisfied that there is reason to suspect that the accused person is suffering from mental illness, psychopathic disorder, severe mental impairment or mental impairment (for the definition of these, see pages 1–3). In addition, the court must be satisfied that it would be impracticable for a report on his/her mental condition to be made if he/she were remanded on bail (see s 35(3)(a) and (b) MHA 1983). It is important to note the requirement to show that bail would render the making of a report impracticable; the use of s 35 is not to be regarded as an alternative to bail.

Before it can make a remand, the court must be satisfied on the basis of written or oral evidence that arrangements have been made for the accused person's admission to a hospital within seven days beginning with the day of remand. This evidence must be provided by the registered medical practitioner responsible for making the report or by some other person who represents the management of the hospital. The remand order empowers a constable, or any other person directed by the court, to take the accused person to the specified hospital within seven days beginning with the date of remand. If the person is not going to be admitted immediately, the court may give directions for him/her to be taken to and detained in a place of safety but for not longer than that seven-day period. Place of safety means any police station, prison, remand centre or hospital the managers of which are willing temporarily to take him/her (s 35(4) and s 55(1) MHA 1983). The managers of the hospital must admit the accused person and detain him/her in accordance with the provisions of the order (s 35(9) MHA 1983).

The initial period of remand is up to twenty-eight days, but this may be extended by further periods of twenty-eight days up to a maximum of twelve weeks (s 35(7) MHA 1983). The further periods of remand are only available if, on the basis of written or oral evidence of the registered medical practitioner responsible for making the report, it appears to the court that a further remand is necessary for completing the assessment. A further remand may be ordered without the accused person being in court if he/she is represented by counsel or a solicitor who is given the opportunity of being heard. (See s 35(6) and (7) MHA 1983.)

Remand is for a specific purpose, namely reporting on his/her mental condition. It does not imply authority to treat the accused person for any mental condition that may be discovered, and the consent to treatment provisions of Part IV MHA 1983 do not apply (s 56(1)(b) MHA 1983; for consent to treatment see pages 91–96). Once the purpose of remand has been achieved, it should cease and any further detention must be justified on another basis. Consequently, under s 35(7) MHA 1983, the court may terminate the remand at any time if it is appropriate to do so; once a hospital has finished its report the case should be taken back to the court. It is open to the accused person to obtain, at his/her own expense, an independent report on his/her mental condition from a registered medical practitioner and use it as the basis for his/her remand to be terminated (s 35(8) MHA 1983). However, the accused person will be subject to the order until terminated by the court. This means that he/she will be liable to be arrested without warrant by a constable if he/she absconds. If arrested, he/she must be brought before the remanding court which may deal with him/her as if no order under s 35 had been made (s 35(10) MHA 1983).

*(b) Remand for treatment*

Section 36 MHA 1983 enables a Crown Court to remand a person

## Admission through the criminal process

to hospital for treatment as an alternative to remanding him/her in custody. Before doing so, the court must be satisfied on the written or oral evidence of two registered medical practitioners that he/she is suffering from mental illness or severe mental impairment of a nature or degree which makes detention in hospital for medical treatment appropriate (s 36(1) MHA 1983; for mental illness and severe mental impairment see pages 1−3). At least one of the practitioners must be approved for the purposes of s 12(2) MHA 1983 by the Secretary of State (see page 19). Written evidence may be received in evidence without proof of signature or requisite qualification. The court may require the signatory to give oral evidence (s 54(2) MHA 1983). As with s 35 remands, the court must be satisfied on the basis of evidence (written or oral) from the registered medical practitioner who would be responsible for treatment, or from the managers of the hospital, that arrangements have been made to admit the accused person within seven days beginning with the date of remand. The same arrangements apply for taking him/her to a place of safety within that seven day period (s 36(3) MHA 1983; see s 35(4) at page 54). Similarly, the same definition of hospital applies to s 36 MHA 1983 (see page 53). Subsections 35(9) and (10) MHA 1983 also apply to remands for treatment under s 36 MHA 1983 (s 36(8) MHA 1983).

The section applies only to accused persons who are in custody awaiting trial before the Crown Court for an offence punishable by imprisonment, and to persons detained in custody during a trial for such an offence at any time before their being sentenced. The section does not apply to offences the penalty for which is fixed by law. The rationale for excluding the offence of murder is that a decision to remand for treatment may well prejudice any decision on the accused person's sanity. (See s 36(2) MHA 1983.)

Remands for treatment may only be made for a period of twenty-eight days. However, further twenty-eight day remands may be made by the court up to a maximum of twelve weeks in total. Further remands may be made without the accused person being in court if he/she is represented by a solicitor or counsel who is given the opportunity of being heard at the hearing. The court may terminate the remand at any time that it considers appropriate to do so. The accused person may, at his/her own expense, obtain an independent medical report which may form the basis of the court's order to terminate the remand. (See s 36(4) −(7) MHA 1983.)

## 2. Hospital orders and guardianship orders

*(a) Orders upon conviction in the Crown Court or magistrates' court*

Both the Crown Court and the magistrates' court have the power to make a hospital admission order or guardianship order in respect of a person convicted of an offence. In the case of the magistrates, it must be an offence punishable on summary conviction with imprisonment (note that any restrictions or prohibitions on imprisoning young offenders do not apply to the exercise of this power − see s 55(2) MHA 1983). This power cannot be used if the person is convicted of an offence the sentence for which is fixed by law (see s 37(1) MHA 1983). Where the court makes a hospital order or guardianship order, it cannot also pass a sentence of imprisonment, impose a fine or make an order under s 7(7)(b) or (c) Children and Young Persons Act 1969 (s 7(7) refers to the court's powers to make supervision orders in respect of children convicted in criminal proceedings). It can, however, make other orders such as compensation orders under s 35 Powers of the Criminal Courts Act 1973 (s 37(8) MHA 1983).

The court may exercise its power if it is satisfied on the written or oral evidence of two registered medical practitioners that the offender is suffering from mental illness, psychopathic disorder, severe mental impairment or mental impairment (for the definition of mental disorder etc, see pages 1−3) and that either:

(i) the mental disorder is of a nature or degree which makes it appropriate for him/her to be detained in hospital for medical treatment and, in the case of psychopathic disorder or mental impairment such treatment is likely to alleviate or prevent a deterioration of his/her condition (for the "treatability test", see page 22); or

(ii) in the case of an offender who has attained the age of sixteen years, the mental disorder is of a degree which warrants his/her reception into guardianship under the MHA 1983; and

the court is of the opinion that the most suitable way of dealing with him/her is by an order under s 37 MHA 1983 (s 37(2) MHA 1983).

The provisions of s 54 MHA 1983 apply to the giving of the medical evidence in the same way that they apply to s 36 MHA 1983 (see page 55). Under s 37(7) MHA 1983, the order must specify the form of mental disorder upon which it is based; both medical practitioners must agree that the offender is suffering from the same form of mental disorder whether or not he/she is also found by one of them to be suffering from an additional form.

In determining the most suitable way of dealing with the offender, the court must have regard to all the circumstances of the case. These include the nature of the offence, the character and antecedents of the offender and alternative methods of dealing with him/her. One important point to note under s 37 MHA 1983 is that the making of a hospital or guardianship order by the court need not be in any way related to the offence with which he/she has been convicted (see *R* v *McBride* (1972)). The court only has to address its mind to whether such an order would be a suitable way of dealing with the offender.

In the case of a hospital order, the court must be satisfied on the basis of oral or written evidence of the registered medical practitioner who would be in charge of treatment, or a representative of the managers of the hospital, that arrangements will be made for admission within twenty-eight days of an order being made. It may request a regional health authority for such information as it has, or may reasonably obtain, with regard to hospitals within its area or elsewhere at which arrangements could be made. Normally the request is directed to the health authority for the region in which the offender resides or last resided; however, it may be addressed to any other health authority which the court considers to be appropriate (for example, an authority for a region in which the offender's relatives live). In Wales the request is directed to the Secretary of State for Wales. The health authority and the Secretary of State for Wales must comply with the request (s 39 MHA 1983). Pending admission within that period, he/she may be taken to a place of safety (s 37(4) MHA 1983; for place of safety see page 54). Problems may arise if, within that twenty-eight day period, the hospital bed ceases to be available to the person subject to the order. Two courses of action are available. Firstly, the Secretary of State may, in cases of emergency or where there are special circumstances, direct that the patient be taken to another hospital (s 37(5) MHA 1983). The person having custody must be informed of the decision. The hospital specified in the direction will be substituted for the one in the original order. Alternatively, the offender can be taken back to the court for a variation of sentence (see s 11(2) Courts Act 1971 and s 142 Magistrates' Courts Act 1980). The Crown Court must direct a prison governor, whose prison is used as a place of safety for an offender, to inform the court if it becomes apparent that the hospital place will not be available on the expiry of twenty-eight days. If it becomes so apparent within the first twenty-one days, the court must be informed within that period; if it becomes apparent after twenty-one days, the court must be informed immediately. The offender can then be brought before the court for re-sentencing. (See Home Office Circular No 66/1980.) Unless one of these courses of action is taken, the offender ceases to be liable to detention at the end of the twenty-eight day period.

Guardianship orders cannot be made unless the court is satisfied that either a local social services authority or an individual is prepared to act as guardian. If the local social services authority is not going to act as guardian, it must approve the person whom the court proposes to appoint. (See s 37(1) and (6) MHA 1983.)

## (b) Orders made where there has not been a conviction

Magistrates' courts have the power to make a hospital or guardianship order without convicting the person charged if they are satisfied that he/she did the act charged. This power is only available if the court could have made an order under s 37(1) MHA 1983 if he/she had been convicted of the offence (s 37(3) MHA 1983). Unlike orders made upon conviction, this power is limited to persons suffering from mental illness or severe mental impairment. As seen at page 186, the magistrates cannot make a finding of disability under s 4 Criminal Procedure (Insanity) Act 1964. If they consider that the person is not fit to stand trial by virtue of mental illness or severe mental impairment, they may make a hospital or guardianship order under s 37(3) MHA 1983, provided they are satisfied he/she did the act. It should be noted that guardianship orders cannot be made under s 4 Criminal Procedure (Insanity) Act 1964, so in this respect the magistrates' powers of disposal are wider.

In *R* v *Lincoln (Kesteven) Magistrates' Court, ex parte O'Connor* (1983), the Divisional Court held that a trial is not necessary before a s 37(3) MHA 1983 order can be made. The accused in this case was charged with assault occasioning actual bodily harm, which is triable either summarily or upon indictment. He was unable to consent to summary trial, so the magistrates committed him to the Crown Court. The Crown Court could have considered his fitness to plead under s 4 Criminal Procedure (Insanity) Act 1964. However, the Divisional Court said that the magistrates in this situation had the power to make a hospital or guardianship order even though there had been no trial.

## Admission through the criminal process

Consequently, s 20 Magistrates' Courts Act 1980 does not apply and an order may be made even though the accused person has not consented to a summary trial. The logic of the *O'Connor* case was applied in *R v Ramsgate Justices, ex parte Kazmarek* (1984). Here, the accused person elected for trial by jury in a case which was triable either way. The Divisional Court held that, even in these circumstances, the magistrates could have made a hospital or guardianship order; the fact that the magistrates had the case before them was sufficient to give rise to the possibility of using s 37 MHA.

There is some doubt whether the magistrates have the power to make an order under s 37 MHA 1983 if the offence is only triable on indictment. In *Kazmarek*, the Divisional Court left this question open. The wording of s 37(3) MHA 1983 suggests that no such power exists. It refers to the court being able to make an order without conviction in respect of a person charged with an offence where it would "have power, on convicting him of that offence, to make an order" under s 37(1) MHA 1983. If the offence is triable only on indictment, the magistrates' court has neither the potential nor the actual power to convict the accused, which means that one of the conditions of s 37(3) MHA 1983 has not been satisfied.

### (c) The legal effects of hospital and guardianship orders

A hospital order is sufficient authority for a constable, approved social worker or other specified person to convey the patient to the specified hospital within twenty-eight days of the order being made. The managers of the hospital have authority to admit him/her within that period and detain him/her in accordance with the provisions of the MHA 1983. (See s 40(1)(a) and (b) MHA 1983.)

Guardianship orders confer upon the named guardian or local authority the same powers as guardianship applications made under Part II MHA 1983 (s 40(2) MHA 1983; for guardianship powers see pages 30–33). A hospital order or guardianship order means that any earlier such order or application under Part II MHA 1983 will cease to have effect. However, if the order is quashed on appeal, the earlier order or application is deemed to continue in force (s 40(5) MHA 1983).

In most respects a person subject to a hospital or guardianship order is treated in the same manner as his/her counterpart under Part II of the MHA 1983 (for Part II MHA 1983, see pages 17–24). However, the MHA 1983 does contain special provisions concerning the jurisdiction of MHRTs (for the jurisdiction of MHRTs, see pages 111–137). In the case of a person subject to a hospital order, the patient or the nearest relative may apply to an MHRT between six months and twelve months after the making of the order, and thereafter during each subsequent period of twelve months (ss 66(1)(f), 69(1)(a) and Sch 1 para 9 MHA 1983). A patient subject to a guardianship order may apply within a period of six months beginning with the date of the order. His/Her nearest relative cannot discharge the patient but may apply to an MHRT within twelve months beginning with the date of the order, and in each subsequent period of twelve months (s 69(b)(i) and (ii) MHA 1983).

## 3. Interim hospital orders

A court may be undecided whether to make a hospital order because it cannot predict how the person will react to hospital treatment. In such circumstances, an interim hospital order under s 38 MHA 1983 may be made so that the person can be assessed with a view to determining whether a full hospital order is appropriate. Once a full hospital order is made, the court ceases to have any control of the person, and if it transpires that hospitalisation is inappropriate there is no power to substitute a sentence of imprisonment. The availability of interim orders avoids this problem. An interim order may be made by the Crown Court where the person is convicted of an offence punishable with imprisonment other than where the sentence is fixed by law. A magistrates' court may make an order if the person is convicted of an offence punishable on summary conviction with imprisonment; this includes a person under twenty-one years even though there may be a statutory prohibition or restriction on actual imprisonment (s 55(2) MHA 1983).

Before an interim order can be made, the court must be satisfied on the written or oral evidence of two registered medical practitioners that:

(a) the offender is suffering from mental illness, psychopathic disorder, severe mental impairment or mental impairment; and

(b) there is reason to suppose that the mental disorder is such that it *may* be appropriate for a hospital order to be made.

(s 38(1)(a) and (b) MHA 1983.)

The exploratory nature of an interim order is emphasised by the

## Admission through the criminal process

use of the word "may". At least one of the medical practitioners must be employed by the hospital which is specified in the court order and at least one must be approved by the Secretary of State under s 12 MHA 1983 (see page 19). Where written evidence is presented, it may be received in evidence without proof of signature or relevant qualifications. However, the court may require the practitioner to attend and give oral evidence (s 55(2)(a) MHA 1983). The nature of the medical evidence differs from that required for a remand for report under s 35 MHA 1983. Under s 35 MHA 1983, the court must be satisfied that *there is reason to suspect* that the accused is suffering from a particular form of mental disorder; section 38 MHA is much less speculative and requires the court to be satisfied that the offender *is suffering* from a particular form of mental disorder.

In addition, the court must be satisfied that arrangements have been made for the admission of the offender to a named hospital within twenty-eight days beginning with the date of the order. It must base this decision on the written or oral evidence of the registered medical practitioner who will be in charge of the offender if an order is made, or of a representative of the managers of the hospital, that arrangements have been made for admission (s 38(4) MHA 1983). If the court is considering an interim order, the provisions of s 39 MHA 1983 apply in the same way that they apply to hospital orders (see page 57). Where the court is satisfied that arrangements have been made, it may give directions that the offender be conveyed to a place of safety pending admission to hospital (for place of safety, see page 54). A constable, or other person directed to do so by the court, must convey the offender to the specified hospital within the time mentioned in the order. The managers of the hospital have authority to detain the offender subject to the provisions of the section (s 40(3) MHA 1983). If the offender absconds whilst in hospital or whilst being conveyed to or from it, he/she may be arrested without warrant by a constable. Upon arrest, he/she should be brought as soon as practicable before the court which made the interim order. The court has the discretion to terminate the interim order and deal with the offender in any way it could have dealt with him/her if the order had not been made (s 38(7) MHA 1983).

An interim order remains in force for not longer than twelve weeks but may be renewed for further periods of twenty-eight days up to a total duration of detention of six months. The court may only renew if it appears on the written or oral evidence of the responsible medical officer that continuation is warranted.

Renewals may be ordered without the offender being brought before the court if he/she is represented by a solicitor or counsel who is given the opportunity of being heard. As an interim order is designed to assess the suitability of the offender for hospital detention, it follows that once it is shown that it is unsuitable the *raison d'être* for the order disappears. Therefore, the court can terminate the order at any time after hearing evidence from the responsible medical officer that the offender should be dealt with in some other way. Upon termination of the order, the court may impose such available penalty as it thinks fit. If, however, it is concluded that hospital treatment would be beneficial and appropriate, the court must terminate the interim order and replace it with a hospital order. An interim order may be replaced by a hospital order without the offender being brought before the court provided he/she is represented by counsel or a solicitor who is given the opportunity of being heard. (See s 38(2), (5) and (6) MHA 1983.)

## 4. Restriction orders

### (a) The power to impose a restriction order

Under s 41 MHA 1983, the Crown Court when making a hospital order may make a further order that the offender is to be subject to special restrictions referred to as a "restriction order". A restriction order may be without limitation of time or for a period specified in the order. (See s 41(1) MHA 1983.)

The power to make restriction orders is not available to the magistrates' court but, as will be seen below, that court may commit an offender to the Crown Court for a restriction order. A normal hospital order places the offender in almost the same position he/she would have been in if admitted under Part II MHA 1983 (see page 17). This means that the period of detention is determined not by the court but by the MHRT or the responsible medical officer (see pages 38 and 111). Whereas in many cases this is perfectly proper, there may be situations which require the imposition of restrictions on the right to discharge the offender. Section 41 MHA 1983 enables the court to impose such restrictions.

In deciding whether or not to make a restriction order, the court must have regard to the nature of the offence, the antecedents of the offender and the risk of him/her committing further offences if discharged from hospital. Taking these factors into consideration, the court must then determine whether it is necessary "for the protection of the public from serious harm" to impose a restriction order (s 41(1) MHA 1983). This is an important limitation on the use of restriction orders. In *R v Birch* (1989), Mustill LJ said that the word "serious" qualified the harm to the public rather than the risk of the offender committing further offences. The harm need not be restricted to personal injury, nor need it relate to the public in general. It would be sufficient if only a single member of the public were thought to be in danger. The potential harm must be serious; a high possibility of a recurrence of minor offences is insufficient. A restriction order cannot be imposed simply because the offender would, if released, be a social nuisance or a pest; therefore, because of the introduction of the serious harm condition, the cases of *R v Toland* (1973) and *R v Eaton* (1976), which indicate the contrary, would be decided differently today. The Court of Appeal has held that where a hospital order with a restriction order without time limit is the appropriate method of dealing with an offender, a judge should not impose a sentence of life imprisonment if a bed is available in a secure hospital (*R v Howell* (1985) and *R v Mbatha* (1985)).

If a person is found not guilty by reason of insanity, or found to be under a disability under the Criminal Procedure (Insanity) Act 1964, he/she will be treated as if he/she were subject to a hospital order together with a restriction order without limitation of time (s 5(1) and Sch 1 para 2(1) Criminal Procedure (Insanity) Act 1964 – see pages 175 and 186). Under s 46 MHA 1983, the Secretary of State may direct that any person who is required to be kept in custody during Her Majesty's pleasure by virtue of an order from a court martial, or an appeal from such a court, may be detained in a specified hospital other than a mental nursing home (see s 16 Courts Martial (Appeals) Act 1968, s 116 Army Act 1955, s 116 Air Force Act 1955 and s 63 Naval Discipline Act 1957). A s 46 direction shall have the same effect as a hospital order with a restriction order without limitation of time, and the person will be treated as having been admitted on the date of the direction.

*(b) The legal consequences of a restriction order*

A number of restrictions are imposed as a consequence of a restriction order. The provisions in Part II MHA 1983 which relate to the duration, renewal and expiry of the authority to detain a patient do not apply if there is a restriction order (see pages 17 and 38). The patient remains liable to be detained by virtue of the hospital order until discharged under s 23 MHA 1983 as amended (see below), or under ss 42, 73, 74 or 75 (see below). The nearest relative cannot apply to the MHRT (s 41(3)(b) MHA 1983). A restricted patient may apply to the MHRT between the end of six months and the end of twelve months beginning with the date of the order; thereafter he/she may apply in any subsequent period of twelve months (s 70 MHA 1983; see below). While a person is subject to a restriction order, the responsible medical officer must examine him/her at such intervals, not exceeding one year, as the Secretary of State may direct. The report of the examination must be given to the Secretary of State (s 41(6) MHA 1983).

Certain powers are only exercisable with the consent of the Secretary of State. These are the power to grant leave of absence (s 17 MHA 1983 – see page 40); the power to transfer a patient (s 19 MHA 1983 – see page 34) and the power to order the discharge of the patient under s 23 MHA 1983 (see page 38). If leave of absence is given under s 17 MHA 1983, the power of recalling the patient lies with the Secretary of State as well as the responsible medical officer. The power of the Secretary of State to recall a restricted patient who is on leave of absence, and the associated power to take such a person into custody (see s 18 MHA 1983 – page 41), may be exercised at any time.

An essential requirement for a restriction order is that it is necessary for the protection of the public from serious harm. If the Secretary of State is satisfied that the patient is no longer such a threat, he/she may direct that the order shall cease to have effect; the relevant hospital order will continue, however, and s 40 applies as if that order had been made on the date of the discharge of the restriction order (s 42(1) and s 41(5) MHA 1983). Alternatively, the Secretary of State may, if he/she thinks fit, discharge the patient from hospital, either conditionally or absolutely (s 42(2) MHA 1983).

Where the discharge is absolute, the patient will cease to be liable to be detained and the restriction order will cease to have effect. If the patient is conditionally discharged, he/she may be recalled at any time during the continuance of the restriction order by the Secretary of State. The recall warrant will specify the hospital to which the patient is to be recalled. If that hospital is not the one from which he/she was conditionally discharged, the hospital order and restriction order have effect as if the "new" hospital replaces the one in the original order. (See s 42(3) and (4)(a) MHA 1983.)

A patient subject to recall will be regarded as if he/she were absent without leave from the hospital mentioned in the recall warrant; the effect of this provision is that he/she may be taken

## Admission through the criminal process

into custody by an ASW, an officer of the staff of the hospital, any constable or by any other person authorised by the hospital (s 42(4)(b) MHA 1983; for s 18 see page 41). If the restriction order ceases to have effect after the patient has been conditionally discharged, and he/she has not been recalled, he/she will cease to be liable to be detained in hospital (s 42(5) MHA 1983).

## 5. Magistrates' power to commit for restriction order

Magistrates' courts do not have the power to include a restriction order in a hospital order. However, s 43 MHA 1983 empowers a magistrates' court to commit to the custody of the Crown Court a person of or over the age of fourteen years who has been convicted by the magistrates of an offence, punishable on summary conviction with imprisonment, in the following circumstances:

(i) the conditions for the making of a hospital order under s 37(1) MHA 1983 are satisfied in respect of the offender; but

(ii) it appears to the court, having regard to the nature of the offence, the antecedents of the offender and the risk of him/her committing further offences if set at large, that if a hospital order is made a restriction order should also be made.

(s 43(1) MHA 1983.)

Where a person is committed under s 43(1), the Crown Court must enquire into the circumstances of the case. The Crown Court may then make a hospital order with or without a restriction order if the statutory provisions for making such orders are satisfied. Alternatively, it may deal with the offender in any other manner in which the magistrates' court could have dealt with him/her. If a hospital order is not made, the Crown Court cannot impose a sentence greater than would have been available to the magistrates unless the offender was also committed under s 30 Magistrates' Courts Act 1980. (See s 43(3) and (5) MHA 1983.) Where a convicted person is committed under s 43, the Crown Court also has the power to make orders under s 35 (remand to hospital for report – see page 52), s 36 (remand to hospital for treatment – see page 54) and s 38 (interim orders – see page 60).

Where the magistrates decide to commit the offender under s 43

MHA 1983, they may, *as an alternative* to committing him/her to custody, direct that he/she be admitted to hospital pending the Crown Court hearing (s 44 MHA 1983). Before doing this, the magistrates must be satisfied on the basis of written or oral evidence that arrangements have been made for his/her admission to a hospital in the event of the Crown Court making a hospital order. The evidence required must be given by the registered medical practitioner who would be in charge of the offender's treatment or by some other person representing the managers of that hospital. Directions may be given regarding such person's attendance at the Crown Court. It is also open to the magistrates' court to include directions that the offender be taken to a place of safety for a period of up to twenty-eight days pending his/her admission to the hospital. If, within that twenty-eight day period, it appears to the Secretary of State that as a result of emergency or other special circumstances it is not practicable to receive the person in the specified hospital, he/she may give directions for admission to another appropriate hospital. He/She must inform the person having custody of the offender of the change of hospital. The order shall have effect as if the new hospital were substituted for the original one. A committal to hospital under s 44 MHA 1983 is sufficient authority for a constable, ASW, or any other person directed by the court to do so, to take the patient to the specified hospital (see ss 44(3) and 40(1) MHA 1983). The duration of this authority is not limited to twenty-eight days. It is also sufficient authority for the hospital managers to admit and detain the person. That authority will last until the case is disposed of by the Crown Court and will have the same effect as if it were a hospital order with a restriction order made without limitation of time (see s 44(1)–(3) MHA 1983). A person admitted to hospital under this section is treated as if he/she were subject to a transfer direction under s 47 for the purposes of s 51(5) and (6) MHA 1983 (see s 51(7) MHA 1983 and below).

## 6. Transfer of prisoners to hospital

The Secretary of State may by warrant direct that a person serving a period of imprisonment (see below) may be removed to and detained in a hospital (not a mental nursing home – see page 72) specified in the direction. Such a transfer is known as a "transfer direction" and it has the same legal effect as a hospital order (see ss 37 and 40 at pages 56 and 59). Before making such a direction, the Secretary of State must be satisfied by reports

## Admission through the criminal process

from at least two medical practitioners (one of whom must be approved for the purposes of s 12 MHA 1983 – see page 19) that:

(i) the prisoner is suffering from mental illness, psychopathic disorder, severe mental impairment or mental impairment; and

(ii) the mental disorder is of such a nature or degree that it is appropriate for him/her to be detained in a hospital for medical treatment and, in the case of psychopathic disorder or mental impairment, the treatment is likely to alleviate or prevent deterioration of his/her condition.

(s 47(1)(a) and (b) MHA 1983.)

Regard must be had to the public interest and all the circumstances of the case, and the Secretary of State must be of the opinion that it is expedient to make a transfer direction. When making a direction, the Secretary of State must specify the particular form or forms of mental disorder in the medical reports; each report must specify at least one form of disorder in common. The direction will cease to have effect after fourteen days if the prisoner is not received into the specified hospital within that period (see s 47(1) – (4) MHA 1983). There is no requirement that the hospital agree to the transfer.

For the purposes of s 47 MHA 1983, reference to a person serving a sentence of imprisonment includes:

(i) a person detained in pursuance of any sentence or order for detention made by a court in criminal proceedings (other than those cases where there has been a finding of insanity in courts martial or on appeal from such a court – see s 46 MHA 1983);

(ii) a person committed to custody under s 115(3) Magistrates' Courts Act 1980 (a person who fails to comply with an order to enter into recognisance to keep the peace or be of good behaviour); and

(iii) a person committed by a court to a prison, or other institution to which the Prisons Act 1952 applies, in default of a payment of any sum adjudged to be payable on his/her conviction.

(s 47(5)(a) – (c) MHA 1983.)

There is also provision for the transfer of certain unsentenced prisoners to hospital. Section 48 MHA 1983 empowers the Secretary of State to direct the transfer of the following types of prisoner to a hospital:

(i) persons detained in prison or a remand centre who are not serving a sentence of imprisonment (s 48(2)(a) MHA 1983);
(ii) persons remanded in custody by a magistrates' court (s 48(2)(b) MHA 1983);
(iii) civil prisoners who are not dealt with under s 47 MHA 1983 (s 48(2)(c) MHA 1983);
(iv) persons detained under the Immigration Act 1971 (s 48(2)(d) MHA 1983);
(For special provisions relating to each of these subsections, see below.)

The criteria for transfer under s 48 are slightly different from those under s 47 MHA 1983. The section only applies to a person who the Secretary of State is satisfied is suffering from mental illness or severe mental impairment. As a consequence of this, the person must be in urgent need of medical attention making it appropriate for him/her to be detained in hospital. In reaching his/her decision, the Secretary of State must be satisfied on the basis of the same type of reports as are used for s 47 MHA 1983. Subsections 47(2)–(4) MHA 1983 apply to a transfer direction under s 48 MHA 1983. (See s 48(1) and (3) MHA 1983.)

Special provisions apply to a transfer direction which has been given in respect of a person who is within s 48(2)(a) MHA 1983 (see above). The direction will cease to have effect as soon as his/her case is disposed of by the court, although this does not prejudice the right of the court to make a hospital order under the provisions outlined earlier.

Where the responsible medical officer, a registered medical practitioner or an MHRT notify the Secretary of State at any time before the case is disposed of that:

(i) the detainee no longer requires treatment in hospital for the mental disorder; or
(ii) no effective treatment can be given for the disorder in the hospital,

the Secretary of State may direct by warrant that the detainee be transferred to a prison or remand centre; in these circumstances, the transfer direction ceases to have effect upon arrival at that place (s 51(3)(a) and (b) MHA 1983). If the Secretary of State has not made a direction under s 51(3) MHA 1983, the court which hears the case may order that the detainee should be transferred to such a place, or released on bail. The transfer direction ceases to have effect upon arrival at that place or release on bail. Before

## Admission through the criminal process

it can make such an order, the court must be satisfied on the written or oral evidence of the responsible medical officer that either of the two conditions mentioned immediately above has been satisfied. (See s 51(4) MHA 1983.)

Where the detainee has not been returned to prison or released on bail under s 51(3) or (4) MHA 1983, the court having jurisdiction to hear his/her case may make a hospital order, with or without a restriction order. The court must be satisfied that:

(i) it is impracticable or inappropriate to bring the detainee before the court;

(ii) on the written or oral evidence of at least two registered medical practitioners (one of whom must be approved under s 12 MHA 1983 – see page 19), the detainee is suffering from mental illness or severe mental impairment of a nature or degree which makes it appropriate for the patient to be detained in hospital for medical treatment; and

(iii) it is proper to make such an order (after consideration of any depositions or other documents sent to the court).

In these circumstances the court may make a hospital order in his/her absence and, in the case of a person awaiting trial, without convicting him/her. (See s 51(5) and (6) MHA 1983.)

Where a transfer direction has been given in respect of a person falling within s 48(2)(b) (see above), s 52 MHA 1983 applies. The transfer direction ceases to have effect when the period of remand expires, unless the accused person is committed into the custody of the Crown Court for trial or disposal. If the accused is committed to the Crown Court and the transfer direction has not been discharged by the magistrates (see below), s 51 MHA 1983 applies as if the direction were one given in respect of a person falling within that section. If the magistrates further remand the accused in custody under s 128 Magistrates' Courts Act 1980, the transfer direction will continue in effect. A further remand may be made in the absence of the accused, provided that he/she has appeared before the court within the previous six months. The magistrates' court may direct that the transfer direction shall cease to have effect even though the period of remand has not expired or the accused has been committed to the Crown Court. Before doing so, the court must be satisfied, on the written or oral evidence of the responsible medical officer, that the accused no longer requires treatment in hospital for the mental disorder, or that no effective treatment can be given in the hospital to which he/she has been removed.

A transfer direction given in respect of persons under s 48(2)(c) or (d) MHA 1983 ceases to have effect when he/she would, but for the fact of being in hospital, no longer be liable to detention in prison. Where a transfer direction and a restriction direction have been made in respect of a person under those subsections, the Secretary of State may by warrant direct that he/she must be remitted to any place where he/she might otherwise have been detained. The Secretary of State must have received notice from the responsible medical officer, any other registered medical practitioner or an MHRT that the person no longer requires treatment in hospital, or that no effective treatment for his/her disorder can be given in the hospital. Once he/she arrives at the place to which he/she has been remitted, the transfer direction and the restriction direction cease to have effect. (See s 53(1) and (2) MHA 1983.)

When making a transfer direction under ss 47 or 48 MHA 1983, a restriction on discharge may, and in some cases must be included by direction of the Secretary of State (s 49(1) MHA 1983). A restriction on discharge, referred to as a "restriction direction", must be included in respect of persons falling within s 48(2) (a) or (b) MHA 1983 (see above); in all other cases it is at the discretion of the Secretary of State (s 49(1) MHA 1983). Restriction directions have the same effect as restriction orders under s 41 MHA 1983 (s 49(2) MHA 1983 – see page 62; for MHRTs see page 111). Where a person is subject to a restriction direction, he/she must be examined by the responsible medical officer at intervals of not greater than twelve months as directed by the Secretary of State, to whom a report must be given (s 49(3) MHA 1983).

Where a transfer direction and restriction direction have been given in respect of a person serving a prison sentence (as defined by s 47(5) MHA 1983 – see above), the responsible medical officer, a registered medical practitioner or an MHRT may notify the Secretary of State of the following:

(i) that the person no longer requires treatment in hospital for mental disorder; or

(ii) that no effective treatment for the disorder may be given in the hospital to which he/she has been removed.

At this point it must be realised that he/she is still subject to a prison sentence. Accordingly, the Secretary of State, upon receiving such notice, may:

(i) by warrant direct that he/she be remitted to any prison or

other institution in which he/she might have been detained if he/she had not been removed to hospital; or
(ii) exercise any power of releasing him/her on licence or discharging him/her under supervision which would have been available if he/she had been detained in a prison or other institution.

(s 50(1)(a) and (b) MHA 1983.)

A restriction direction imposed upon a person serving a sentence of imprisonment will cease to have effect at the end of that sentence. His/Her sentence ends on the date on which he/she would cease to be liable to detention after taking into account any remission and any periods during which he/she was unlawfully at large. (See s 50(2)–(4) MHA 1983.)

## Chapter 3

# Institutional care and treatment

## 1. Introduction

Chapters 1 and 2 considered the procedure for patients who may be compulsorily admitted and detained in hospital. However, many people are in hospital on a voluntary basis in consequence of a mental disorder. This chapter considers the various types of institutional care that are available for the purposes of both compulsory and informal admission. The growing provision by the private sector is considered and the procedure for registration explained. In addition, the question of consent to treatment is discussed.

## 2. Hospitals, special hospitals and managers

*(a) Definition*

For the purposes of the MHA 1983, "hospital" means any health service hospital within the meaning of the National Health Service Act 1977 and any accommodation provided by a local authority and used as a hospital or on behalf of the Secretary of State under that Act (s 145(1) MHA 1983). The 1977 Act defines "hospital" as follows:

    (i) any institution for the reception and treatment of persons suffering from illness;

    (ii) any maternity home;

    (iii) any institution for the reception and treatment of persons during convalescence or persons requiring medical rehabilitation.

    (s 128(1) National Health Service Act 1977.)

Included in the definition of hospital are the four special

## Institutional care and treatment

hospitals (see below). Under s 1 of the 1977 Act, the Secretary of State has a duty to continue the promotion of a comprehensive health service in England and Wales in order to secure improvement in the physical and mental health of the people.

"Special hospital" is defined by s 4 National Health Service Act 1977. Under that section the Secretary of State has a duty to provide and maintain establishments:

> "for persons subject to detention under the MHA 1983 who in his opinion require treatment under conditions of special security on account of their dangerous, violent or criminal propensities."

The Secretary of State is the manager of the four special hospitals at Rampton, Broadmoor, Park Lane and Moss Side (s 145(1) MHA 1983), although some of his/her functions are carried on by special health authorities set up for that purpose. They may be used for the detention of patients subject to the criminal and the civil process of admission under the MHA 1983. The provisions of the MHA 1983 apply to special hospitals in the same way that they apply to other hospitals within the meaning of the Act, although special provisions apply to the correspondence of patients detained in such a hospital (see page 87). The definition of hospital for the purposes of Parts II and III MHA 1983 includes mental nursing homes which are registered as being able to receive patients detained under the MHA 1983 (see page 79). This extended definition applies, unless otherwise expressly provided. (See ss 34(2) and 55(5) MHA 1983.)

For the purposes of the MHA 1983, "managers" means in relation to a hospital as defined in the 1977 Act the district health authority or special health authority responsible for the administration of the hospital. In relation to a special hospital it means the Secretary of State, and in relation to a mental nursing home the person or persons registered in respect of the home. (See s 145(1) MHA 1983.)

### (b) Informal patients

Limited provision in the MHA 1983 is made for informal patients, that is persons suffering from mental disorder who are in hospital but not subject to any of the powers of detention under Parts II and III MHA 1983. Nothing in the MHA 1983 must be construed as preventing a patient requiring treatment for a mental disorder being admitted to any hospital or mental nursing home as an informal patient rather than subject to the powers of detention. Similarly, a patient who ceases to be liable to detention under the MHA 1983 may continue to stay in the hospital as an informal patient. (See s 131(1) MHA 1983.)

Admission as an informal patient may represent the least restrictive alternative where the patient is not unwilling to be admitted; it does not have to be shown that he/she is positively willing to enter as an informal patient. A minor who has attained the age of sixteen years and is capable of expressing his/her own wishes may decide for himself/herself whether or not he/she will be admitted as an informal patient. He/She may do this notwithstanding any right of custody or control vested by law in his/her parent or guardian. An informal admission in respect of a minor under the age of seventeen years may be subject to challenge through the wardship jurisdiction. It is also theoretically possible to achieve an informal admission in respect of such a person through wardship, although the court in such a case might well conclude that a statutory framework for admission exists and should be used.

None of the provisions relating to review, access to MHRTs and correspondence apply to informal patients. However, one section which does apply to them is s 57 MHA 1983, which regulates treatment requiring both consent and a second opinion (see page 92). It is also possible to make an application in respect of an informal patient under s 5 MHA 1983. Section 117 MHA 1983, which imposes a duty to provide after-care for patients who cease to be detained, does not apply to informal patients. However, many of the other statutory provisions which provide for community care of persons leaving hospital will be applicable (see page 165).

## 3. Nursing homes and mental nursing homes

### (a) Definitions

The Registered Homes Act 1984 ("RHA 1984") provides for the registration and regulation of nursing homes and mental nursing homes run by the private sector. Only mental nursing homes can accommodate persons subject to detention under MHA 1983; however, persons suffering from mental disorder may be residents in nursing homes. Under s 21(1) RHA 1984 "nursing home" is defined, *inter alia*, as:

> "(a) any premises used, or intended to be used, for the reception of, and the provision of nursing for, persons suffering from any sickness, injury or infirmity."

## Institutional care and treatment

This may include nursing homes which take in elderly persons who may be mentally confused, but not considered to be suffering from a mental disorder within the MHA 1983. It might also cover homes which accommodate persons with a mental handicap. Certain premises are excluded from the definition of nursing home. These include hospitals, school sanatoriums (provided they are used exclusively by pupils, staff and families), doctors' surgeries, and premises used wholly or mainly as a private dwelling. Also excluded are mental nursing homes. Section 22(1) RHA 1984 defines "mental nursing home" as:

> "any premises used, or intended to be used, for the reception of, and the provision of nursing or other medical treatment (including care, habilitation and rehabilitation under medical supervision) for one or more mentally disordered patients (meaning persons suffering, or appearing to be suffering from mental disorder), whether exclusively or in common with other persons."

"Mental nursing home" does not include a health service hospital within the National Health Service Act 1977, nor accommodation provided by a local authority and used as a hospital under that Act (s 22(2) and (3) RHA 1984). Also excluded are premises managed by a government department or provided by a local authority (s 22(2) RHA 1984). "Mental disorder" has the same meaning as it does under s 1(2) MHA 1983 (s 55 RHA 1984; see page 1).

### (b) Registration

Nursing homes and mental nursing homes must be registered under the RHA 1984; failure to register is a criminal offence (s 23(1) RHA 1984). The RHA 1984 also makes it a criminal offence to hold out, with intent to deceive, that premises are a nursing home or a mental nursing home unless they are registered in accordance with the Act (s 24 RHA 1984). The Secretary of State has delegated the registration duties under the RHA 1984 to district health authorities ("registration authorities"). An application for registration must be made in writing to the registration authority and accompanied by the appropriate fee. If registration as a mental nursing home is sought, the application must specify whether or not it is proposed to receive in the home patients who are liable to be detained under the MHA 1983. (See s 23(3) RHA 1984.)

When making an application, the Nursing Homes and Mental

Nursing Homes Regulations 1984, SI No 1578 ("NH & MNHR 1984") require the applicant to provide the following particulars:

(i) the name, telephone number and professional/technical qualifications of the applicant;

(ii) if the applicant is a company, society, association or body, the address of its registered office/principal place of business and the full names, addresses and technical/ professional qualifications of the directors/partners;

(iii) the address of any other home, residential care home, voluntary care home, or children's home under the CA 1989 in which the applicant has an interest (the nature and extent of any interest must be stated);

(iv) the situation of the home and the form of its construction;

(v) the telephone number of the home;

(vi) the accommodation available and the equipment and facilities provided, or to be provided, in the home;

(vii) the date on which the home was established or is to be established;

(viii) whether any other business will be carried out on the same premises as the home, and whether the premises are, have been, or are proposed to be registered as a residential care home under Part I RHA 1984;

(ix) the type of home (nursing home or mental nursing home);

(x) the number of patients for whom the home is proposed to be used (different categories must be identified and the age range within each category);

(xi) the full names, ages, qualifications and experience of persons employed in the management of the home and whether they are or will be resident in the home;

(xii) the arrangement for the management and control of the home (details of the arrangements or proposed arrangements must be included);

(xiii) the full names and qualifications of any resident or non-resident employed medical practitioner plus the number of hours to be worked;

(xiv) the full names and any qualifications of the nursing and other professional, technical, administrative and ancillary staff employed or proposed to be employed in the home plus the number of hours to be worked (a

*Institutional care and treatment*

        distinction must be drawn between resident and non-resident);
- (xv) the arrangements made for the supply of blood and blood products;
- (xvi) the arrangements made for the provision of pathology and radiology services.

(r 4(2) and Sch 2 NH & MNHR 1984.)

The applicant must also provide such other information, including any comments made by the fire authority in relation to the home, as the registration authority may reasonably require.

If the registration authority proposes to grant an application, it must give written notice of its proposal and of any conditions which it is imposing under s 29 RHA 1984 (s 31(1)(a) and (b) RHA 1984). A condition must be included which stipulates the maximum number of persons who may be kept at any one time in the home. This number will be specified on the certificate of registration (s 29(1) RHA 1984). In addition, the registration authority has a discretion to include a condition regulating the age, sex or other category of person who may be received in the home (s 29(2) RHA 1984). Regulation 6 NH & MNHR 1984 allows for the variation of conditions attached to registration. The registration authority must give written notice to the registered person of its intention to vary a condition (r 6(1) NH & MNHR 1984). It must specify a date, which is reasonable in the circumstances, on which the proposed variation is to take place (r 6(2) NH & MNHR 1984). If the variation reduces the maximum number of persons who may be received into the home, transitional provisions apply (r 6(3) NH & MNHR 1984). The original maximum continues to apply for as long as all the patients resident in the home were so resident at the time the notice was given. However, no new residents can be accepted until the number falls below the new maximum, and then only up to that figure. If a condition is not complied with, the person carrying on the home will be guilty of an offence (r 29(4) NH & MNHR 1984). Notice must also be given of an intention by the registration authority to impose an additional condition (s 31(3)(c) RHA 1984).

Where the registration authority proposes to refuse an application, it must give the applicant notice of, and the reasons for, its proposal (s 31(2) and (4) RHA 1984). Registration may be refused on one or more of the following grounds:

- (i) the applicant or any person employed, or proposed to be employed, is not a fit person to be involved in a home of the type named in the application;

(ii) for reasons connected with the situation, construction, state of repair, accommodation, staffing or equipment, the home or premises used in connection with the home are not fit for the purpose;

(iii) the home or any premises used in connection with it are used, or proposed to be used, for purposes which are in any way improper or undesirable in the case of such a home;

(iv) the home or any premises used in connection with it consist of, or include works executed in contravention of s 12(1) Health Services Act 1976;

(v) the home or any premises used in connection with it are in contravention of an authorisation under s 13 Health Services Act 1976;

(vi) the home is not, or will not be, in the charge of a person who is either a registered medical practitioner or a qualified nurse;

(vii) failure or inability to fulfil the condition in a notice by the registration authority to the applicant as to the number and qualifications of the nursing staff required to be on duty in the home at such times as may be specified in the notice.

(s 25(1)(a)–(g) RHA 1984.)

"Qualified nurse" means a nurse possessing such qualifications as the registration authority may specify in a notice served on the applicant (s 29(2) RHA 1984). In preparing such a notice, and a notice mentioned in (vii) above, the registration authority must have regard to the class and the number of patients for whom nursing care is to be provided in the home (s 25(3) RHA 1984).

When issuing a notice under s 31 RHA 1984, the registration authority must give the reasons for its proposals (s 31(4) RHA 1984). The notice must also state that the applicant may, in writing and within fourteen days of notice being served, require the registration authority to give him/her the opportunity to make representations on any matter which he/she wishes to dispute. After it has served notice of its proposals, the registration authority cannot finally determine the matter until one of the following is satisfied:

(i) the person on whom notice was served has made representations; or

(ii) the fourteen day period has expired and no request has been made by the applicant; or

## Institutional care and treatment

    (iii) the applicant asked to make representations, and the registration authority has allowed a reasonable time within which they could be made but no representations have been made.

(s 32(2) and (3) RHA 1984.)

Representations may be made in writing or orally. If the applicant wishes to make oral representations, he/she may be given the opportunity of making them before a person appointed by the registration authority. (See s 32(4) and (5) RHA 1984.)

Where the registration authority decides to adopt the proposal, it is required to serve notice in writing on any person entitled to notice under s 31 RHA 1984. The notice must be accompanied by a note explaining the right of appeal conferred by s 34 RHA 1984 (see below). Where the decision to grant registration is subject to conditions agreed with the applicant, or where there is a refusal to register, the decision of the registration authority takes effect immediately. In all other cases, implementation is delayed until the end of a period of twenty-eight days if no appeal is brought (see s 34(3) RHA 1984 below) or, if an appeal is brought, until it is determined or abandoned. (See s 33(1)–(3) RHA 1984.)

An appeal may be made against any decision of the registration authority acting under the powers outlined above. Appeals lie to the Registered Homes Tribunal (s 34(1) RHA 1984). The appeal must be made by notice in writing to the registration authority within twenty-eight days of receipt of the notice under s 33 RHA 1984. The tribunal may confirm the registration authority's order or direct that it shall not have effect. It also has the power to:

    (i) vary any condition which is for the time being in force;
    (ii) direct that such a condition shall cease to have effect;
    (iii) direct that any such condition as it thinks fit shall have effect.

The registration authority must comply with any directions given by the tribunal during an appeal against its decision. (See s 34(2) – (7) RHA 1984.)

If the registration authority decides to register the applicant in respect of the home named in the application, it must issue a certificate of registration. This must be displayed in a conspicuous place in the home; failure to do so is a criminal offence. (See s 23(4) and (6) RHA 1984.)

Where the person is registered in respect of a mental nursing home and it is proposed to receive into the home patients liable to be detained under the MHA 1983, that fact must be stated in the certificate and the particulars entered into a separate part of the register by the registration authority (s 23(5) RHA 1984).

If the sole registered person in respect of a mental nursing home dies at a time when any patient is liable to be detained in the home under the MHA 1983, registration may continue in force for a limited period. It will continue in force until the expiry of two months from the date of his/her death, or until the patient ceases to be so liable, or until another person is registered in respect of the home, whichever is the earlier. The registration will continue in force for the benefit of the personal representative of the deceased as from the time of the grant of representation, and until that grant for the benefit of any person approved by the registration authority. The person for whose benefit the registration will continue is treated as the person registered in respect of the home. (See s 36(3)–(5) RHA 1984.)

*(c) Cancellation of registration*

The RHA 1984 provides a general and an urgent procedure for cancelling registration of a nursing home or mental nursing home. Section 28 RHA 1984 outlines the general procedure. Under s 28 RHA 1984, the registration authority may at any time cancel registration of any person in respect of a nursing home or mental nursing home. The grounds upon which such a cancellation may be made are as follows:

(i) any of the grounds upon which it could have refused registration under s 25(1)(a)–(g) RHA 1984 (see page 77);
(ii) the registered person has been convicted of any offence under Part II RHA 1984 relating to any nursing home or mental nursing home;
(iii) any other person has been convicted of an offence in respect of the nursing home or mental nursing home in question;
(iv) any condition of registration in respect of the home has not been complied with;
(v) the person has been convicted of an offence against regulations made under ss 26 or 27 RHA 1984 (see page 81);
(vi) the annual fee has not been paid on or before the due date.

(s 28(a)–(e) RHA 1984.)

*Institutional care and treatment*

Sections 31–33 apply to cancellations under s 28 RHA1984 (see page 77). The registration authority has a discretion whether to cancel registration in the above circumstances. It may alternatively decide to impose additional conditions or vary existing ones.

Special provisions apply in respect of a mental nursing home whose registration is cancelled under s 28 RHA 1984 (s 36 RHA 1984). If registration is cancelled at a time when any patient is liable to be detained in the home under the MHA 1983, the registration shall continue in force until the expiry of a two month period beginning with the date of cancellation, or until any such patient ceases to be liable to be so detained, whichever is the earlier (s 36(2) RHA 1984).

An urgent procedure for cancelling registration is found in s 30 RHA 1984. This requires the registration authority to apply to a justice of the peace for an order:

(i) cancelling the registration of a person in respect of a home;

(ii) varying any condition for the time being in force in respect of the home;

(iii) imposing an additional condition.

(s 30(1)(a) RHA 1984.)

If it appears to the justice of the peace that there will be a serious risk to the life, health or well-being of the patients in the home unless an order is made, he/she may make the appropriate order. The order must be in writing and has effect from the date on which it is made. An application under this procedure may be made *ex parte* and it must be supported by a written statement of the registration authority's reason for making it. (See s 30(1)–(3) RHA 1984.) As soon as is practicable after the making of the order, the registration authority must serve on the registered person a notice of the making of the order and a copy of its written statement of the reasons for making the application (s 30(4) RHA 1984). The appeals procedure outlined above applies to cancellations under ss 28 and 30 RHA 1984. In the case of an appeal against an order under s 30 RHA 1984, the Registered Homes Tribunal may confirm the order or direct that it shall cease to have effect (s 34(5) RHA 1984).

*(d) Regulation of nursing homes and mental nursing homes*

Sections 26 and 27 RHA 1984 empower the Secretary of State to make regulations in relation to nursing homes and mental nursing homes. These regulations are found in NH & MNHR 1984. Regulation 7 NH & MNHR 1984 imposes a duty on the person registered to keep records. He/She must keep the following records:

   (i) a register of all the patients, including the particulars mentioned in Sch 4 Part 1 of NH & MNHR 1984 (see below);
   (ii) details of surgical operations carried out and use of specially controlled techniques;
   (iii) a register of each patient including an adequate daily statement of his/her health and condition, and details of any investigation made, surgical operation performed and treatment given;
   (iv) a record of all staff employed (including details of qualifications of all nursing staff);
   (v) a record of fire practices, fire alarm tests and results (including action taken to remedy defects), and the procedure to be followed in the event of fire;
   (vi) a record of maintenance carried out on medical, surgical and nursing equipment.
   (r 7 NH & MNHR 1984.)

Records under (i) and (ii) must be retained for a period of not less than one year beginning with date of the last entry, and those under (iii) for at least one year from the date at which the patient ceases to be a patient in the home.

Part 1 of Sch 4 requires the following particulars to be included in the register maintained under (i) above:

   (i) name, address, date of birth and marital status of each patient;
   (ii) name, address and telephone number of the patient's next of kin or any person authorised to act on the patient's behalf;
   (iii) the name, address and telephone number of the patient's medical practitioner;
   (iv) where the patient is a child, the name and address of the school which he/she attends or attended before entering the home;
   (v) where the patient has been received into guardianship under the MHA 1983, the name, address and telephone

## Institutional care and treatment

number of the guardian, and if the guardian is a local social services authority the same details in respect of any officer of the authority required to supervise the welfare of the patient;
(vi) the name and address of any public body which arranged the patient's admission to the home;
(vii) the date the patient entered the home;
(viii) if the patient has left the home, the date on which he/she left;
(ix) if the patient is transferred to hospital, the date of and the reasons for the transfer and the name of the hospital to which he/she is transferred;
(x) if the patient has died in the home, the date, time and cause of death.

The NH & MNHR 1984 also require certain facilities and services to be provided in a nursing or mental nursing home. In determining the level of provision, the person registered must have regard to the size of the home and the number, age, sex and condition of the patients (see generally r 12(1) and (2) NH & MNHR 1984). Adequate professional, technical and ancillary support staff must be provided. The patient must have adequate accommodation space along with furniture, bedding and, where appropriate, screens and floor covering. Adequate toilet and washing facilities (including hot and cold water) must be provided as must heat, light and ventilation in all parts of the home used by the patients. Day room facilities should be provided where appropriate.

As far as the structure of the home is concerned, the NH & MNHR 1984 require the registered person to keep it in good repair, clean and reasonably decorated. Precautions against the risk of accidents must be taken. Necessary precautions against the risk of fire, including means of escape and early detection, must be taken. The staff and, so far as is practicable, the patients must know the procedure for evacuation in the event of fire. Consultation must take place with the fire authority on the fire precautions in the home. Kitchens must be adequately equipped and have sufficient cutlery, crockery and facilities for storing and preparing food. Patients must have an adequate supply of food. Facilities for laundry must be provided.

The registered person is also responsible for the provision of adequate medical, surgical and nursing equipment, and adequate treatment facilities. Arrangements must be made for medical and dental services (National Health or otherwise) to be available to patients; consultation must take place with the health authority over provision in cases of medical emergency. The disposal of swabs, soiled dressings, instruments and similar substances and materials must be properly controlled. Proper arrangements for the recording, safe-keeping, handling and disposal of drugs must be made. In order to prevent infection, toxic conditions or the spread of infection in the home, the registered person must make adequate arrangements.

Provision must be made for the general training, occupation or recreation of patients, including play and education facilities for any children. Facilities for visitors and for interviews in private must be made available. The home must also be connected to the public telephone service.

## 4. Protection of detained patients

The MHA 1983 contains many safeguards for patients who are detained in hospital under its provisions. A specific duty is imposed upon the Secretary of State to keep under review the exercise of the powers and duties under the MHA 1983 so far as they relate to the detention of patients and their subsequent care in hospital. This duty has been delegated to the Mental Health Act Commission under s 121(2)(b) MHA 1983. The Commission may authorise persons to visit and interview on its behalf patients detained under the MHA 1983 in hospitals or mental nursing homes. Such interviews should take place in private (see s 120(1) (a) MHA 1983). Furthermore, the Commission must make arrangements for authorised persons to investigate any complaint made by a person in respect of any matter which occurred while he/she was detained and which he/she considers has not been satisfactorily dealt with by the managers of the hospital or mental nursing home (s 120(1)(b)(i) MHA 1983). Any other complaints (either by the patient or some other person such as the nearest relative or Member of Parliament) relating to the exercise of any other powers and duties under the MHA 1983 in respect of a person who is or has been detained may also be investigated (s 120(1)(b)(ii) MHA 1983). If the complaint is made by a Member of Parliament, the Commission must ensure that the results of the investigation are communicated to him/her (s 120(3) MHA 1983). Only complaints in respect of a period when the patient was subject to detention can be investigated under these subsections. The Commission may exclude certain matters from investigation under s 120(1) MHA 1983. It may also decline to investigate a complaint, or to continue an investi-

*Institutional care and treatment*

gation, where it considers it appropriate to do so (s 120(2) MHA 1983); this covers situations where the complaint is being, or would more appropriately be investigated by some other person such as a Health Service Commissioner (see DHSS Memorandum – Mental Health Act 1983, para 263).

To enable investigations to take place, or to enable the Commission to review the working of the legislation, any authorised person may visit and interview a patient detained in a hospital or mental nursing home. If the authorised person is a registered medical practitioner, he/she may examine the patient in private. In addition to visiting and interviewing, the authorised person may require the production of, and inspect, records relating to the patient's detention or treatment (see s 120(4) MHA 1983). To enable the proper carrying out of these duties, health authorities and special health authorities (see page 73) are required to make arrangements to ensure the following:

(i) records required to be made under MHR 1983 which relate to the detention or treatment of a patient in hospital are to be kept for a period of five years commencing on the date when he/she ceases to be a patient;

(ii) that any person:

- authorised by the Mental Health Act Commission under s 120 MHA 1983; or
- who is a person appointed by the Commission for the purposes of s 57(2)(a) MHA 1983 (see page 93); or
- who is a registered medical practitioner appointed by the Commission for the purposes of Part IV or s 118(2) MHA 1983 (a registered medical practitioner appointed for the purpose of the Code),

is able, at any reasonable time:

- to visit and interview the patient in accordance with s 120(4) MHA 1983;
- if he/she is a registered medical practitioner or person appointed by the Commission, to require the production of, and inspect, any records relating to the treatment of the patient in hospital; and
- in any other case, to require the production of and inspect any records relating to the detention or treatment of any person who is, or has been, detained in a hospital for which the authority is responsible.

(See DHSS Circular HC(83)19.)

Inspection of premises and the visiting of patients in mental nursing homes are covered by s 35 RHA 1984. Any person authorised by the registration authority may at any time enter and inspect premises which are used, or which he/she has reasonable cause to believe are being used, as a mental nursing home. An inspection may be made on such occasions and at such intervals as the registration authority may decide. However, every home must be inspected not less than twice a year (r 11 NH & MNHR 1984). He/She may be required to produce some duly authenticated document showing that he/she is so authorised. Upon entry, the authorised person may inspect any records required to be kept under s 27(b) RHA 1984. (See s 35(1) RHA 1984.)

The authorised person has the right to interview the patient in private for the purpose of investigating any complaint as to his/her treatment. Similarly, an interview in private may be conducted if the authorised person has reasonable cause to believe that the patient is not receiving proper care. If the authorised person is a medical practitioner, he/she may examine the patient in private and require the production of any medical records relating to the patient's treatment in that home. (See s 35(2)(a) and (b) RHA 1984.)

It is an offence for any person to obstruct the authorised person in the exercise of his/her functions; this includes refusing a request to withdraw in order that an interview or examination in private can be conducted. (See s 35(5) and (6) RHA 1984.)

Inspection of nursing homes is authorised by r 11 NH & MNHR 1984. A person authorised by the registration authority may enter and inspect any premises which are used, or which he/she reasonably believes are being used, as a nursing home. There is no reference to entry at "any time" as in s 35 RHA 1984. If asked, the authorised person must produce an authenticated document showing that he/she is duly authorised. When inspecting the nursing home, he/she may require the production of records if they may reasonably be required for the purpose of the inspection. However, only a medical practitioner in the service of the Crown or a health authority may have access to and inspect clinical records relating to patients in the home. Nursing homes should be inspected at least twice every year.

## 5. Duty of managers to provide information

The managers of hospitals or mental nursing homes in which

## Institutional care and treatment

patients are detained under the MHA 1983 are under a duty to provide information to the patient and the nearest relative. Section 132 MHA 1983 requires the managers to take such steps as are practicable to ensure that the patient understands the provision of the Act under which he/she is detained and its effect, and what rights he/she has to apply to an MHRT. This provision applies to all forms of detention under the MHA 1983 including a nurse's holding power under s 5(4) MHA 1983 (see page 26). Where the authority for detention changes, the patient must be informed of this fact and of the effect of the new form of detention. The patient must be given this information as soon as possible after the commencement of his/her detention in the hospital or mental nursing home. (See s 132(1)(a) and (b) MHA 1983.)

It is also incumbent upon the managers to ensure, in so far as it is practicable, that the patient is aware of the provisions of ss 23, 25 and s 66(1)(g) (power of discharge – see pages 38, 39 and 113), ss 56–64 (consent to treatment – see page 91), s 118 (the Code of Practice), s 120 (protection of patients – see page 84) and s 134 MHA 1983 (correspondence of patients – see below). (See s 132(2) MHA 1983.)

Information given under s 132 MHA 1983 must be given both in writing and orally (s 132(3) MHA 1983). Unless the patient objects, the managers must, so far as is practicable, take such steps to furnish the person (if any) appearing to be the nearest relative with the information given to the patient under s 132 MHA 1983. This should be done at the same time the patient is given the information, or within a reasonable time thereafter. (See s 132(4) MHA 1983.)

The managers must also provide information to the nearest relative concerning the discharge of the patient. Where a patient is to be discharged, other than by the nearest relative under s 25 MHA 1983, the managers must take such steps as are practicable to inform any person who appears to be his/her nearest relative. If practicable, this information should be given at least seven days before the date of discharge. However, this provision does not apply if the patient or the nearest relative has requested that information about discharge should not be given (s 133(1) and (2) MHA 1983).

## 6. Correspondence of patients

Correspondence by and to a detained patient may be examined

and withheld under s 134 MHA 1983. The MHA 1983 gives hospital managers the power to withhold a postal package to see if it is one to which the section applies and, if it is, to determine whether or not it should be withheld. This power to withhold a package includes the power to withhold anything contained in it. The managers' functions under the section may be performed on their behalf by a person on the staff of the hospital appointed for that purpose; different persons may be appointed to perform different functions. If a package is withheld under the section, the managers must record that fact in writing.

A postal packet which is addressed to any person by a detained patient and is delivered by the patient for dispatch may be withheld from the Post Office in one of two sets of circumstances. The first situation is where the addressee has requested that communications addressed to him/her by that patient should be withheld (s 134(1)(a) MHA 1983). Any such request must be made by notice in writing given to the managers of the hospital, the registered medical practitioner in charge of the patient's treatment or the Secretary of State. The second situation is where the hospital is a special hospital (see page 72) and the managers consider that the postal package is likely:

(i) to cause distress to the addressee or any other person (not being a member of staff of the hospital); or

(ii) to cause danger to any person.

(s 134(1)(b)(i) and (ii) MHA 1983.)

Postal packages addressed to a person detained *in a special hospital* may be withheld from the patient if, in the opinion of the managers, it is necessary to do so in the interests of the patient or for the protection of other persons (s 134(2) MHA 1983).

However, ss 134(1)(b) and (2) MHA 1983 do not apply to postal packages sent by, or to, the following:

(i) a Minister of the Crown or any member of either House of Parliament;

(ii) the Master or any other officers of the Court of Protection or any of the Lord Chancellor's visitors;

(iii) the Parliamentary Commissioner for Administration, the Health Service Commissioner for England, the Health Service Commissioner for Wales, or a Local Commissioner within Part III Local Government Act 1974;

(iv) a Mental Health Review Tribunal;

## Institutional care and treatment

- (v) a health authority within the National Health Service Act 1977, a local social services authority, a community health council or a probation and after-care officer;
- (vi) the managers of the hospital in which the patient is detained;
- (vii) any legally qualified person instructed to act as the patient's legal adviser;
- (viii) the European Commission of Human Rights or the European Court of Human Rights.

(s 134(3) MHA 1983.)

If a postal package is withheld under s 134(1) or (2) MHA 1983, the managers of the hospital must record that fact in writing (s 134(5) MHA 1983). Where, after inspection, nothing is withheld, the person inspecting it must record in writing that the package has been inspected and opened, and that nothing has been withheld; and he/she must also provide on the record the name of the hospital (r 17(1) MHR 1983). Before resealing the package, he/she must place the record inside it. If the package or item contained in it is withheld, the person responsible must record in a register kept by the hospital the following details:

- (i) that the packet or anything contained in it has been withheld;
- (ii) the date on which it was so withheld;
- (iii) the grounds upon which it was so withheld;
- (iv) a description of the contents of the packet withheld or any item withheld; and
- (v) his/her name.

(r 17(2)(a) MHR 1983.)

If anything contained in the package is withheld under s 134(1) or (2) MHA 1983, but the package is allowed to proceed minus that item, he/she must record the following in writing:

- (i) that the packet has been inspected and opened;
- (ii) that an item or items contained in the packet have been withheld;
- (iii) a description of any such item;
- (iv) his/her name and the name of the hospital;
- (v) in any case to which s 134(1)(b) or (2) MHA 1983 applies, the further particulars required by s 134(6) (see below).

(r 17(2)(b)MHR 1983.)

Before resealing the packet, the person must place the record in it.

Section 134(6) requires that notice must be given where a postal package or anything contained in it is withheld under s 134(1)(b) or (2) MHA 1983. Where a postal package, or anything contained it it, has been withheld under either of these subsections the manager must, within seven days of the event, give notice to the patient and, if under s 134 (2), the person by whom the package was sent (s 134(6) MHA 1983). The notice must state the grounds on which the contents are being withheld, the name of the person appointed who took the decision, and the name of the hospital (r 17(3)(a) MHR 1983). Furthermore, the notice must contain a statement as to the right to apply to the Commission under s 121(7) and (8) MHA 1983 (see below). If only part of the contents of a package has been withheld and the remainder has been delivered to the addressee, the record to be inserted under r 17(2)(b) MHR 1983 shall, provided the other information required by s 134(6) is included, be sufficient notice under that subsection (r 17(3)(b) MHR 1983).

The Mental Health Act Commission may review a decision under s 134(1)(b) or (2) MHA 1983 to withhold a package, or anything contained in one. An application may be made by the patient in respect of s 134(1)(b), and either by the patient or by the person to whom the package was sent in respect of cases under s 134(2). Applications must be made within six months of the notice under s 134(6) being received by the applicant. (See s 121(7) MHA 1983.)

There is a considerable degree of flexibility as to how an application for review can be made. Under r 18(1) MHR 1983, an application can be made in any manner that the Commission may accept as being sufficient in the circumstances. It may be made other than in writing if necessary and should be made, delivered or sent to an office of the Commission. An applicant must, however, provide the Commission with the notice under s 134(6) MHA 1983, or a copy of that notice. In determining the application, the Commission may direct the production of such documents, information and evidence as it may reasonably require. (See r 18(2) and (3) MHR 1983.) If the Commission directs that the postal package or anything contained in it shall not be withheld, the managers must comply with such a direction (s 134(8) MHA 1983).

*Institutional care and treatment*

## 7. Consent to treatment

Consent to treatment is a particularly controversial area of mental health law. The need or otherwise for consent to treatment depends upon the category of person being considered. Different principles apply when considering patients detained under the MHA 1983, persons subject to guardianship, voluntary in-patients and people with a mental handicap.

*(a) Patients liable to detention under the MHA 1983*

Part IV MHA 1983 deals with consent to treatment for a mental disorder by most categories of patient detained under Part II or III of the Act. The MHA 1983 does not deal with consent to treatment other than for mental disorder; thus it does not include a sterilisation operation or an abortion on a person with a mental disorder (*T* v *T* (1988)). It applies to all detained patients other than the following:

   (i) a patient who is liable to be detained under an emergency application under s 4 MHA 1983 where no second medical recommendation has been provided;
   (ii) a patient liable to be detained under:
   - s 5(2) or (4) MHA 1983 – short-term detention of in-patients (see page 26);
   - s 35 MHA 1983 – remand to hospital for report on accused's mental condition (see page 52);
   - s 37(4) MHA 1983 – detention in a place of safety pending admission under a hospital order (see page 57);
   - s 135 MHA 1983 – person detained in a place of safety after issue of a warrant to search for and remove (see page 15);
   - s 136 MHA 1983 – mentally disordered person found in a public place and detained in a place of safety (see page 16);
   (iii) a patient who has been conditionally discharged under s 42(2), s 73 or s 74 MHA 1983 (see pages 64, 122 and 124).
   (s 56(1) MHA 1983.)

The MHA 1983 deviates from the common law principles of consent to treatment (see page 96). It envisages two categories of treatment for a mental disorder. The first category covers the more serious types of treatment that may be used to treat detained patients; this type of treatment requires the consent of the patient *and* a second opinion. The second category covers some other forms of treatment which require the consent of the patient *or* a second opinion.

## Treatment requiring consent and a second opinion

Section 57 MHA 1983 requires that certain types of medical treatment for a mental disorder can only be carried out if the patient has consented and a second opinion has been obtained. The serious nature of the treatment covered by s 57 means that its provisions also apply to informal patients (s 56(2) MHA 1983). It applies to the following types of treatment:

(i) any surgical operation for destroying brain tissue or for destroying the functioning of the brain tissue;
(ii) *surgical* implantation of hormones for the purpose of reducing the male sex drive.

(s 57(1)(a) and (b) MHA 1983 and r 16(1)(a) MHR 1983.)

Treatment falling within these categories cannot be given (unless falling within s 62 MHA 1983 – see page 95) until s 57(2) and (3) MHA 1983 have been satisfied. The surgical implantation of hormones was considered in *R* v *Mental Health Act Commission ex parte W* (1988). In this case a paedophile sought medical help for his condition, and *goserlin* was administered to him by means of a syringe. The Court of Appeal held that "surgical implantation" was a matter of interpretation, but use of a conventional hypodermic syringe could not be described as surgical. Also the word "hormone" in r 16(1)(a) MHR 1983 was intended to include synthetic equivalents to the normally occurring substance; *goserlin* was not a synthetic equivalent of naturally occurring hormone. The treatment did not fall within s 57 MHA 1983.

Under s 57(2) MHA 1983, the patient must have consented to the treatment. If the patient does not consent either out of choice or incapacity the treatment cannot proceed. The consent must be given by the patient and not on his/her behalf, for example by the nearest relative or the ASW. Nor can the consent be implied. Consent must be real consent, the patient being told, in terms which he/she is capable of understanding, the nature, purpose and likely effects of the treatment. In order to ensure that proper consent has been given, the MHA 1983 requires that a registered medical practitioner and two other persons (not being registered

## Institutional care and treatment

medical practitioners), all appointed by the Mental Health Act Commission, must certify in writing that the patient is capable of understanding the nature, purpose and likely effects of the treatment in question, and that he/she has consented to it (s 57(2)(a) MHA 1983). The registered medical practitioner must not be the responsible medical officer. To assist the persons appointed by the Commission under the subsection, they must be allowed to interview the patient in private and have access to any relevant medical or other records or documents. It is an offence under s 129 MHA 1983 to obstruct anybody in the performance of this duty. (See ss 120 and 121 MHA 1983.)

In addition, the registered medical practitioner appointed by the Commission under s 57(2)(a) MHA 1983 must certify in writing that the treatment should be given. He/She should have regard to the likelihood of the treatment alleviating or preventing a deterioration of the patient's condition. Before certification, the registered medical practitioner must consult two other persons who have been professionally concerned with the patient's medical treatment. One of those persons must be a nurse and the other a person who is not a nurse or registered medical practitioner. (See s 57(2)(b) and (3) MHA 1983.)

### Treatment requiring consent or a second opinion

Certain forms of treatment for a mental disorder in a detained patient require either the consent of the patient *or* a second opinion (s 58 MHA 1983). This section does not apply to informal patients who are covered by the common law rules of consent. The types of treatment covered by this section are:

(i) administration of medicine to a patient by any means at any time during a period for which he/she is liable to be detained, if three months or more have elapsed since the first occasion in that period when medicine was administered to him/her by any means for the mental disorder (s 58(1)(b) MHA 1983); or

(ii) electro-convulsive therapy (the three month period does not apply – see r 16(2)(a) MHR 1983).

Under (i), the period of three months commences on the date when the particular treatment for the mental disorder is first given during the time that the patient is liable to compulsory detention. Detention under any of the provisions in s 56 MHA 1983 does not count for this purpose. As the section refers to the patient being "liable to be detained", it does not matter if there is a change in the authority for the detention, provided that there is a *continuous* three month period of detention. Thus, the three months may commence when the patient is subject to detention under s 2 (note that s 2 does allow for assessment and treatment) and can continue if he/she becomes liable to detention under s 3 MHA 1983. During the three month period, treatment for the mental disorder may be given without consent and without the need for a second opinion.

Unless s 62 MHA 1983 applies (see page 95), the above treatment cannot be given to a detained patient except in the following circumstances:

(i) he/she has consented to that treatment and either the responsible medical officer or a registered medical practitioner appointed for the purpose by the Mental Health Act Commission has certified in writing that the patient is capable of understanding its nature, purpose and likely effect, and has consented to it (s 58(3)(a) MHA 1983); or

(ii) a registered medical practitioner (appointed for the purpose by the Mental Health Act Commission, but not the responsible medical officer) has certified in writing that the patient is not capable of understanding the nature, purpose and likely effect of the treatment or has not consented to it, but having regard to the likelihood of it alleviating or preventing a deterioration of his/her condition, the treatment should be given (s 58(3)(b) MHA 1983).

Before certifying under (ii), the registered medical practitioner concerned must consult two other persons who have been professionally involved with the patient's treatment. One of those persons must be a nurse, the other must be a person who is neither a nurse nor a registered medical practitioner (s 58(4) MHA 1983).

*Plans of treatment, withdrawal of consent, reviews and urgent treatment*

Consent under s 57 or 58 MHA 1983 may relate to a single act of treatment or to a plan of treatment. A plan may involve one or more forms of treatment as defined by the appropriate section. It may also specify a period within which the treatment can be administered (see s 59 MHA 1983). The patient may withdraw his/her consent to further treatment under the plan at any time (s 60(1) MHA 1983). Similarly, the patient may withdraw

## Institutional care and treatment

consent to treatment under ss 57 and 58 MHA 1983 which is not given under a plan. Such a withdrawal may be made at any time before the completion of the treatment (s 60(1) MHA 1983). However, the provisions relating to withdrawal are subject to s 62 MHA 1983 (see below).

If consent to treatment or a plan of treatment under ss 57 and 58 MHA 1983 is withdrawn, the responsible medical officer may order its continuance pending compliance with those sections if he/she considers that discontinuance would cause *serious* suffering to the patient (s 62(2) MHA 1983). Once discontinuance would cease to have that effect, treatment must cease. Thus treatment may be withdrawn gradually if this is necessary to protect the patient. In the case of a withdrawal of treatment under s 58 MHA 1983, the treatment can only be recommenced if the patient is persuaded to give another consent or the provisions of s 58(3)(b) are complied with.

Provision is made for the review of a patient's treatment under s 57(2) and s 58(3)(b) MHA 1983 by the Mental Health Act Commission. A report on the treatment and the patient's condition must be given by the responsible medical officer to the Commission on the next occasion when he/she makes a s 20(3) MHA 1983 report on the patient (s 61(1)(a) MHA 1983 – see page 23). The Commission may also request such a report at any other time (s 61(1)(b) MHA 1983). Where the patient is subject to a restriction order or direction (see pages 62 and 70) the report to the Commission must be made at the end of the first six months if treatment was given in that period, and after that on the next occasion a report is made under ss 41(6) or 49(3) MHA 1983 (s 61(2)(a) and (b) MHA 1983 – see pages 64 and 70). The Commission may give notice at any time to the responsible medical officer directing him/her that a certificate under s 57(2) or s 57(3)(b) MHA 1983 shall cease to have effect after a particular date. In these circumstances, it will be necessary to go through the s 57 or s 58 procedure again before treatment can recommence. (See s 61(3) MHA 1983.) However, s 61(3) MHA 1983 is subject to s 62 and, in particular, to the provision that treatment should not cease immediately if the responsible medical officer considers that discontinuance would cause serious suffering to the patient (see above s 62(2) MHA 1983).

In order to deal with emergencies that may arise, s 62(1) MHA 1983 makes provision for urgent treatment. The subsection only applies to the categories of treatment covered by ss 57 and 58. Other forms of treatment are covered either by the common law or s 63 MHA 1983 (see page 96). Subsection 62(1)

states that ss 57 and 58 do not apply to the following treatment:
   (i) treatment immediately necessary to save a patient's life;
   (ii) treatment (not being irreversible) which is immediately necessary to prevent a serious deterioration of his/her condition;
   (iii) treatment (not being irreversible or hazardous) which is immediately necessary to alleviate serious suffering by the patient; or
   (iv) treatment (not being irreversible or hazardous) which is immediately necessary and represents the minimum interference necessary to prevent the patient from behaving violently or being a danger to himself/herself or to others.

(s 62(1)(a)–(d) MHA 1983.)

Note that the test is one of *immediate* necessity and not just necessity. For the purposes of the subsection, treatment is irreversible if it has "unfavourable irreversible physical or psychological consequences". This definition does not include irreversible consequences which are deemed to be favourable. Treatment is hazardous if it entails "significant physical hazard". (See s 62(3) MHA 1983.)

*Treatment which does not require consent*

Section 63 MHA 1983 enables treatment to be given to a detained patient without his/her consent. It only applies to treatment for a mental disorder and not for physical disability. Furthermore, the treatment proposed must not be of the types falling within ss 57 and 58 MHA 1983. The treatment must be given by or under the direction of the responsible medical officer. Treatment under s 63 includes psychological and social therapies.

*(b) The common law*

The common law rules on consent to treatment apply to informal patients other than where the treatment falls under s 57 MHA 1983 (see page 92). They also apply to detained patients in respect of treatment which does not come within ss 57, 58, 62 and 63 MHA 1983, such as treatment for physical illness. The common law is based on the fundamental principle that every person's body is inviolate. Exceptions to this principle have developed; for example, physical interference is lawful if the person has consented provided that it is not contrary to the public

## Institutional care and treatment

interest. Thus a person may consent to being examined by a doctor and to receiving treatment for an ailment. Consent in such cases must be real consent. In *Chatterton* v *Gerson* (1981), Bristow J said that "once the patient is informed in broad terms of the nature of the procedure which is intended, and gives her consent, that consent is real".

In cases of adult patients, no other person is capable of consenting on his/her behalf; consent in respect of children may be given by a parent or guardian, or through the wardship jurisdiction of the High Court (see below). Difficulties arise where the patient is unable to give consent, where he/she is unconscious, for example, as a result of a road accident and requires urgent life-saving treatment. The doctor in such a situation is able to do what is reasonably required in the best interests of the patient. This is the medical application of the doctrine of necessity. It must be borne in mind that, in determining what is reasonably required, regard must be had to whether the patient will recover consciousness and therefore be able to consent to further treatment.

These considerations are relevant when deciding whether treatment should be given to a person who is unable to consent in consequence of some form of mental disorder. It must, of course, be remembered that the fact that a person has a mental disorder does not always mean that he/she is rendered incapable of consenting to treatment. Indeed the law will require that consent be given if the person is capable of understanding in broad terms the effects of his/her consent. If the law sought higher standards of comprehension, not only would it apply different standards between those with a mental disorder and others, but it would also deny such people the right to maximum control over their own bodies. When considering the question of consent by people who lack mental capacity, a distinction must be made between minors and adults.

The consent of a minor, who has attained the age of sixteen years, to any surgical, medical or dental treatment is as effective as if he/she were of full age, that is eighteen years (s 8(1) Family Law Reform Act 1969). Consent of a parent or guardian is not necessary. Thus the competence of a minor between sixteen and eighteen years will be assessed as if he/she were an adult. However, until he/she attains the age of eighteen years, the wardship jurisdiction (see below) will be available and may override the wishes of the minor. For minors who have not attained the age of sixteen years, parental or guardian consent to treatment may be necessary. Whether or not parental consent is necessary depends upon the test laid down in the case of *Gillick* v *West Norfolk and Wisbech Area Health Authority and the DHSS* (1985). In that case, Lord Scarman in the House of Lords said:

> "... that as a matter of law the parental right to determine whether or not their minor child below the age of sixteen will have medical treatment terminates if and when the child achieves a sufficient understanding and intelligence to enable him or her to understand what is proposed. It will be a question of fact whether a child seeking advice has sufficient understanding of what is involved to give a consent valid in law. Until the child achieves the capacity to consent, the parental right to make the decision continues save only in exceptional circumstances."

Examples of exceptional circumstances given by Lord Scarman include emergency, parental neglect and an inability to find the parents. If the child in question has a mental disability, this will be one of the facts referred to in order to determine whether he/she has sufficient understanding to give consent.

The wardship jurisdiction of the High Court "is founded on the obvious necessity that the law should place somewhere the care of individuals who cannot take care of themselves, particularly in cases where it is clear that some care should be thrown around them". (See Lord Eldon LC in *Wellesley* v *Duke of Beaufort* (1827).) No important decision concerning a minor who is a ward of court (for example, consent to medical treatment) may be taken without the consent of the court. A minor may be made a ward of court specifically to determine whether or not he/she should undergo a particular form of medical treatment. In determining whether to sanction treatment, the court must regard the welfare of the child as being the paramount consideration (s 1(1) Children Act 1989). Furthermore, the court must have regard to the understanding and intelligence of the minor in accordance with the *Gillick* principle.

The principles applying to the use of wardship in cases of consent to the treatment of a minor with a mental disorder were discussed in two sterilisation cases, *Re D (A Minor)(Wardship: Sterilisation)* (1976) and *Re B (A Minor)(Wardship: Sterilisation)* (1988). In *Re D*, the child was an eleven year old who was born with Sotos syndrome. She was epileptic, had behavioural problems and some impairment of intelligence. Her mother and the paediatrician formed the opinion that D should be sterilised because they were afraid that she would be seduced and give birth to an abnormal child. Heilbron J held that the case was an appropriate one for the wardship jurisdiction. After stressing that the welfare principle applied to the case, she held that an operation for non-therapeutic purposes, such as the one proposed, could not be within the doctor's sole clinical judgment. The evidence showed that her mental and physical conditions and attainment had improved and that future prospects were unpredictable. Although at present she could not give valid consent, the likelihood was that in later years she would be able to make her own choice. On the basis of this evidence the judge held that it would not be in D's best interest for the operation to be performed. To sterilise D would be to deny her one of her basic human rights.

In *Re B,* the House of Lords had to determine whether a seventeen year old woman who had a moderate degree of mental handicap but limited intellectual development should be sterilised. Her ability to understand speech was that of a six year old, and her ability to express herself that of a two year old; she was incapable of giving valid consent. The evidence showed that B was becoming sexually aware. Contraception would be very difficult to supervise and pregnancy would be very traumatic for her. She had no maternal instincts and would be unable to care for any child. B was made a ward of court and Bush J gave leave for the operation to be carried out. The Official Solicitor, acting as her guardian *ad litem*, appealed to the Court of Appeal which dismissed the appeal. On appeal, the House of Lords held that the operation would be in B's best interests. Lords Hailsham LC, Oliver and Bridge stressed that the decision had nothing to do with eugenic theory or with any attempt to lighten the load of those responsible for the care of B. B's welfare was the first and paramount consideration. Lord Templeman felt that a sterilisation operation on a person under the age of eighteen years should only be carried out with the leave of a High Court judge under the wardship jurisdiction. A doctor carrying out such an operation with the consent of a parent or guardian might still be liable in criminal or civil proceedings. Only the court through wardship proceedings could authorise such a drastic step and only after a full and informed investigation.

These cases indicate that each situation should be judged on its own facts and that there is a danger in applying a uniform solution to the problems. Furthermore, they show that where serious treatment is involved, particularly irreversible treatment, the wardship jurisdiction should be used rather than relying solely on parental consent or the opinion of doctors.

When considering adults who lack capacity to consent to

treatment, there is no equivalent to the wardship jurisdiction. In *F* v *West Berkshire Health Authority* (1989), the House of Lords considered the case of an adult woman aged thirty-six years who suffered from a serious mental disability taking the form of an arrested or incomplete development of mind. She was a voluntary patient in a mental hospital and had a general mental capacity of a child of four or five. F formed a relationship with another patient in the hospital and sexual intercourse took place approximately twice a month. The evidence was that F could not cope with pregnancy nor could she care for a baby if she had one. The ordinary means of contraception would not, for a variety of reasons, be effective. It was proposed to sterilise F by ligation of her fallopian tubes. The case eventually came before the House of Lords. A number of arguments were put before the House of Lords aimed at providing a basis for the jurisdiction. It was firstly argued that the ancient prerogative jurisdiction *parens patriae* existed. Under this jurisdiction the court had the power and the duty to protect the property and person of those unable to do so on their own behalf. It was held that, other than the wardship jurisdiction in respect of minors, this ancient jurisdiction had been abolished by the Mental Health Act 1959. Secondly, it was suggested that the jurisdiction of the Court of Protection included matters relating to the person of the patient (see page 190). This again was rejected; the House was of the opinion that the Court of Protection jurisdiction was confined to property and financial matters. The House did, however, confirm that the courts have jurisdiction to make a declaration on the lawfulness of the operation. Lord Bridge succinctly stated the principle at issue in the following manner:

> "... that the court has jurisdiction to declare the lawfulness of such an operation proposed to be performed on the ground that it is, in the circumstances, in the best interests of the woman and that, although such a declaration is not necessary to establish the lawfulness of the operation, in practice the court's jurisdiction should be invoked whenever such an operation is proposed to be performed."

The House of Lords was anxious to avoid the situation where the common law operated to deny proper treatment to people with mental disabilities in cases where they were unable to consent. It was also aware of the practical problems that would arise if every case had to be referred to the courts before treatment could lawfully proceed. In its judgment, the House of Lords decided that the common law provides that "a doctor can lawfully operate on, or give other treatment to, adult patients who are incapable for one reason or another, of consenting to his doing so, provided that the operation or other treatment concerned is in the best interests of such patients" (per Lord Brandon). The consent or approval of the court is not necessary provided that the proposed course of action meets the "best interests" test. Wherever practicable, relatives' views should be sought, but their opinion would not be binding on the doctors. Lord Brandon considered that it would be in the patient's best interest if carried out in order either to save life, or to ensure improvement or prevent deterioration in physical or mental health. Lords Bridge and Goff referred to the principles laid down in *Bolam* v *Friern Hospital Management Committee* (1957). This case makes it clear that we cannot expect absolute perfection from the medical profession. Instead we have to rely upon the test of:

> ". . . the ordinary skilled man exercising and professing to have that special skill. A man need not possess the highest expert skill at the risk of being found negligent. It is a well-established principle that it is sufficient if he exercised the ordinary skill of an ordinary man exercising that particular art."
> (per McNair J.)

Thus the doctor will be required to act in accordance with a responsible and competent body of relevant medical opinion.

However, the members of the House of Lords did express concern over the extreme nature of a sterilisation operation. They felt therefore that as a matter of good practice the court's jurisdiction to make a declaration should be invoked when such an operation was proposed. It was left open whether there were other categories of treatment to which this practice should also apply.

## 8. Residential care homes

A residential care home is defined as:

> "any establishment which provides or is intended to provide, *whether for reward or not*, residential accommodation with both board and personal care for persons in need of personal care by reason of old age, disablement, past or present dependence on alcohol or drugs, or past or present mental disorder."
> (s 1(1) RHA 1984.)

Although the section refers to "mental disorder", any patient subject to detention under Part II or III MHA 1983 must be detained in a mental nursing home registered for that purpose and not in a residential care home (see page 75). However, any person with a mental disorder but not subject to detention under the MHA 1983 may be accommodated in a residential care home. This may include, but is by no means limited to, persons subject to guardianship. Persons with a mental handicap may also be accommodated in a residential care home.

The distinction between a residential care home and a mental nursing home depends upon the type of care that is being provided. A residential care home provides "residential accommodation with both board and personal care". "Personal care" includes assistance with bodily functions if such assistance is required (s 20(1) RHA 1984). The provision of direct and constant professional medical attention is not envisaged; personal care is the type of physical and emotional care that the person may receive from his/her own relatives or close friends. A mental nursing home provides "nursing or other medical treatment (including care, habilitation and rehabilitation under medical supervision) . . ." (see page 75). The crucial difference is that the type of care provided in a mental nursing home is related to professional nursing and medical skills.

A residential care home, other than one which provides accommodation for fewer than four people, must register under Part I of the RHA 1984 (s 1(4) RHA 1984). If fewer than four people within s 1(1) RHA 1984 are to be accommodated, but the home is registered under Part II as a nursing home or mental nursing home, there is an option to register under s 1 RHA 1984 (s 4(1) and (2) RHA 1984). Where the option is exercised, the provisions of Part I RHA 1984 apply to the registered person. It is a criminal offence to carry on a residential care home without registration, and both the manager and the person in control will be liable (ss 2 and 3 RHA 1984). Establishments exempt from registration include schools; hospitals under s 128 National Health Service Act 1977 or as defined by s 145(1) MHA 1983; and voluntary homes, children's homes or community homes within CA 1989. Also excluded are establishments which are used solely as nursing homes or mental nursing homes. (See s 1(5) RHA 1984.)

For the purposes of the RHA 1984, the "registration authority" is the local social services authority for the area in which the residential care home is situated. Applications must be made to the registration authority and accompanied by a registration fee (s 5(1) RHA 1984 – see r 3(1) and (2) Residential Care Homes Regulations 1984 ("RCHR 1984") as amended by 1988 SI No

1192). The RCHR 1984 outline the details which must accompany an application:

*Applicant is manager/intended manager and he/she is not in/to be in control (as owner or otherwise):*
- (i) name, date of birth, address and telephone number;
- (ii) details of professional/technical qualifications/experience of running a home;
- (iii) name and addresses of two previous employers and two referees;
- (iv) name and address and telephone number of the home in respect of which registration is sought;
- (v) if the registration authority so requests, a report by a registered medical practitioner on the state of the applicant's health.

(Sch 1 para 1 RCHR 1984.)

Note that in this situation both the manager and the person who is in control must register.

*Applicant is the person having control/or will have control:*
- (i) the same information as required in the above category;
- (ii) the address of any other residential care home, nursing home, mental nursing home or voluntary home in which he/she has or had a business interest, and the nature of that interest;
- (iii) the location of the home, its form of construction and, where requested by the registration authority, any comments made by the local fire authority, or local environmental health authority;
- (iv) details of accommodation available for residents and employees;
- (v) date upon which the home is to be established;
- (vi) whether any other business will be carried out from the premises;
- (vii) whether registration under Part II RHA 1984 (see page 74) is required;
- (viii) the number, sex, and categories of resident for whom the home is proposed;
- (ix) names, dates of birth, qualifications and experience of any person other than the manager who will be employed in the management of the home, and whether they will live-in;

(x) names, dates of birth, qualifications and experience of any other staff (excluding teaching staff), distinguishing between resident and non-resident and between full-time and part-time staff (including hours of work for the latter category);
(xi) statement of objectives of the home, of the care and attention to be provided, and of any arrangements for the supervision of the residents;
(xii) details of equipment, facilities and services to be provided, and of any special provision for a particular category of resident (eg persons with a mental disorder);
(xiii) arrangements for medical and dental supervision and for nursing care in cases of minor ailments;
(xiv) details of scales of charges to be paid by residents.

(Sch 1 para 3(a) – (n) RCHR 1984.)

*Applicant is a company, society, association or other body or firm:*

(i) the address of the registered or principal office of the firm or body, the full names of the chairperson and secretary of the company, or other responsible persons or partners of the firm;
(ii) if the registration authority so requests, details of their professional or technical qualifications, and experience of running a home.

(Sch 1 para 2(b) RCHR 1984.)

The registration authority may attach conditions to the registration. One condition which *must* be included is that the persons for whom accommodation is provided do not exceed a specified number. Other conditions may regulate the age, sex or category of person who may be residents (s 5(3) RHA 1984). Under RCHR 1984, the categories of residents are as follows:

- old age;
- mental disorder, other than mental handicap, past or present;
- mental handicap;
- alcohol dependence, past or present;
- drug dependence, past or present;
- physical disablement.

(Sch 1 para 3(g) RCHR 1984.)

## Institutional care and treatment

Applicants must specify if residents are over sixty-five years of age or a child. The power to attach conditions is limited to the specific matters mentioned in s 5(3) RHA 1984; conditions relating to other matters cannot be imposed. If it proposes to grant the application, the registration authority must give notice of its proposal to the applicant; the notice must specify the reasons for the proposals. Notice is unnecessary if it is proposed to grant the application subject to conditions which the applicant specified or with which he/she has agreed (s 12(1), (2) and (5) RHA 1984).

An application may be refused on one or more of the following grounds:

(i) the applicant or any person concerned in the running of the home is not fit to do so (s 9(a) RHA 1984);

(ii) for reasons connected with their situation, construction, state of repair, staffing or equipment, the premises are not fit to be used as a residential care home (s 9(b) RHA 1984);

(iii) the way in which it is intended to carry on the home is such as not to provide the services or facilities reasonably required (s 9(c) RHA 1984).

Notice of a proposal to refuse an application must be given by the registration authority (s 12(3) and (5) RHA 1984).

If the registration authority serves a notice under s 12 RHA 1984, it must state that the recipient may, within fourteen days of service, make a written request for an opportunity to make representations in respect of the proposal (s 13(1) RHA 1984). Representations may be written or oral. The registration authority may not finally decide upon registration until the recipient has either made representations or the fourteen day period has expired. If the recipient has asked to make representations but failed to do so within a reasonable time, the registration authority may proceed to a decision (s 13 RHA 1984). Where the registration authority decides to adopt a proposal, it must serve notice to that effect on the applicant informing him/her of the right to appeal to the Registered Homes Tribunal (s 14 RHA 1984).

A certificate of registration must be issued; it must be displayed in a conspicuous place in the residential care home (s 5(6) RHA 1984). A registration authority must keep a register of residential care homes which it has registered. Schedule 3 RCHR 1984 requires the following details to be recorded in the register:

(i) the full name and address of person/persons registered in respect of a residential care home;

(ii) if the registered person is a company, society, association or other body or firm, the full name and address of its registered or principal office, and the full names and addresses of the directors or other persons responsible for the management of the body, or the partners of the firm;

(iii) the name, address and telephone number of the residential care home;

(iv) the number, sex and category of residents indicating the various categories by reference to a code;

(v) the date of registration and the issue of the certificate, and, where applicable, the date of cancellation;

(vi) details of any conditions imposed and any subsequent additional conditions or variations.

Registration of a residential care home may be cancelled by the registration authority on one of the following grounds:

(i) any ground that would entitle the authority to refuse registration;

(ii) non-payment of the annual fee;

(iii) the registered person has been convicted of an offence under Part I RHA 1984 or the regulations in respect of that, or any other, residential care home;

(iv) any other person has been convicted of such an offence in respect of that residential care home;

(v) any condition attached to the registration has not been complied with.

(s 10(c)(i)–(iii) RHA 1984.)

The procedure for notices of cancellation and the right to make representations is the same as for notices under s 12 RHA 1984 (see above).

In an emergency, the registration authority may make an *ex parte* application to a single justice of the peace for an order cancelling, varying or imposing an additional condition. If it appears that there will be "serious risk to the life, health or well-being of the residents unless the order is made", he/she may make an order in writing which will have immediate effect (s 11(1)(b) RHA 1984). In *East Sussex County Council* v *Lyons* (1988) the Court of Appeal held that the justice could not make an order under s 11 RHA 1984 unless he/she was satisfied that there was a risk to life, health or well-being; this principle applied even though the

## Institutional care and treatment

registered person might be considered by the justice to be an unsuitable person to run the home. The court said that there was no reason why, if an authority had before it evidence which might justify a s 11 order, it should not at the same time make use of the slower, but wider provisions of s 12 RHA 1984 as a back-up should the emergency application fail.

An appeal against a registration authority's decision or against a decision of a justice of the peace under s 11 RHA 1984 may be made to the Registered Homes Tribunal (s 15(1) RHA 1984). Written notice must be given to the registration authority; the appeal must be brought within twenty-eight days of the service of notice, or of the date on which the s 11 order was made (s 15(3) RHA 1984). In addition to confirming or not confirming the registration authority's decision or the justice's order, the tribunal may:

(i) vary any condition in force in respect of the home;
(ii) direct that a condition shall cease to have effect;
(iii) direct that such conditions as it thinks fit shall have effect in respect of the home.

(s 15(6) RHA 1984.)

Under the RCHR 1984, the registered person is required to conduct the home so as to make proper provision for the welfare, care and, where appropriate, treatment and supervision of the residents. He/She must ensure that corporal punishment is not used as a sanction in relation to any child in the home (r 9(4) RCHR 1984 as amended by 1988 SI No 1192). First consideration must be given to the need to safeguard and promote the welfare of the resident when reaching a decision in respect of him/her. Good relations must be fostered between the registered person, the employees and the residents. (See r 9(1)–(3) RCHR 1984.)

Suitable facilities must be made for visits by friends, relatives or other visitors. These include facilities for visits by an officer of the local authority under a duty to supervise the resident, for example, his/her guardian under the MHA 1983. Provision must be made for such visits to be held in private (r 11(1) and (2) RCHR 1984). Rule 10(1) RCHR 1984 imposes certain specific duties on the registered person relating to the physical environment of the home (for example, wash basins, heat, light etc); fire precautions; kitchen and catering arrangements; laundry arrangements; arrangements for the receipt of medical attention; arrangements for the recording, safekeeping and disposal of drugs; and arrangements for the training, occupation and recreation facilities for residents. Rules 14–16 RCHR 1984 require that notice be given to the registration authority in the event of certain occurrences such as the absence of the manager, death, theft or accidents.

Records must be kept by the registered person; these must be available for inspection and kept for a minimum period of three years from the date of the last entry (r 6 RCHR 1984). These records must include the statement of the aims of the home, of the care and attention to be provided and of any arrangements made for the supervision of the residents which were submitted to the registration authority at the time of the application. A daily register must also be kept which must include the following particulars:

- the name, address, date of birth and marital status of the resident and whether he/she is subject to any court order or other process;
- the name, address and telephone number of the resident's next of kin or of any person authorised to act on his/her behalf;
- the name, address and telephone number of the resident's registered medical practitioner and of any officer of a local social services authority whose duty it is to supervise the welfare of that person;
- the date on which the resident entered the home;
- the date on which the resident left the home;
- if the resident is transferred to a hospital or nursing home, the date of, and reasons for, the transfer and the name of the hospital or nursing home to which he/she has been transferred;
- if the resident died in the home, the date, time and cause of death;
- if the resident is a child in the care of a local social services authority, the name, address and telephone number of the care authority, or any officer of the authority whose duty it is to supervise the welfare of the child, and of the child's independent visitor (if any);
- if the resident is an adult subject to guardianship of a local social services authority, the name, address and telephone number of that authority and of any officer of the authority whose duty it is to supervise his/her welfare;
- the name and address of any authority, organisation or other body which arranged the resident's admission to the home;

## Institutional care and treatment

- if the resident is a child, the name of any school which he/she is attending or any other place where he/she may be receiving education or vocational training.

(See Sch 2 para 2 RCHR 1984.)

Each patient must have a case record which will contain details of any special needs, any medical treatment required by him/her and any information which may be relevant (for example, details of any periodic review of his/her health, welfare, conduct and progress). Where the home is used to accommodate children, there must be a statement of the sanctions used to control bad behaviour and a record of any sanction administered. Corporal punishment may no longer be administered. There must also be a register within which the date of each child's arrival was notified to the district health authority and the local education authority (Sch 1 para 4 RCHR 1984). A record must also be kept in respect of any child having special educational needs within s 1 Education Act 1981 and the special educational provision being made for him/her (Sch 1 para 5 RCHR 1984; see page 158). Other matters which must be recorded are as follows:

- all medicines kept in the home for a resident, and their disposal when no longer required;
- dates of visits by persons authorised by the Secretary of State or the registration authority;
- food provided for residents in sufficient detail to enable a judgment to be made as to whether the diet is satisfactory;
- fire practice, drills or fire alarm tests, and action taken to remedy defective equipment;
- the procedure to be followed in the event of a fire;
- the procedure to be followed in the event of accidents or a resident going missing;
- details of persons employed in the home to provide personal care (dates of birth, qualifications, experience and number of hours worked);
- a record of any relatives of the registered person, or persons employed at the home, who are residents;
- statements of facilities provided in the home for residents, and of arrangements made for visits by their parents, guardians, friends and other visitors;
- a copy of any report made following an inspection;
- the scale of charges applicable, including any extra

services not included by that scale, and the amounts paid by or in respect of each resident;
- a record of all money or other valuables deposited by a resident for safekeeping or received on his/her behalf and the date upon which they were returned.

(Sch 2 paras 5–17 RCHR 1984.)

The Secretary of State and the registration authority may authorise a person to enter and inspect any premises which are used, or which that person suspects are being used, as a residential care home. Entry may take place "at all times" and not necessarily "reasonable times". Notice need not be given. An inspection must take place at least twice in every twelve months (r 18(1) RCHR 1984 as amended by 1988 SI No 1192). The power of inspection covers records kept by the residential care home. The person registered must give the authorised person such information relating to the running of the home as he/she reasonably requires. Evidence of authorisation must be produced if requested. Obstructing such a person in the exercise of his/her duty is an offence.

# Chapter 4

# Mental Health Review Tribunals

## 1. Introduction

Mental Health Review Tribunals were first established under the Mental Health Act 1959. Their current statutory basis is s 65(1) MHA 1983 which provides for a tribunal known as a Mental Health Review Tribunal ("MHRT") for every regional health authority region and for the whole of Wales. The purpose of MHRTs is to deal with applications and references under the provisions of the MHA 1983. MHRTs have a duty to act judicially in the discharge of their functions. However, for the purposes of the law of contempt, it has been held that they are not courts of law (*Attorney-General* v *Associated Newspaper Group plc and others* (1988)). In hearing applications and references, an MHRT is not acting as an appellate body against the original decision to admit a patient. It is instead reviewing the evidence at the date of the hearing to see whether continued detention or guardianship is still justified. If it is felt that the original admission was in any way unlawful, an application may be made for *habeas corpus*, although it is highly unlikely that the High Court will question the professional judgement of those involved in the admission. The Council of Tribunals must keep under review the working of all MHRTs. Part V MHA 1983 deals with the jurisdiction and powers of MHRTs; in addition, the Mental Health Tribunal Rules 1983 deal with the procedure to be followed at MHRTs.

Under Sch 2 MHA 1983, each MHRT consists of the following:

(i) the legal members — appointed by the Lord Chancellor as having such legal experience as he/she considers suitable;

(ii) the medical members — registered medical practitioners appointed by the Lord Chancellor after consultation with the Secretary of State;

THE LAW OF MENTAL HEALTH

(iii) other members – persons appointed by the Lord Chancellor after consultation with the Secretary of State who have experience in administration, knowledge of social services or other such qualifications or experience as the Lord Chancellor considers suitable.

Members hold and vacate office under the terms of the instrument under which they are appointed. They may resign office by written notice to the Lord Chancellor. A member ceasing to hold office is eligible for re-appointment. One of the legal members for each MHRT will be appointed by the Lord Chancellor as chairperson of the tribunal. The jurisdiction of an MHRT may be exercised by three or more of its members (s 65(3) MHA 1983). Members of an MHRT for the purpose of particular proceedings or group of proceedings are appointed by the chairperson of the tribunal, or by another person appointed by him/her for that purpose. Of the members appointed, one or more must be a legal member, one or more must be a medical member, and one or more must be neither a legal nor medical member. If the chairperson is appointed for particular proceedings, he/she will be the president of the tribunal; in other cases the president will be one of the appointed legal members nominated by the chairperson. However, where the MHRT is considering the application or reference in respect of a restricted patient (see page 62), the choice of president is restricted to those legal members who have been approved for that purpose by the Lord Chancellor.

An MHRT may, and if required by the court must, state a case for determination by the High Court on any question of law which may arise before it (s 78(8) MHA 1983). The procedure for stating a case is found in the Rules of the Supreme Court Order 56.

## 2. Applications and references in respect of Part II patients

*(a) Applications*

An application may be made to an MHRT in any of the following cases:

*Admission for assessment under s 2 MHA 1983*

The patient may apply where he/she is subject to detention under s 2 MHA 1983 (see page 17). An application should be made within fourteen days beginning with the day of admission to hospital (s 66(1)(a) MHA 1983).

## Admission for treatment under s 3 MHA 1983

The patient may apply where he/she is detained for treatment under s 3 MHA 1983 (see page 21). An application should be made within the first six months beginning with the date of admission to hospital (s 66(1)(b) MHA 1983).

## The patient is received into guardianship

The patient may apply if he/she is received into guardianship under s 7 MHA 1983 (see page 30). The application should be made within the first six months beginning with the day on which the application is accepted (s 66(1)(c) MHA 1983).

## Report furnished under s 16 MHA 1983

Where a report is made under s 16 MHA 1983 concerning the reclassification of the patient, an application may be made by the patient or by his/her nearest relative (see page 33). The application should be made within twenty-eight days beginning with the day on which the applicant is informed that the report has been furnished (s 66(1)(d) MHA 1983).

## Transfer from guardianship to hospital under s 19 MHA 1983 regulations

If the patient has been transferred from guardianship to hospital, he/she may apply (see page 36). The application should be made within six months beginning on the day of the transfer (s 66(1)(e) MHA 1983).

## Section 20 MHA 1983 report furnished and the patient is not discharged

The patient may apply if authority for detention or guardianship is renewed under s 20 MHA 1983 (see page 23). An application should be made within the period for which the authority for detention or guardianship is renewed by virtue of the report (s 66(1)(f) 1983).

## Section 25 MHA 1983 report which prevents discharge by the nearest relative of a patient detained under an application for admission for treatment

Where the discharge of a patient detained under an application for treatment has been prevented by virtue of a s 25 MHA 1983 report, the nearest relative may apply to the tribunal (see page 39). Note that the patient cannot apply. An application must be made within twenty-eight days beginning on the day on which the applicant was informed that the report had been furnished (s 66(1)(g) MHA 1983).

*Section 29 MHA 1983 order is made in respect of a patient who is or subsequently becomes liable to be detained or subject to guardianship*

Where the court makes an order appointing an acting nearest relative in respect of a patient, the nearest relative (that is, the nearest relative determined under s 26 MHA 1983 – see page 8) may apply to the MHRT within twelve months beginning with the date of the order, and in any subsequent period of twelve months during which the order continues in force (s 66(1)(h) MHA 1983).

(See s 66(1) and (2) MHA 1983.)

*(b) References*

The Secretary of State has a general discretion to refer to an MHRT any patient who is liable to be detained or subject to guardianship under Part II MHA 1983. For the purpose of obtaining information necessary for such a reference, any registered medical practitioner authorised by or on behalf of the patient may visit and examine him/her in private. The registered medical practitioner may require the production of and inspect any records relating to the treatment or detention of the patient in any hospital. (See s 67(1) MHA 1983.)

Under s 68 MHA 1983, a hospital manager has a duty to refer the case of certain patients to an MHRT. This duty arises in respect of a patient who is admitted for treatment or is transferred from guardianship to hospital and does not exercise his/her right to apply to an MHRT under s 66(1)(b) or (e) MHA 1983. Once the period within which such an application must be made has expired, the hospital manager must refer the patient's case to the tribunal unless an application has been made under s 66(1)(d), (g) or (h) MHA 1983, or a reference made under s 67(1) MHA 1983. (See s 68(1) MHA 1983.)

A hospital manager must also make a reference where authority for detention has been renewed under s 20 MHA 1983 and a period of three years has elapsed since the case was last considered by an MHRT (s 68(2) MHA 1983). Where the patient has not attained the age of sixteen years, the period is one year.

Any registered medical practitioner authorised by or on behalf of the patient may at any reasonable time visit and examine the

## Mental Health Review Tribunals

patient in private for the purpose of providing information in respect of a case referred by a hospital manager. The medical practitioner may require the production of and inspect any records relating to the detention or the treatment of the patient in any hospital. (See s 68(3) MHA 1983.)

## 3. Applications and references in respect of Part III patients

### (a) Applications

An application may be made to an MHRT in respect of a patient who is subject to a hospital or guardianship order (see pages 56–59). Section 66 MHA 1983 applies with some modifications to patients subject to hospital or guardianship orders; the following subsections apply to this category of patient:

(i) s 66(1)(d) MHA 1983 – a report furnished under s 16 MHA 1983:

(ii) s 66(1)(e) MHA 1983 – transfer from guardianship to hospital under s 19 MHA 1983;

(iii) s 66(1)(f) MHA 1983 – a report made under s 20 MHA 1983 and the patient is not discharged.

(s 40(4) and Sch 1 para 9 MHA 1983; note that references to ss 16, 19 and 20 are to the modified sections.)

It should be noted that the nearest relative of a hospital or guardianship order patient cannot apply for discharge under s 23 MHA 1983 (Sch 1 paras 2 and 8 MHA 1983). Nor can a patient subject to a hospital order apply to an MHRT within the first six months of detention; but he/she may apply between six and twelve months after the making of the order, and thereafter during each subsequent period of one year. (Sch 1 paras 2 and 9 MHA 1983.)

The justification for preventing the patient from applying to an MHRT within the first six months of a hospital order being made is that, unlike civil admission, a court has recently examined the evidence of the two registered medical practitioners. It follows that where there is no judicial consideration of this evidence, the patient should be allowed to apply within that period. Under s 69(2) MHA 1983, the following patients may apply to an MHRT in the six month period beginning with the date of the order or direction:

THE LAW OF MENTAL HEALTH

    (i) a patient who was originally detained subject to a restriction order and who remains in hospital after it expires as if he/she were subject to a hospital order made on the date the restriction order expired (see s 41(5) MHA 1983 and page 64);

    (ii) a patient who was originally detained under the legislation in force in Northern Ireland, the Channel Islands, the Isle of Man or Scotland and is transferred to a hospital in England or Wales under that legislation (see ss 82 and 85 MHA 1983 and s 77(2) Mental Health (Scotland) Act 1984);

    (iii) a patient admitted to hospital under an order made under s 5(1) Criminal Procedure (Insanity) Act 1964 (see page 180);

    (iv) a patient subject to a direction under ss 46(3), 47(3) or 48(3) MHA 1983 (see pages 63 and 68).

(s 69(2)(a) and (b) MHA 1983.)

In addition to applications under s 66 MHA 1983 (as modified by Sch 1), an application may also be made under s 69(1) MHA 1983. The nearest relative of a patient admitted to hospital in pursuance of a hospital order may apply to an MHRT in the period between six and twelve months after the making of the court order. Thereafter, the nearest relative may apply within any subsequent period of twelve months (s 69(1)(a) MHA 1983). Where the patient is subject to a guardianship order, he/she may apply within the first six months of the order; the nearest relative may also apply within the first twelve months of the order and in each subsequent twelve month period (s 69(1)(b) MHA 1983).

A restricted patient who is detained in hospital may apply to an MHRT between six and twelve months after the making of the order or the direction, and in any subsequent period of twelve months (s 70(a) and (b) MHA 1983). "Restricted patient" covers the following persons:

    (i) a person subject to a restriction order under s 41 MHA 1983 (see page 62);

    (ii) a person subject to a restriction direction under s 49 MHA 1983 (see page 70);

    (iii) a person subject to a direction under s 46(3) MHA 1983 (see page 63);

    (iv) a person who is treated as subject to a hospital order and restriction order under s 5(1) Criminal Procedure (Insanity) Act 1964 or ss 6 or 14(1) Criminal Appeal Act 1968;

(v) a person who is treated as subject to a hospital order and a restriction order or a transfer direction and restriction direction by virtue of s 82(2) (transfer from Northern Ireland), s 85(2) (transfer from Channel Islands or Isle of Man) or s 77(2) Mental Health (Scotland) Act 1984 (transfer from Scotland).

(s 79 MHA 1983.)

Where a restricted patient has been conditionally discharged and is later recalled to hospital, he/she may make an application to an MHRT within the period between six and twelve months from the date of recall, and thereafter in any subsequent period of twelve months (s 75(1)(b) MHA 1983; for conditional discharge see page 64). If he/she is conditionally discharged but is not recalled to hospital, he/she may apply to an MHRT within the period between twelve months and two years from the date of that discharge and in any subsequent two year period (s 75(2)(a) and (b) MHA 1983). When hearing an application under s 75(2) MHA 1983, ss 73 and 74 do not apply (see pages 121–124). Instead, the MHRT may:

(i) vary any condition to which the patient is subject in connection with his/her discharge;

(ii) impose any condition which might have been imposed in connection with his/her discharge;

(iii) direct that the restriction order or restriction direction to which he/she is subject shall cease to have effect (the patient will cease to be liable to be detained under the relevant hospital order or transfer direction).

(s 75(3)(a) and (b) MHA 1983.)

*(b) References*

The provisions of s 67 MHA 1983 (references to an MHRT by the Secretary of State – see above page 114) and s 68 MHA 1983 (references to an MHRT by the managers of hospitals – see above page 114) apply to patients subject to a hospital order without restriction under s 37 MHA 1983 (s 40(1)(b), (4) and Sch 1 Part 1 MHA 1983).

The Secretary of State has a general discretion to refer the case of a restricted patient to an MHRT (s 71(1) MHA 1983; for the definition of "restricted patient" see page 62). If the patient has been conditionally discharged and not recalled to hospital (see page 64), the reference is to be made to the tribunal for the area in which he/she is residing. There is a duty on the Secretary of State to refer the case of a restricted patient if it has not been considered by an MHRT within the last three years (s 71(2) MHA 1983). The Secretary of State must also refer the case of a person who is, by virtue of an order under s 5(1) Criminal Procedure (Insanity) Act 1964, treated as a restricted patient and who has not exercised his/her right to apply to an MHRT within the six month period beginning with the making of the order (s 71(5) MHA 1983). If such a person makes an application but then withdraws it, he/she shall be treated as if no application had been made. Where the withdrawal takes place after the expiry of the six month period, the reference must be made as soon as possible after that date. (See s 71(6) MHA 1983 and page 180.)

## 4. The powers of a Mental Health Review Tribunal

### (a) General power to discharge and reclassify unrestricted patients

Section 72 MHA 1983 gives an MHRT the power to discharge patients other than those subject to restriction orders. For the purposes of this section, and ss 73 – 75 MHA 1983, "discharge" means release from hospital *(Secretary of State for the Home Department v MHRT for the Mersey Regional Health Authority; Same v MHRT for Wales* (1986)). The section applies both to applications and to references by the hospital managers or the Secretary of State (s 72(6) MHA 1983). It covers patients admitted to hospital or subject to guardianship under Parts II and III MHA 1983, but does not apply to restricted patients other than as provided for in ss 73 and 74 MHA 1983 (s 72(7) MHA 1983 – see below). Where an application or reference is made, an MHRT has a general discretion to discharge a patient detained in hospital under the MHA 1983. In addition, the patient must be discharged by the MHRT if certain conditions (see below) are satisfied. When exercising this power, the MHRT is not reviewing the validity of the original admission. Ackner LJ in *R v Hallstrom, ex parte W* (1985) stressed that the jurisdiction of the MHRT under s 72 MHA 1983 is limited to entertaining applications by a person "liable" to be detained under the Act; the tribunal cannot consider the underlying validity of the admission which gave rise to the liability to be detained.

The circumstances in which an MHRT is required to discharge a patient depends upon the particular form of admission. These will be considered in turn:

*Admission for assessment:* an MHRT must direct that a patient liable to be detained under s 2 MHA 1983 must be discharged if satisfied:

(i) that he/she is not then suffering from mental disorder or from mental disorder of a nature or degree which warrants detention in hospital for assessment (or assessment followed by medical treatment) for at least a limited period; or

(ii) that his/her detention under s 2 MHA 1983 is not justified in the interests of his/her own health or safety or with a view to the protection of other persons.

(s 72(1)(a)(i) and (ii) MHA 1983.)

*Admission other than under s 2 MHA 1983:* an MHRT must discharge a patient liable to detention other than under s 2 MHA 1983 if satisfied:

(i) that he/she is not then suffering from mental illness, psychopathic disorder, severe mental impairment or mental impairment or from any of those forms of disorder of a nature or degree which makes it appropriate for him/her to be liable to be detained in a hospital for medical treatment (s 72(1)(b)(i) MHA 1983); note that "medical treatment" includes nursing, care, habilitation and rehabilitation under medical supervision and not just treatment designed to alleviate or prevent deterioration of the patient's condition – see *R* v *Mersey Mental Health Review Tribunal, ex parte D* (1987); or

(ii) that it is not necessary for the health or safety of the patient or for *the protection* of other persons that he/she should receive such treatment (s 72(1)(b)(ii) MHA 1983); or

(iii) in the case of an application under s 66(1)(g) MHA 1983 (see page 113), that the patient would not be likely to act in a manner *dangerous* to other persons or to himself/herself (note that this is a much narrower provision than (ii) – it appears to require probable physical injury rather than the more general forms of conduct coming within (ii)) (s 72(1)(b)(iii) MHA 1983).

It is important that an MHRT, when considering an application in respect of a patient, should bear in mind the difference between the various grounds for discharge. In *R* v *Mental Health Tribunal, ex parte Pickering* (1986), Forbes J said that an MHRT must clearly identify whether it reached its conclusions on the basis of ground (i), (ii) or (iii). This is particularly important as the doctor in charge of the patient, and the patient himself/herself, should know the reasons why an application has been turned down.

As noted above, an MHRT has a general discretion to discharge a patient when an application is made. When considering the exercise of this general discretion with regard to patients liable to be detained other than under s 2 MHA 1983, it must "have regard" to certain matters; it is not obliged to take these matters into consideration, but will invariably do so. Firstly, the MHRT must have regard to the likelihood of the medical treatment alleviating or preventing a deterioration in the patient's condition. This is another example of the treatability test (see page 22), although unlike admission under s 3 MHA 1983 it applies to both minor and major forms of mental disorder (see the use of the treatability test when renewing authority for detention — page 24). Secondly, in the case of a patient suffering from mental illness or severe mental impairment, the MHRT must have regard to the likelihood of him/her, if discharged, being able to care for himself/herself, obtaining the care that he/she needs or guarding himself/herself against serious exploitation. (See s 72(2) MHA 1983.)

It may be necessary to make arrangements for the reception of a patient back into the community if he/she is discharged by an MHRT. An immediate return may be detrimental to the patient and also to his/her carers. Consequently, an MHRT may direct that the patient be discharged under s 72(1) MHA 1983 at some specified future date during the period within which he/she may be lawfully detained (s 72(3) MHA 1983). Where an MHRT decides not to discharge a patient under s 72(1) MHA 1983, it may recommend under the Act that he/she be granted leave of absence or transferred to another hospital or into guardianship with a view to facilitating his/her eventual discharge. It must be emphasised that these are recommendations and not directions. When making such a recommendation, an MHRT must specify the period after which it will further consider the case in the event of non-compliance (r 24(4) Mental Health Review Tribunal Rules 1983). If the recommendation is not complied with, the MHRT may reconvene and give further consideration to his/her case. Under r 25(2) Mental Health Review Tribunal Rules 1983, an MHRT may, at the end of the specified period for compliance, make enquiries of the responsible authority to see whether the statutory recommendation has been complied with. If not, it may give the parties not less than fourteen days' notice of its intention to reconvene the proceedings. (See s 72(3)(a) and (b) MHA 1983.)

*Guardianship:* an MHRT has a general discretion to discharge a patient from guardianship when an application is made by him/her or on his/her behalf. It must discharge the patient if satisfied that:

(i) he/she is not suffering from mental illness, psychopathic disorder, severe mental impairment or mental impairment; or

(ii) it is not necessary in the interests of the patient, or for the protection of others, that the patient should remain subject to guardianship.

(s 72(4) MHA 1983.)

*Reclassification of patients:* where an application is before an MHRT *under any of the provisions of the MHA 1983* and the tribunal decides not to discharge the patient, it may reclassify the patient. It can do so if satisfied that the patient is suffering from a form of mental disorder other than the one specified in the application, order or direction under which the patient is detained or subject to guardianship (s 72(5) MHA 1983 – for reclassification see page 33). The wording of this subsection includes restricted patients, although in practice such reclassification is exceptionally rare.

*(b) Power to discharge restricted patients*

Section 72(1) MHA 1983 does not apply to restricted patients except as provided in ss 73 and 74. Section 73(1) MHA 1983 enables an MHRT, upon an application or a reference, to discharge absolutely a restricted patient who is subject to a restriction order under s 41 MHA 1983 (see page 62). Unlike s 72 MHA 1983, there is no general discretionary power to discharge such patients. Instead, the MHRT must be satisfied regarding the matters stated in s 72(1)(b)(i) or (ii) MHA 1983 (see page 119), and also that it is not appropriate for the patient to remain liable to be recalled to hospital for further treatment (s 73(1)(a) and (b) MHA 1983). If it is so satisfied, the MHRT must direct the absolute discharge of the patient; it is not a matter for discretion. Where the patient is absolutely discharged, he/she ceases to be liable to be detained by virtue of the relevant hospital order and the restriction order shall cease to have effect (s 73(3) MHA 1983).

If an MHRT is satisfied in respect of a restricted patient

regarding the matters stated in s 72(1)(b)(i) or (ii), but is not satisfied that it is inappropriate for him/her to remain liable to recall, it must direct the conditional discharge of the patient (s 73(2) MHA 1983). The provisions of s 73(2) MHA 1983 are mandatory; once an MHRT is satisfied that either condition has been met, it is obliged to make the order which is final, subject only to the power to defer under s 73(7) MHA 1983 (see page 123 and *R v Oxford Regional Mental Health Tribunal, ex parte Secretary of State for the Home Department* (1987)). A patient who is conditionally discharged may be recalled to hospital by the Secretary of State under s 42(3) as if he/she had been conditionally discharged under s 42(2) MHA 1983 (s 73(4) MHA 1983; see page 64; for the right of a recalled patient to apply to an MHRT see page 117).

In *R v Merseyside MHRT ex parte Kay* (1989), the applicant argued that as a tribunal had found that he was no longer suffering from a mental disorder, he ceased to be a "patient" and should not therefore be subject to a conditional discharge which allowed for recall. This argument was rejected by the Court of Appeal who said that it was out of step with the philosophy of the MHA 1983. Section 73 MHA 1983 gave the tribunal power to impose a conditional discharge and retain residual control over a patient not then suffering from mental disorder, or not to a degree requiring continued hospital detention. It was designed to ensure proper community care for the patient and protection for the public and should not be lightly set aside in the absence of clear words.

It is open to the MHRT at the time of discharge, and to the Secretary of State at any subsequent time, to impose conditions on the patient. The Secretary of State may from time to time vary any conditions whether imposed by him/her or by the MHRT (s 73(4) and (5) MHA 1983). The type of condition that may be imposed normally relates to accommodation and contact with, for example, social services and doctors (note that there is no power to require the patient to undergo medical treatment – see page 91).

In *Secretary of State for the Home Department v MHRT for the Mersey Regional Health Authority; Same v MHRT for Wales*, the MHRT imposed a condition that the patient should continue to reside in hospital because he required "treatment" in the form of supervision and guidance as to personal hygiene and social rehabilitation. This treatment was not, argued the MHRT, "medical treatment" as defined in s 145(1) MHA 1983. This line of argument was rejected on appeal. The Queen's Bench Division held that as "discharge" meant discharge from hospital it was unlawful to impose a condition that a patient must reside in hospital. The treatment envisaged was medical treatment within s 145(1) MHA 1983, so the MHRT was wrong in concluding that s 72(1)(b)(i) MHA 1983 had been satisfied. For the right of a conditionally discharged patient to apply to an MHRT, see page 117.

Under s 73(7) MHA 1983, an MHRT may defer a final direction for the conditional discharge (but not the absolute discharge) of a patient until necessary arrangements have been made for the patient's after-care. The arrangements must meet with the approval of the MHRT, although under r 25(1) Mental Health Review Tribunal Rules 1983, there is no need for another hearing in order to make any further decision. In *R* v *Oxford Regional Mental Health Tribunal, ex parte Secretary of State for the Home Department* (above), the House of Lords said that MHRTs only had power to defer under s 73(7) MHA 1983 for the necessary arrangements for the patient's discharge to be made. Before they make such an order they must be satisfied that s 73(2) MHA 1983 is satisfied; if they are, the conditional discharge is mandatory and there is no power to reconsider the decision at some later date. Lord Bridge of Harwich said that there was no power under s 73(7) to defer to a fixed date as it was impossible for an MHRT to assess how long it will take to make the necessary arrangements. The decision should simply state that the direction is deferred until the MHRT is satisfied that the arrangements are suitable — and the MHRT should specify what arrangements are required. It is also unlawful to defer under s 73(7) in order to allow arrangements to be made to transfer the patient to another hospital — this would be inconsistent with the intention of returning him/her into the community.

The provisions of s 73 MHA 1983 as outlined above are without prejudice to the powers of the Secretary of State under s 42 in respect of restricted patients (s 73(8) MHA 1983; for s 42 see page 64).

*(c) Restricted patients subject to restriction directions*

Special provisions apply to restricted patients who are subject to restriction directions (see page 70). In these cases, the final say as to whether a patient should be absolutely or conditionally discharged lies with the Secretary of State (the Home Secretary) and the MHRT's role is one of notifying him/her of what it would do if the case came before it under s 73 MHA 1983. When hearing an application or reference in respect of such a patient:

(i) it shall notify the Secretary of State whether, in its opinion, the patient would if subject to a restriction order be entitled to be absolutely or conditionally discharged under s 73 MHA 1983 (s 74(1)(a) MHA 1983); and

(ii) if it does notify the Secretary of State that the patient would be entitled to absolute or conditional discharge, it may recommend that, in the event of him/her not being discharged, he/she should continue to be detained in hospital (s 74(1)(b) MHA 1983).

The effect of this notification depends upon whether the patient was originally a remand prisoner transferred under s 48 MHA 1983 (see page 67). If he/she is not such a person, then where the MHRT gives notification that the patient would be entitled to be absolutely or conditionally discharged the Secretary of State may, within ninety days, notify the MHRT that he/she may be so discharged. The MHRT must then direct the absolute or conditional discharge of the patient (s 74(2)(a) and (b) MHA 1983). Subsections 73(3)–(8) MHA 1983 (see page 121) apply as if the references to hospital order and restriction order are to transfer direction and restriction direction (s 74(6) MHA 1983). If, at the end of the ninety day period, the MHRT has not been notified that the patient may be discharged, the managers of the hospital must transfer him/her to a prison or other institution in which he/she might have been detained if he/she had not been transferred to hospital. However, the patient cannot be transferred in these circumstances if the MHRT has made a recommendation under s 74(1)(b) MHA 1983 that in the event of non-discharge he/she should remain in hospital. (See s 74(3) MHA 1983.)

If the patient is a remand prisoner who has been transferred under s 48 MHA 1983, different rules apply. Where the MHRT notifies the Secretary of State that the patient would, if within s 73, be entitled to absolute or conditional discharge, the patient must be returned to prison or other institution unless a recommendation has been made under s 74(1)(b) that he/she should remain in hospital. The reason for this is that the patient is still subject to the jurisdiction of the court and it must then determine his/her guilt or innocence; such matters are not to be determined by the Secretary of State. (See s 74(4) MHA 1983.)

## 5. Procedure before a tribunal

*(a) Applications*

The procedure for applications and conducting a case before an MHRT is governed by the Mental Health Review Tribunal Rules 1983 ("MHRTR 1983"). Any irregularity resulting from a failure to comply with the MHRTR 1983 before the MHRT has determined the application will not in itself render the proceedings void. However, the MHRT may and, if it considers that the irregularity has prejudiced any person, must take such steps as it thinks fit to cure the irregularity. This may include amending documents or giving any notice (r 28 MHRTR 1983). Applications may be made to an MHRT by the patient, a person authorised by him/her, his/her representative, or the nearest relative within the time limits prescribed by the MHA 1983 (see page 131 for the special provisions that apply to assessment applications; references by the Secretary of State, the Home Secretary or the hospital managers are considered at page 133). They must be in writing (no particular form is prescribed) and addressed to the tribunal for the area in which the hospital or mental nursing home in which the patient is detained is located, or for the area in which a patient subject to guardianship is residing (s 77(3) MHA 1983). An application must, wherever possible, include the following information:

(i) the name of the patient;
(ii) the patient's address, which shall include:
   – the address of the hospital or mental nursing home where he/she is detained;
   – the name and address of the patient's private guardian;
   – in the case of a conditionally discharged patient or one to whom leave of absence has been given under the MHA 1983 (see pages 40 and 122), the address of the hospital or mental nursing home where he/she was last detained, or is still liable to be detained, together with his/her current address;
(iii) if the applicant is the nearest relative, his/her name and address and his/her relationship to the patient;
(iv) the section of the MHA 1983 under which the patient is detained, or is liable to be detained;
(v) the name and address of any representative authorised under r 10 MHRTR 1983 – if none has been authorised,

there should be a statement as to whether or not the applicant intends to authorise a representative or conduct his/her own case (for r 10 see page 134).

(r 3(2)(a)–(e) MHRTR 1983.)

If any of the above information is not included, the tribunal may request the responsible authority or, in the case of a restricted patient, the Secretary of State to provide it so far as they can practicably do so. In the case of a patient liable to be detained under the MHA 1983, the responsible authority are the managers of the hospital or mental nursing home in which he/she is detained. For patients subject to guardianship, the responsible authority is the local social services authority as defined by s 34(3) MHA 1983.

When it receives the application, the tribunal must send notice to the responsible authority, the patient if he/she is not the applicant, and the Secretary of State if the patient is a restricted patient (r 4(1)(a)–(c) MHRTR 1983). Within three weeks of receiving such notice, the appropriate authority must provide the tribunal and, in the case of a restricted patient, the Secretary of State with a statement under r 6(1) MHRTR 1983. Such a statement must contain, so far as it is within the knowledge of the responsible authority, the following information:

(i) the patient's full name;
(ii) the age of the patient;
(iii) the date of admission to the current hospital or mental nursing home, or reception into guardianship;
(iv) if the patient is treated in a mental nursing home under a contractual arrangement with a health authority, the name of that authority;
(v) the statutory basis of the authority for detention or guardianship and any renewal or changes in that authority;
(vi) the form of mental disorder from which the patient is recorded as suffering in the authority for detention, including any amendments under s 16 or s 72(5) MHA 1983, but excluding cases within s 5 Criminal Procedure (Insanity) Act 1964 (see pages 32, 121 and 180);
(vii) the name of the responsible medical officer (see page 28) and the period of time for which the patient has been under his/her care;
(viii) if another registered medical practitioner is, or has recently been, largely concerned with the patient's

treatment, the name of that practitioner and the period of time for which the patient has been under his/her care;

(ix) dates of all previous tribunal hearings, decisions reached and the reasons given;

(x) details of any Court of Protection hearings and of any receivership order made in respect of the patient;

(xi) the name and address of the nearest relative or anybody exercising that function;

(xii) the name and address of any other person taking a close interest in the patient;

(xiii) details of any leave of absence granted in the past two years (including duration of such leave and particulars of the arrangements made for the patient's residence while on leave).

(r 6(1)(a) and Sch 1 Part A MHRTR 1983.)

In addition to the above, the appropriate authority must provide an up-to-date medical report which has been prepared for the tribunal. This report must include all the relevant medical history and a full report on the patient's mental condition (r 6(1)(b) and Sch 1 Part B para 1 MHRTR 1983). Wherever reasonably practicable, the appropriate authority should also supply the tribunal with an up-to-date social report on the patient including his/her home and family circumstances, employment and housing opportunities, community and medical support and the patient's financial circumstances. The authority should also give its views on the patient's suitability for discharge along with any other information or observations it may wish to make on the application. (See r 6(1)(c) and Sch 1 Part B paras 2 – 4 MHRTR 1983.)

If the patient is a restricted patient, the Secretary of State must, within three weeks of receiving the authority's report, send to the tribunal a statement containing any further information which he/she considers may be relevant (r 6(2) MHRTR 1983).

Slightly different provisions apply where the application is made in respect of a conditionally discharged patient (see page 122). Instead of the above statement and reports being provided, the Secretary of State must, so far as it is within his/her knowledge, send to the tribunal within six weeks of receiving notice of the application a statement containing the following information:

(i) the full name of the patient;

(ii) the patient's age;

(iii) the history of the patient's present liability to detention including details of his/her offence, dates of the original order or direction and of the conditional discharge;

(iv) the form of mental disorder from which the patient is recorded as suffering in the authority for detention (not applicable to cases within s 5 Criminal Procedure (Insanity) Act 1964);

(v) the name and address of any medical practitioner responsible for the care and supervision of the patient in the community and the period which the patient has spent under the care of the practitioner;

(vi) the name of any social worker or probation officer responsible for the care and supervision of the patient in the community and the period which the patient has spent under the care of that person.

(r 6(3)(a) Sch 1 Part C MHRTR 1983.)

He/She must also provide certain reports so far as is practicable. Where there is a medical practitioner responsible for the care and supervision of the patient in the community, an up-to-date medical report should be prepared for the tribunal. Similarly, if a social worker or probation officer is responsible for the patient's community care and supervision, an up-to-date report should be prepared for the tribunal on his/her progress in the community since discharge. A report should also be made on the patient's home circumstances. Finally, the Secretary of State should also express any views which he/she may have on the suitability of the patient for absolute discharge along with any other observations on the application which he/she wishes to make. (See r 6(3) and Sch 1 Parts C and D MHRTR 1983.)

Copies of any of the above statements received by the tribunal must be sent to the applicant and also to the patient if he/she is not the applicant. If, when making any of the above statements, the appropriate authority or the Secretary of State feels that part of them should be withheld from the patient on the ground that disclosure would adversely affect his/her health or welfare, or that of other persons, that part should be made in a separate document (r 6(4) MHRTR 1983). Reasons should be given why it is felt that the disclosure of the information in question would have such a detrimental effect. When copies of the statement are sent to the applicant or the patient, information contained in such a separate document is excluded. (See r 6(5) MHRTR 1983.)

On receiving a statement from the authority or the Secretary of

State, the tribunal is required to give notice of proceedings to the following persons:

  (i) if the patient is liable to be detained in a mental nursing home, the registration authority of that home (see page 75);
  (ii) where the patient is subject to the guardianship of a private guardian, that guardian;
  (iii) where the patient's financial affairs are under the control of the Court of Protection, the court;
  (iv) where any person other than the applicant is named in the authority's statement as exercising the function of the nearest relative, that person;
  (v) where a health authority has a right to discharge the patient under s 23(3) MHA 1983, that authority;
  (vi) any other person who, in the opinion of the tribunal, should have an opportunity to be heard.

(r 7(a) – (f) MHRTR 1983.)

The chairperson of the tribunal must then appoint the members who will hear the application. Certain persons are not qualified to serve on a tribunal because of a potential conflict of interests between them and the patient. Thus a member or officer of the responsible authority or a health authority having a power of discharge under s 23(3) MHA 1983 is not qualified to sit on the tribunal. In addition, any person who has a personal connection with the patient, or has recently treated him/her in a professional medical capacity, is also disqualified from sitting on the tribunal dealing with the patient's case. Where the application or reference relates to a restricted patient, the persons qualified to serve as president of the tribunal are restricted to those persons approved for that purpose by the Lord Chancellor. The tribunal must give at least fourteen days' notice of the date, time and place fixed for the hearing to all the parties and, in the case of a restricted patient, the Secretary of State. It is open to the parties to consent to a shorter period of notice. (See r 20 MHRTR 1983.) Subject to the MHRTR 1983, the tribunal may give such directions as it thinks fit to ensure a speedy and just determination of the application (r 13 MHRTR 1983).

In certain circumstances the hearing of an application may be postponed by the tribunal if it considers it to be in the interest of the patient. The power of postponement applies where the application by or in respect of a patient has recently been heard and determined by another tribunal in the same or any other area. Consideration of the application may be postponed until such date as the tribunal may direct; however, it cannot be later than the expiry of the current period of detention or six months from the determination of the previous hearing, whichever is the earlier. If a tribunal postpones a hearing of the application, it must give, in writing, the reasons for its decision and the period of postponement. Copies must be sent to the parties and, in the case of a restricted patient, the Secretary of State. Not less than seven days before the end of the period of postponement, the tribunal must send the notices required under r 4 MHRTR 1983 (see above). The application must then be heard unless it has been withdrawn before the period of postponement expires, or is deemed to be withdrawn under r 19 MHRTR 1983 (see below), or has been determined under r 9(6) MHRTR 1983. Rule 9(6) MHRTR 1983 states that where a new application which is not postponed under these provisions is made in respect of the patient, the tribunal may direct that any earlier postponed applications should also be determined at the same hearing.

The power to postpone does not apply to the following applications:

(i) applications under s 66(1)(d) MHA 1983 (report furnished under s 16 MHA 1983 – see page 113);

(ii) applications under s 66(1)(f) MHA 1983 (patient is not discharged after a report under s 20 MHA 1983 – see page 113) unless the previous application was made to the tribunal more than three months after the patient's admission to hospital or reception into guardianship;

(iii) applications under s 66(1)(g) MHA 1983 (report furnished under s 25 MHA 1983 in respect of a patient detained in pursuance of an application for treatment – see page 113);

(iv) an application where the previous application was determined before a break or change in the authority for the patient's detention or guardianship.

(r 9(2) MHRTR 1983.)

For the purposes of (iv), a break or change in the authority for detention or guardianship occurs only in the following situations:

- on the admission of the patient to hospital in pursuance of an application for treatment or a hospital order without an order restricting discharge;

## Mental Health Review Tribunals

- on the patient's reception into guardianship in pursuance of a guardianship application or a guardianship order;
- on the application to him/her of the provisions of Parts II and III MHA 1983 as if he/she had been so admitted or received following the making of a transfer direction, the ceasing of effect of a transfer direction or an order or direction restricting his/her discharge (see page 66);
- on his/her transfer from guardianship into hospital in pursuance of regulations under s 19 MHA 1983 (see page 36).

(r 9(7) MHRTR 1983.)

An application may be withdrawn at any time at the request of the applicant provided that it is made in writing and the tribunal agrees. If the patient ceases to be detained or subject to guardianship, an application to an MHRT is deemed to have been withdrawn. In both situations the MHRT must inform the parties to the case and, in the case of a restricted patient, the Secretary of State. (See r 19(1)–(3) MHRTR 1983.)

Any document required or authorised by the MHRTR 1983 to be sent or given to any person may be sent by prepaid post or delivered:

(i) in the case of a document directed to the tribunal or chairperson, to the tribunal office;

(ii) in any other case, to the last known address of the person to whom the document is directed.

(r 27 MHRTR 1983.)

### (b) Assessment applications

The above applications procedure applies with some modification to assessment applications. An assessment application is an application by a patient who is detained for assessment under s 2 MHA 1983 and is entitled to apply, or has already applied, under s 66(1)(a) MHA 1983. The twenty-eight days' maximum duration, and the fourteen days within which the application must be made, necessitate the following changes to the rules outlined above. Assessment applications must be made to the tribunal in writing signed by the patient or some person authorised by him/her to do so on his/her behalf. Where it is made by somebody on behalf of the patient, that fact must be stated on the application. Wherever possible, the application must include the following information:

(i) the name of the patient;
(ii) the address of the hospital or mental nursing home in which he/she is detained;
(iii) the name and address of the patient's nearest relative and his/her relationship with the patient;
(iv) the name of any representative authorised under r 10 MHRTR 1983 or, if none, whether the patient intends to authorise such a representative or to conduct his/her own case.

(r 30(2)(a) – (d) MHRTR 1983.)

If any of this information is not provided in the application, it will be provided, so far as is practicable, by the responsible authority at the request of the tribunal. The tribunal must then fix a date for the hearing which is not later than seven days after receiving the application; it must also determine the time and venue. Notice of date, time and venue must be given to the patient, the appropriate authority, the nearest relative (where practicable) and any other person whom the tribunal considers should have an opportunity to be heard. (See r 31 MHRTR 1983.)

At this stage the chairperson of the tribunal should appoint the members who are going to deal with the case (see r 8 MHRTR 1983 for the procedure). Upon receiving a notice of an assessment application from a tribunal, or a request for information if earlier, the responsible authority must provide the tribunal with copies of the admission papers. It must also provide the tribunal with such information as is within its knowledge as specified in Part A, and such reports specified in Part B of Schedule 1 MHRTR 1983 as can reasonably be provided within the time available (r 32(1) MHRTR 1983; see above). The appropriate authority may indicate to the tribunal that any part of the documents submitted should, in its opinion, be withheld from the patient on the grounds that disclosure would adversely affect his/her health or welfare, or that of others (r 33(2) MHRTR 1983). Copies of the admission papers or other documents should be made available to the patient by the tribunal. It may, however, exclude any part which the appropriate authority considers should be withheld under r 33(2) MHRTR 1983 (r 33(3) MHRTR 1983).

Rules 5, 8, 10 – 19 and 21 – 28 MHRTR 1983 apply to assessment applications subject to the following modifications:

(i) rule 12 applies as if the reference to a document being withheld in accordance with r 6 were a reference to part

## Mental Health Review Tribunals

of the admission papers or other documents supplied in accordance with r 32 being withheld;

(ii) rule 16 applies with the substitution for the reference to fourteen days' notice of a reference to such notice as is reasonably practicable;

(iii) rule 24 applies as if the period of time specified therein were three days instead of seven days.

(r 33 MHRTR 1983.)

*(c) References*

As noted above, references to an MHRT may be made by the Secretary of State, the Home Secretary or the hospital managers (see pages 114 and 117). Rules 3, 4 and 19 MHRTR 1983 do not apply to references. Upon receipt of the reference, the tribunal shall send notice of it to the patient and to the responsible authority. However, if the reference has been made by the responsible authority, the tribunal shall request a statement from the authority rather than give it notice. The provisions of rr 5 – 7 MHRTR 1983 then apply as though the reference in r 6(1) MHRTR 1983 to notice of application were to a notice of reference or a request for the authority's statement. Where the Secretary of State makes a reference, but is not obliged by the MHA 1983 to do so, he/she may withdraw it at any time before it is considered by the tribunal. The tribunal must then inform the patient and other parties that the application has been withdrawn. (See r 29(a) – (d) MHRTR 1983.) The power to postpone contained in r 9 MHRTR 1983 also applies to references (see (a) above).

## 6. Disclosure and representation

*(a) Disclosure of documents*

As soon as it is practicable, the tribunal must send copies of all documents it receives which are relevant to the application to the applicant, the patient (if not the applicant), the responsible authority and, in the case of a restricted patient, the Secretary of State. Any of those people may submit comments in writing to the tribunal. As seen above, the appropriate authority or the Secretary of State may withhold certain information from the patient on the ground that disclosure would adversely affect his/her health or welfare, or that of some other person (see r 6(4) and (5) MHRTR 1983 – page 128). The tribunal must consider whether disclosure of such information would have the effect claimed by the authority or the Secretary of State. If it is satisfied that disclosure would have that effect, it must record in writing its decision not to disclose the information. However, if the applicant or the patient has an authorised representative the tribunal must, as soon as is practicable, disclose the withheld information to the representative if he/she is a barrister or solicitor, a registered medical practitioner, or a person the tribunal considers to be suitable by virtue of experience or professional qualification. (See r 12(2) and (3) MHRTR 1983.) The authorised representative must not directly or indirectly disclose the information to the applicant, the patient if he/she is not the applicant, or any other person, without the authority of the tribunal. The information is not to be used otherwise than in connection with the application to the tribunal.

## (b) Representation

Any party may either conduct his/her own case, or somebody may act as representative on his/her behalf. Legal aid may be available depending upon whether the applicant satisfies the criteria. He/She may be represented by any person whom he/she has authorised to act on his/her behalf, provided that such person is not liable to be detained or subject to guardianship under the MHA 1983, or is not receiving treatment for a mental disorder in the same hospital or nursing home as the patient (r 10(1) MHRTR 1983). A representative authorised under r 10(1) must notify the tribunal of his/her authorisation and his/her postal address. Where a patient does not wish to conduct his/her own case and has not authorised anybody to act on his/her behalf, the tribunal may (not must) appoint somebody to act as authorised representative (r 10(3) MHRTR 1983).

The tribunal must send authorised representatives copies of all notices and documents which it is required to send the person he/she is representing. However, this is subject to r 12(3) MHRTR 1983 which limits disclosure of certain documents (see above). For the purposes of the proceedings, the representative may do everything which the person he/she represents is required or authorised to do by the MHRTR 1983. Furthermore, sending a document under the MHRTR 1983 to the authorised representative of a party shall be deemed to be the same as sending it to the party himself/herself (r 10(5) MHRTR 1983).

## 7. The conduct of the hearing

If there is more than one application pending in respect of the same patient (for example by the patient and his/her nearest relative, or two applications made by the patient), the tribunal may consider them at the same time. It may adjourn a hearing where it is necessary to organise the hearing of the two or more applications. Where a tribunal hears more than one application in respect of a patient at the same time, each applicant has the same rights under the MHRTR 1983 as if he/she were the only applicant. (See r 18(1) and (2) MHRTR 1983.)

Tribunal hearings are normally in private, although it is open to the patient to request a public hearing. If such a request is made, the tribunal must be satisfied that a public hearing would not be contrary to the interests of the patient. Where a request for a public hearing is refused by the tribunal, or where it directs that a public hearing should be continued in private, the tribunal must record in writing, and inform the patient of, the reasons for its decision. The tribunal does have the power to admit a person who is not a party to a private hearing if it considers it appropriate; however, it may specify terms and conditions of admission. It is open to the tribunal to exclude from either a public or a private hearing any person or class of persons other than a representative to whom documents would be disclosed under r 12(3) MHRTR 1983 (see above). This gives a wide power to the tribunal which can result in the patient or the applicant being excluded from the hearing. Where a person is excluded from the hearing, the tribunal must inform him/her of the reasons and record them in writing. This power of exclusion does not apply to a member of the Council of Tribunals who is acting in that capacity; however, he/she must take no part in the proceedings or the deliberations of the tribunal. Unless the tribunal directs otherwise, information about the proceedings or the names of any person concerned in them must not be made public. (See r 21(1)–(6) MHRTR 1983.)

Wherever appropriate, the tribunal should seek to avoid formality in the conduct of the hearing. It should conduct it in the manner which is most suitable, having taken into consideration the health and interests of the patient. The president must at the start of the hearing explain the manner of the proceedings which the tribunal proposes to adopt. Any party may appear at the hearing and take part in the proceedings as the tribunal considers proper unless he/she has been excluded under the provisions outlined in the above paragraph. Similarly, any other person may appear with the permission of the tribunal and take such part as it thinks proper. The MHRTR 1983 place particular emphasis on the need to hear and take evidence from the applicant, the patient (if not the applicant), and the responsible authority. Each may hear the other's evidence and put questions to each other. Questions may also be put to any other witness or person appearing before the tribunal. Once all the evidence has been given, the applicant and the patient (if not the applicant) are to be given a further opportunity to address the tribunal. Before the application is determined, the tribunal, or any one or more of its members, may interview the patient. If the patient requests an interview, one must be granted. Interviews may, and if requested by the patient must, be conducted in the absence of any other person. (See r 22(1)–(5) MHRTR 1983.)

A tribunal has the power to adjourn a hearing if it considers it necessary in order to obtain further information or for some other appropriate reason. In order to avoid unnecessary delay, the tribunal when adjourning may give such directions as it thinks fit for ensuring prompt consideration of the application. An adjourned hearing may be resumed if the applicant, or the patient (if he/she is not the applicant), or the responsible authority so request, but the tribunal must only comply if it is satisfied that to do so would be in the interests of the patient. The tribunal, when adjourning the hearing, may fix a date upon which it will be resumed; if it does not do so, then it must give to all parties (and the Secretary of State in the case of a restricted patient), not less than fourteen days' notice of the date, time and place of the resumed hearing. The parties may, however, consent to a shorter period of notice being given. (See r 16(1)–(4) MHRTR 1983.)

If a case has not been disposed of by the members of a tribunal appointed for that purpose, and the chairperson is of the opinion that it is not practicable or possible without undue delay for them to do so, he/she may arrange for it to be completed by other members of the tribunal (r 17(1) MHRTR 1983). A transfer is also possible where the patient in respect of whom the proceedings are pending moves to the area of another tribunal. In these circumstances the chairperson may direct that the hearing be transferred to that other tribunal. Notice of the transfer must be given to the parties and, in the case of a restricted patient, the Secretary of State. (See r 17(2) MHRTR 1983.)

Tribunal decisions are by majority with the president having a casting vote in the event of a tie. A written record of the decision must be made by the tribunal and signed by the president. Reasons for a decision must be given, and where the tribunal relies on matters specified in s 72(1) or (4) or s 73(1) or (2) MHA 1983, it must state its reason for being satisfied as required by those subsections. The tribunal's decision may be announced by the president immediately after the hearing of the case. The written decision of the tribunal, and the reasons for that decision, must be sent to all the parties within seven days of the hearing; if the patient is a restricted patient, the Secretary of State must also be informed in writing. There may be cases where full disclosure of the reasons for a decision would adversely affect the health and welfare of the patient or some other person. In these circumstances the tribunal may communicate its decision to the patient in such a manner as it considers to be appropriate. Disclosure to the other parties may be subject to such conditions as the tribunal considers necessary, bearing in mind the nature of the communication to the patient. Where the patient was represented by a person who would receive documents under r 12(3) MHRTR 1983 (see page 134), that person is entitled to receive the fully recorded grounds for the decision; the tribunal may, however, make such a disclosure subject to any conditions regarding disclosure to the patient.

The above requirements for communication also apply if the decision is provisional or is accompanied by a recommendation. A "provisional decision" includes a deferred direction for conditional discharge under s 73(7) MHA 1983 and a notification to the Secretary of State under s 74(1) MHA 1983 (see r 2 MHRTR 1983 and pages 123 and 124). Where a provisional decision has been made, any further decision in the proceedings may be made without another hearing of the case (r 25(1) MHRTR 1983). A "decision with recommendations" is a decision in accordance with s 72(3)(a) MHA 1983 (r 2 MHRTR 1983 and page 120). Where a tribunal makes a decision with recommendations, the decision must specify the period within which the conditions must be met. At the end of that period the tribunal should make enquiries of the responsible authority to see whether the recommendations have been complied with. A failure to comply with a recommendation within that period will result in the tribunal reconsidering the case (r 24(4) MHRTR 1983). Not less than fourteen days' notice must be given by the tribunal to all parties of a reconvened hearing following a failure to comply with a recommendation. Such notice must also be given to the Secretary of State if the patient is a restricted patient. It is open to the parties to consent to a shorter period of notice.

# Chapter 5

# Community care

## 1. Introduction

Care in the community of the mentally ill or persons with mental handicap is, wherever possible, a more desirable alternative than institutional care. When considering the making of an application under Part II MHA 1983, an ASW should always consider the least restrictive alternative and endeavour to minimise the legal intrusion into the life of the person with the mental disorder. Care in the community may maximise the enjoyment and satisfaction they get through contact with a familiar environment and an opportunity to participate in employment and social life. However, in order to be effective, community care must be planned and have the benefit of professional support as well as that of the informal carers such as family and friends. The statutory framework of community care for those with a mental disability has developed in a rather haphazard way. Much of it also applies to persons with physical disabilities and the elderly. Other statutory provisions are aimed exclusively at those with a mental disorder, for example community care through guardianship. This chapter examines the statutory framework of community care. In addition to the support available from local social services authorities, it will also consider community support from central government through the social security system.

## 2. Guardianship

Guardianship is a form of community care which envisages supportive assistance for the patient either through a private guardian or the local social services authority (for applications for guardianship see page 30). Upon being received into guardianship, any previous application by virtue of which the patient was subject to guardianship or liable to be detained in hospital ceases to have effect (s 8(5) MHA 1983). Guardianship will cease if the patient is subsequently admitted for treatment under s 3 MHA 1983, but will continue if he/she is admitted for assessment. Under s 8(1) MHA 1983, a guardian has the following powers:

"(a) the power to require the patient to reside at a place specified by the authority or person named as guardian;

(b) the power to require the patient to attend at places and times so specified for the purpose of medical treatment, occupation, education or training;

(c) the power to require access to the patient to be given, at any place where the patient is residing, to any registered medical practitioner, approved social worker or other person so specified."

(s 8(1)(a)–(c) MHA 1983.)

These powers are exercisable to the exclusion of any other person. It should be noted that they are limited. For example, the guardian cannot compel the patient to undergo medical treatment, only to attend a place where such treatment is available (*T v T* (1988)). Nor can the guardian consent to medical treatment on behalf of the patient. The consent to treatment provisions of the MHA 1983 do not apply to a patient subject to guardianship (see page 91). There is no power over the property of the patient (but see Chapter 7). However, a person subject to guardianship who absents himself/herself from the place where the guardian requires him/her to live may be taken into custody and returned to that place (s 18(3) MHA 1983; see page 42). In certain circumstances a person subject to guardianship may be transferred to hospital (see page 36). It is an offence for any individual to ill-treat or wilfully neglect a mentally disordered patient who is for the time being subject to guardianship or otherwise in his/her custody or care.

In addition, a private guardian has the following duties:

(i) to appoint a registered medical practitioner to act as the nominated medical attendant for the patient;

(ii) to notify the responsible local social services authority of the address of the nominated medical attendant;

(iii) in the exercise of his/her powers under the MHA 1983, to comply with such directions as the responsible local social services authority may give;

(iv) to furnish the authority with reports or information concerning the patient as it may from time to time require;

(v) to notify the authority:
- on the reception of the patient into guardianship of his/her name and address;
- of any permanent change of address within the area of the authority before, or not later than seven days after, the change takes place;

(vi) where the patient moves into the area of another local social services authority, to notify that authority of:
- his/her address and that of the patient;
- the particulars mentioned in (ii) above;

and then send the original authority a copy of the notice;

(vii) in the event of the patient's death, or the termination of guardianship through discharge, transfer or otherwise, to notify the responsible local social services authority as soon as is practicable.

(r 12(a)–(g) MHR 1983.)

The responsible local social services authority must arrange for every patient received into guardianship to be visited at intervals of not more than three months. At least once a year, a visit must be made by a practitioner approved by the Secretary of State (see page 19; r 13 MHR 1983). Guardianship is a form of community care that has not been widely used. Its success or otherwise may depend more upon the availability of some of the other services outlined below, rather than on the limited powers of the guardian.

## 3. After-care upon leaving hospital

Section 117 MHA 1983 makes special provision for those patients who leave hospital after being detained under s 3, are admitted under a s 37 hospital order, or are transferred to hospital through a transfer direction under s 47 or s 48 MHA 1983 (see pages 21, 66 and 67). A duty is imposed upon the district health authority and the local social services authority, in co-operation with voluntary agencies, to provide after-care services until satisfied that the person is no longer in need of them. The relevant health authority and local authority are the ones for the area in which the person concerned is resident or to which he/she is sent upon discharge from hospital. (See s 117(1)–(3) MHA 1983.) The MHA 1983 gives no further guidance as to what form of assistance may be provided. The DHSS Memorandum – Mental Health Act 1983 states that s 117 MHA 1983 "reinforces" the duty imposed by other health and social services legislation (see below); it does not envisage a clearly defined role under the section (para 251). This would fit in with the government view that the section is unnecessary as sufficient statutory powers and duties already exist. The distinct advantage of this interpretation is that it avoids having to define the circumstances when a person is liable to be detained as required by s 117 MHA 1983. For example, is a person who is conditionally discharged from hospital still liable to be detained? If he/she is, then s 117 does not apply. Similar considerations apply to a person on leave of absence. The "official" interpretation would render such discussion otiose as the relevant question would be whether or not he/she comes within the particular statutory provision under consideration (see below).

However, in a limited way the section does impose some obligations over and above those found in the other statutory provisions. Firstly, it imposes a duty to provide after-care rather than a discretion as in a number of the other statutes. Secondly, it also imposes a duty upon the local social services authority and the health authority to co-operate in making such provision. Enforcement of either of these duties may be difficult given the uncertainty as to what can be expected under s 117 MHA 1983; however, failure to perform these duties may initiate the default powers of the Secretary of State under s 124 MHA 1983. Finally, s 117 requires both bodies to keep the individual's case under review with a view to determining whether such after-care is still required. However, in practice such differences may be of little, if any, effect.

## 4. National Health Service Act 1977

Under s 21 and Sch 8 para 2 National Health Service Act 1977 ("NHSA 1977"), local social services authorities may make provision for the prevention of illness and for the care and after-care of persons suffering from illness. "Illness" includes mental illness as defined in the MHA 1983 (s 128(1) NHSA 1977). A local social services authority may with the approval of the Secretary of State, or in accordance with his/her directions, make arrangements for persons falling within the scope of s 21 NHSA 1977. Normally arrangements cannot include the payment of money. Until the implementation of the CA 1989, a money payment may be made to a person suffering from a mental disorder within the MHA 1983 provided he/she is under sixteen years of age and is in accommodation provided under the arrangements. The payment may be of an amount which the local authority thinks fit in respect of his/her occasional personal expenses where it appears that a payment would not otherwise be made (Sch 8 para 2(2)(b) NHSA 1977 – but see Sch 15 CA 1989).

Formal arrangements under the NHSA 1977 have been made by the Secretary of State for mentally disordered people and are found in the DHSS Circular LAC 19(74). In the Appendix to LAC 19(74), the Secretary of State has approved the following arrangements for the prevention of mental disorder, or for assisting those who are or have been suffering from mental disorder:

(i) the provision of accommodation (including residential homes, hostels, group homes, minimum support facilities or other appropriate accommodation – the premises may be managed by the authority or otherwise) and care for persons ordinarily resident in the area of the authority and for those in that area who have no settled residence;

(ii) the provision of similar accommodation for persons ordinarily resident in the area of another authority who, following discharge from hospital, become ordinarily resident in its area;

(iii) the payment of pocket money under Sch 8 para 2(2)(b) NHSA 1977 (see above);

(iv) the provision of centres (including training centres and day centres) or other facilities (including domiciliary facilities) whether in premises managed by the authority or by some other body and used for the training or occupation of such people;

(v) the provision of meals, and the remuneration of such people who are engaged in suitable employment under the arrangements;

(vi) the provision of social and recreational activities;

(vii) the exercise by the authority of its functions under the MHA 1983 in respect of persons placed under guardianship (including those placed under private guardianship);

(viii) the provision of social work and related services to help in the identification, diagnosis, assessment and social

*Community care*

treatment of mental disorder and to provide social work support and other domiciliary and care services to people living in their homes and elsewhere;
(ix) the appointment of ASWs under the MHA 1983.
(Appendix para 1(a)–(j) LAC 19(74).)

The Secretary of State has directed local authorities to make arrangements for residential accommodation for ordinary residents (i), training and occupation facilities (iv), provisions for guardianship (vii) and general social work support (viii), and appointment of ASWs (ix) (para 4 LAC 19(74)).

In making the above arrangements, the authority may wish to use suitable accommodation, facilities and services provided by another authority, voluntary body or other person on agreed conditions. However, the authority should bear in mind the need for such provision being made available as near to the person's home as is practicable. If the authority wishes to provide such services to a person who is an alcoholic, drug addict or a homeless single person whose way of life exposes him/her to the risk of mental disorder, it should not be dissuaded from doing so simply because of doubts as to the precise definition of mental disorder (Appendix para 2 LAC 19(74)).

In deciding what provision to make for a person coming within s 21 NHSA 1977 who is living at home and receiving a substantial amount of care from another person, the local authority must have regard to the ability of that person to care for him/her (s 8(1) Disabled Persons (Services, Consultation and Representation) Act 1986).

## 5. Provision of accommodation by local authorities

A local authority *may* provide:

"residential accommodation for persons [aged eighteen or over] who by reason of age, infirmity or any other circumstances are in need of care and attention which is not otherwise available to them."
(s 21(1)(a) NAA 1948 as amended by Sch 13 para 11(1) CA 1989 – words in square brackets inserted by CA 1989.)

Such accommodation is usually referred to as "Part III accommodation" (see Part III NAA 1948). When making any arrangements, the authority must have regard to the welfare of the person for whom accommodation is to be provided.

Particular regard should be had to the need to provide different types of accommodation for the different categories of people mentioned in s21(1) NAA 1948 (s 21(2) NAA 1948). The following people may benefit under s 21(1) NAA 1948:

- any person having his/her *ordinary residence* in the area of the authority;
- any person in the area of the local authority who has no settled residence, or is not ordinarily resident there, but is in urgent need of accommodation;
- a person in a hospital vested in the Secretary of State is deemed to be ordinarily resident in the area where he/she was so resident prior to admission.

(s 24 NAA 1948.)

Accommodation may be provided on premises managed by the local authority or managed by another local authority. If provided by another authority, the terms of reimbursement and other matters should be agreed between the two authorities (s 21(4) NAA 1948). Alternatively, accommodation may be provided on premises managed by a voluntary organisation (including a housing association) or in a home registered under the Registered Homes Act 1984. In both cases, the terms of payment should be agreed with the local authority. (See s 26 NAA 1948 and para 3(f) DHSS LAC (74) 13.)

Although the NAA 1948 gives the local authority a *power* to make provision, the Secretary of State by direction requires authorities to make arrangements for the following purposes:

(i) the provision of accommodation for persons ordinarily resident in the local authority's area, *or for other persons in urgent need,* who by reason of age, infirmity or other circumstances are in need of care and attention which is not otherwise available to them;

(ii) the provision of temporary accommodation for those in urgent need as a result of circumstances which could not reasonably have been foreseen, or in such circumstances as the authority may in any particular case determine;

(iii) the provision of welfare for all persons for whom it provides accommodation and for the supervision of the hygiene of that accommodation;

(iv) enabling residents in provided accommodation to obtain medical and nursing attention and the benefit of National Health Service provisions;

## Community care

(v) the provision of other services, amenities and requisites as the authority considers necessary in connection with any accommodation provided.

In addition, the Secretary of State has approved the making of the following arrangements:

(i) the provision of accommodation, referred to in (i) or (ii) above, in premises managed by another local authority;

(ii) the provision of such accommodation, to an extent which it considers desirable, for persons ordinarily resident in the area of another authority;

(iii) the provision of such accommodation, by making arrangements with voluntary organisations or persons in charge of a home registered under RHA 1984;

(iv) so far as it is appropriate, the provision of transport to and from such accommodation.

(para 3 DHSS LAC (74) 13.)

An authority must regularly review the above provisions and make any necessary improvements.

Section 22 NAA 1948 provides for charges to be made in respect of the provision of Part III accommodation. Each local authority should fix a standard charge which should represent as closely as possible the true economic cost of the provision (s 22(2) NAA 1948). However, if the person for whom accommodation is provided satisfies the authority that he/she is unable to pay that full rate, his/her ability to pay shall be assessed by the authority (s 22(3) NAA 1948). The NAA 1948 provides a formula for assessment which makes use of Part III of Sch 1 to the Supplementary Benefits Act 1976. Paragraph 32(2) of Sch 10 to the Social Security Act 1986 will remain in force for this specific purpose despite the introduction of income support. In making an assessment, the authority must assume that the person will need a sum of money for his/her own personal requirements – this sum is prescribed by the Secretary of State in regulations (s 22(4) NAA 1948). If it thinks fit, a local authority managing premises in which Part III accommodation is provided has the power to limit a person's payment to the minimum amount for the first eight weeks (s 22(5A) NAA 1948). This may be done regardless of that person's means. The section is primarily intended for short-term provision, although it can be used when accommodation is provided on a number of separate occasions. (See DHSS Circular LAC (78)8 for charging provision under the NAA 1948.) Any sum of money which is due under these provisions may be recovered summarily as a civil debt within three years of the sum being due. (See s 56(1) and (2) NAA 1948.)

The Secretary of State may request a local authority to provide information on the number of persons under sixty-five years who are in premises, or in part of premises, used to accommodate persons over that age – s 18(1) Chronically Sick and Disabled Persons Act 1970. The authority must also supply the Secretary of State with such information on the working of these provisions as he/she may require.

In deciding what provision to make for a person coming within s 21 NAA 1948 who is living at home and receiving a substantial amount of care from another person, the local authority must have regard to the ability of that person to care for him/her (s 8(1) Disabled Persons (Services, Consultation and Representation) Act 1986).

## 6. Section 29 National Assistance Act 1948

Section 29 NAA 1948 gives local authorities the power to promote the welfare of:

> "persons [aged eighteen or over] who are blind, deaf or dumb, or who suffer from mental disorder of any description, and other persons [aged eighteen or over] who are substantially and permanently handicapped by illness, injury, or congenital deformity or such other disabilities as may be prescribed by the Minister."
>
> (s 29(1) NAA 1948 as amended by Sch 13 para 11(2) CA 1989 – words in square brackets inserted by CA 1989.)

Such provision must be with the approval of the Secretary of State or in accordance with any direction which he/she may make. Local authorities are required to keep a register of persons in their areas to whom s 29 NAA 1948 applies (s 29(4)(g) NAA 1948 and paras 8 and 9 DHSS Circular LAC 13(74)). Some of the services provided under s 29 NAA 1948 overlap with those provided under s 21 NHSA 1977. Those people who have a mental disorder within the meaning of MHA 1983 may still be registered under this provision. However, local authority provision is generally made under the NHSA 1977 rather than the 1948 Act (see para 14 DHSS Circular LAC 17(74)). Section 8(4) MHA 1959 makes it clear that a local authority is not required to make the same provision for the same purpose under both Acts in respect of one person.

*Community care*

Under s 29 NAA 1948, the Secretary of State has approved the following provisions:

(i) social work service and such advice and support as may be needed to support a person in their own home or elsewhere*;

(ii) facilities, at centres or elsewhere, for social rehabilitation and adjustment to disability including assistance in overcoming mobility or communications problems*;

(iii) facilities, at centres or elsewhere, for occupational, social, cultural and recreational activities and, where appropriate, the making of payments to persons for work undertaken by them*;

(iv) hostels for persons undertaking training or employment and the provision of holiday homes;

(v) free or subsidised travel for all or any persons who do not receive concessionary travel from some other source;

(vi) assistance in the finding of suitable and supportive lodgings;

(vii) contribution to the cost of employing a warden in warden-assisted housing schemes;

(viii) warden services for occupiers of private housing;

(ix) arranging for the provision of such services by another local authority or voluntary organisation;

(x) payment of any specialist fees in respect of advice given as to whether a person is within s 29*;

(xi) maintenance of a register to whom the section applies*.

(para 8(a)−(1) LAC 13(74) − those marked with an asterisk are directions by the Secretary of State.)

Section 29 NAA 1948 has been modified by the Chronically Sick and Disabled Persons Act 1970 ("CSDPA 1970") and the Disabled Persons (Services, Consultation and Representation) Act 1986 ("DP(SCR)A 1986"). Under s 1 CSDPA 1970, each local authority is under a duty to inform itself of the number of persons in its area to whom s 29 NAA 1948 applies and the need to make arrangements under the section. Information should be published from time to time by each authority on the s 29 provision which it makes. Any person within s 29 who makes use of local authority services should also be informed of other services which are available which are considered to be relevant to his/her needs. If the authority has in its possession details of relevant services provided by another authority or organisation, it must inform the person. (See s 1(2)(a) and (b) CSDPA 1970.)

The obligations under the CSDPA 1970 also apply with respect to disabled children, in relation to whom a local authority has duties under Part III CA 1989, in the same way as to persons within s 29 NAA 1948 (Sch 9 para 16 CA 1989).

Section 4 DP(SCR)A 1986 imposes a duty on local authorities to assess the needs of a disabled person who comes within s 29 NAA 1948. It must do so if requested by the disabled person, his/her authorised representative or any person who provides him/her with a substantial amount of care on a regular basis. Where, in the case of a person to whom s 29 NAA 1948 applies and who is ordinarily resident in its area, an authority is satisfied that it is necessary to meet the need of a person who has been assessed, it has a duty to make the following arrangements in the exercise of its s 29 functions:

(i) the provision of practical assistance for that person in the home;

(ii) the provision for that person of, or assistance in obtaining, wireless, television, library or similar recreational facilities;

(iii) the provision for that person of lectures, games, outings or other recreational facilities outside his/her home, or assistance to that person in taking advantage of educational facilities that may be available;

(iv) the provision for that person of facilities for, or assistance in, travelling to and from home for the purpose of participating in services provided under s 29 NAA 1948, or any similar service provided by the authority;

(v) the provision of assistance for that person in arranging for the carrying out of adaptations in his/her home, or the provision of additional facilities designed to secure his/her greater safety, comfort or convenience;

(vi) facilitating the taking of holidays by that person;

(vii) the provision of meals for that person at home or elsewhere;

(viii) the provision of, or assistance in obtaining, a telephone for that person.

(s 2(1) CSDPA 1970.)

In deciding what provision to make for a person coming within s 29 NAA 1948 who is living at home and receiving a substantial

*Community care*

amount of care from another person, the local authority must have regard to the ability of that person to care for him/her (s 8(1) DP(SCR)A 1986).

## 7. Provision for children

*(a) Introduction*

The CA 1989 has made many changes to the law relating to the care and protection of children. The Government White Paper, *The Law on Child Care and Family Service* (Cm 62) proposed the unification of child care law (which provides for children to be supported in the family) and health and welfare legislation (which enables services to be provided for children such as those with a mental handicap or physical disability). In making this recommendation, the White Paper recognised the concern that flowed from the perception that taking children into care was often associated with parental shortcomings. However, the intention was to ensure that children should receive a proper standard of care and protection through voluntary partnership between statutory bodies and parents. It was proposed that local authorities should have a broad "umbrella" power to provide services and promote care and upbringing of children. This would help to prevent the breakdown of the family and the necessity for a care order. The type of care envisaged includes community care and short or long periods away from home, either with foster parents or in a children's home. Part III CA 1989 sets out local authority responsibility towards children and their families.

*(b) Local authority duty to provide services for children and their families under Part III CA 1989*

In addition to other statutory duties, local authorities now have a duty to safeguard and promote the welfare of children in need who are in their area and, so far as is consistent with that duty, to promote the upbringing of the child by his/her family. "Family" includes any person who has parental responsibility for a child and any other person with whom he/she may be living (s 17(10) CA 1989). Where a child in need is living apart from his/her family (and he/she is not being looked after by the local authority), the local authority must take reasonable steps to enable him/her to live with the family, or to promote contact with the family through, for example, visits (Sch 2 Part I para 9

149

CA 1989). To this end they should make available a range of services appropriate to the needs of such children. (See s 17(1) CA 1989.)

A child is to be regarded as being in need if:

(a) "he is unlikely to achieve or maintain, or to have the opportunity of maintaining, a reasonable standard of health or development without the provision for him of services by a local authority under this Part;

(b) his health or development is likely to be significantly impaired, or further impaired, without the provision of such services; or

(c) he is disabled."

(s 17(10)(a)–(c) CA 1989.)

"Disabled" is defined as a child who is:

"blind, deaf or dumb or who suffers from mental disorder of any kind or who is substantially and permanently handicapped by illness, injury or congenital deformity or such other disability as may be prescribed."

(s 17(11) CA 1989.)

"Development" means physical, intellectual, emotional, social or behavioural development. "Health" means physical or mental health (s 17(11) CA 1989).

Section 17(2) CA 1989 and Part I of Sch 2 CA 1989 outline the provision of services for families with children who are in need. Every local authority must take reasonable steps to identify the extent to which there are children in need within its area. In addition, it must publish information about any services it provides under the CA 1989 and take reasonably practicable steps to ensure that people who might benefit are aware of them (Sch 2 Part I para 1(1) and (2) CA 1989). Any of the available services may be provided for the family of a particular child in need if it is made with a view to safeguarding or promoting that child's welfare (s 17(3) CA 1989). A local authority must open and maintain a register (on computer if desired) of disabled children within its area. Where it appears that a child within its area is in need, it *may* (not must) assess his/her needs for the purpose of Part III at the same time as any assessment under the CSDPA 1970 (see page 147), the Education Act 1981 (see page 158), the DP(SCR)A 1986 (see page 148) or under any other legislation.

*Community care*

There is a direct duty upon local authorities to provide services which are designed to minimise the effect on disabled children living in their areas of their disabilities. These services must give such children the opportunity of leading lives which are as normal as is possible (Sch 2 Part I para 6 CA 1989). In the case of children living with their families, the following provision shall, as far as is appropriate, be available:

(i) advice, guidance and counselling;
(ii) occupational, social, cultural or recreational activities;
(iii) home help (including laundry facilities);
(iv) facilities for, or assistance with, travelling to and from home for the purpose of taking advantage of any other service provided under the CA 1989 or any similar service;
(v) assistance to enable the child concerned and his/her family to have a holiday.

(Sch 2 Part I para 8 CA 1989.)

An authority must take steps designed to reduce the need for bringing care, wardship or similar proceedings in respect of a child in need (Sch 2 Part I para 7 CA 1989).

In order to assist the family and the child in need, each local authority must provide such family centres as it considers appropriate for its area. These centres may be for the use of a child (not only the child with the disability), parents, any person who is not a parent but who has parental responsibility or any other person looking after the child. Such centres may provide occupational, social, cultural or recreational activities; advice, guidance or counselling; or accommodation while a person is receiving advice, guidance or counselling. (See Sch 2 Part I para 8 CA 1989.)

In discharging the above functions, a local authority must facilitate provision by others of services it is empowered to provide. Particular mention is made of the voluntary organisations which may be able to provide support. It will also include the private sector such as, for example, residential care homes. Arrangements may be made for any person to act on behalf of the authority in the provision of any such service or facility (see s 17(5) CA 1989). Services provided include assistance in kind or, in exceptional circumstances, in cash. Assistance may be unconditional or subject to conditions as to repayment, unless income support or family credit is being received. However, before it gives any assistance, the local authority must have regard to the means of the child concerned and of each of his/her parents. (See s 17(6)–(8) CA 1989.)

### (c) Provision of accommodation for children

Under the Child Care Act 1980, a local authority could under s 2 receive a child into "voluntary care" in certain circumstances. The CA 1989 adopts a similar idea; however it is now to be seen in a wider context as being part of the range of services which a local authority can offer to parents of children who are in need. As the White Paper puts it, "(Such) a service should, in appropriate circumstances, be seen as a positive response to the needs of families and not as a mark of failure on the part of the family or those professionals and other workers supporting them. An essential character of this service should be its voluntary character, that is it should be based clearly on continuing parental agreement and operate as far as possible on a basis of partnership and co-operation between the local authority and parents." (See para 21 White Paper.) This approach is adopted in the CA 1989.

A local authority must provide accommodation for any child in need within its area who appears to require it as a result of:

(i) there being no person who has parental responsibility for him/her;
(ii) the child being lost or abandoned; or
(iii) the person who has been caring for him/her being prevented (whether or not permanently, and for whatever reason) from providing him/her with suitable accommodation or care.

(s 20(1)(a)–(c) CA 1989.)

Category (iii) may, in addition to those children with a disability, include cases where a parent has been admitted to hospital under the MHA 1983 and is, therefore, unable to look after his/her children. The provision of accommodation under s 20 CA 1989 may be helpful in providing a temporary period of respite for the parents of a disabled child. In the case of a child in need who has reached the age of sixteen years, accommodation must be provided by the authority if his/her welfare will be seriously prejudiced if it is not provided (s 20(3) CA 1989). A disabled child who has reached the age of sixteen years but is under twenty-one years may be accommodated in a community home if it is provided for children who have reached sixteen years (s 20(5)(b) CA 1989).

## Community care

Accommodation may be provided, even though the person with parental responsibility is able to make provision, if the authority considers that to do so would safeguard or promote that child's welfare. However, the authority may not provide accommodation if the person with parental responsibility objects and is able to provide accommodation; such a person may remove a child from accommodation unless the child has reached the age of sixteen years and agrees to his/her being looked after in local authority accommodation. The twenty-eight days' notice period for children who were in voluntary care for more than six months no longer applies. Before providing accommodation a local authority should, so far as is practicable and consistent with the child's welfare, ascertain and give due regard to the wishes of the child. (See s 20(6),(7),(8), (9) and (11) CA 1989.)

A child in need for whom accommodation is provided under s 20 CA 1989 is regarded as being "looked after" by the local authority (s 22(1)(b) CA 1989). It is the duty of that authority to safeguard and promote the child's welfare and make use of such facilities and services as are available for children who are cared for by their parents. Before making any decisions with regard to the child, the authority should, so far as is reasonably practicable, ascertain the wishes of the child, his/her parents and any person who is not a parent but who has parental responsibility. Due consideration must be given to the wishes and feelings of the child (having regard to his/her age and understanding), the wishes of the parent or person having parental responsibility, and to the child's religious persuasion, racial origin and cultural background. These obligations do not apply if the authority considers it necessary to deviate from them for the purpose of protecting members of the public from serious injury. Similarly, the Secretary of State may give directions to a local authority concerning the exercise of the above powers with regard to a particular child if necessary for the protection of members of the public. The authority must comply with those directions even though they may be inconsistent with their duties under the CA 1989. (See s 22(3)–(7) CA 1989.) Any accommodation provided will invariably be done in partnership with the parent or person having parental responsibility, and will be done with a view to returning the child to the home environment as soon as is practicable.

Accommodation for a child being looked after by a local authority may be provided in any one of the following ways:

    (i) a family, relative or other suitable person;

(ii) accommodation in a community home;
(iii) accommodation provided by a voluntary organisation;
(iv) a registered children's home;
(v) a home provided by the Secretary of State under s 82(5) CA 1989 on such terms as he/she may determine;
(vi) in any other manner as seems appropriate to the authority and complies with regulations made by the Secretary of State.

(s 23(2) CA 1989.)

Section 82(5) CA 1989 enables the Secretary of State to provide, equip and maintain homes for the accommodation of children who are in need of particular facilities which are unlikely to be readily available in community homes. Such homes may make special provision for children who are mentally ill or who have a mental handicap. Regulations may be made by the Secretary of State for the placing of children with foster parents and the provision of any accommodation under (vi) above (Sch 2 Part II paras 12 and 13 CA 1989).

When accommodation is provided, the authority shall ensure that, so far as is reasonably practicable and consistent with the child's welfare, it shall be near his/her home (s 23(7) CA 1989). Similarly, the authority must endeavour to promote contact between the child and his/her parents or the person having parental responsibility, and any other person connected with him/her. Where accommodation is provided for a child who is disabled, the authority should have regard to any special needs he/she may have. Payments may be made in respect of expenses incurred as a consequence of visiting a child looked after by a local authority. It must appear to the authority that the visit could not otherwise be made without undue financial hardship and that the circumstances warrant the making of the payment. A payment may be made to a parent or a person having parental responsibility, or any other person connected with the child, in respect of expenses incurred in visiting the child. Payment to the child may be made in respect of expenses incurred in his/her visiting any such person. (See Sch 2 Part II paras 15 and 16 CA 1989.)

If contact by the parent or person with parental responsibility with the child is infrequent, or the child has not been visited or lived with them for the last twelve months, the local authority has a duty to appoint an independent visitor for the child. This person will be responsible for visiting, advising and befriending the child. He/She may recover reasonable expenses incurred in performing these duties. Regulations on the independent nature of a visitor may be made by the Secretary of State. (See Sch 2 Part II para 17 CA 1989.)

Where a child is being looked after by a local authority, it has a duty to advise, assist and befriend him/her with a view to promoting his/her welfare when he/she returns to the home environment (s 24(1) CA 1989). Special provision is made for a child who is under twenty-one years and who was at any time after reaching sixteen years of age, but below the age of eighteen years, looked after by a local authority, accommodated by a voluntary organisation or in a registered children's home, or privately fostered. Where such a person is no longer so accommodated or fostered and is living in the community, if:

(i) it appears to the authority that the person is in need of advice and being befriended; or

(ii) the person by whom he/she is currently being looked after does not have the necessary facilities for advising or befriending; or

(iii) the person has asked for help of a kind that the authority can give under s 24(2) CA 1989,

the authority must (where he/she was previously accommodated by the authority or by or on behalf of a voluntary organisation) or may (in any other case) advise, befriend and give assistance to him/her (s 24(2) and (5) CA 1989). This provision also applies where the child was accommodated by a health authority, education authority, or in a home under the RHA 1984 for at least three months (s 24(2)(d) and (3) CA 1989).

The local authority within whose area the child proposes to live must be informed of a child who has reached the age of sixteen years who is leaving accommodation provided other than directly by the authority. Assistance given under the above provision may include help in kind or, in exceptional circumstances, cash. It may be conditional or unconditional as to the repayment in whole or in part. Regard must be had to the means of the child concerned and of each of his/her parents. (See s 20(7) CA 1989.)

Where it is reasonable to do so, the authority may require a contribution to be made towards the upkeep of a child for whom accommodation is provided. Contributions may be sought from a parent or person with parental responsibility, or from a child if he/she has reached the age of sixteen years. A parent in receipt of income support or family credit under the Social Security Act 1986 will not be required to make a contribution. Liability to pay is determined by the procedure outlined in Part III of Sch 2 of the CA 1989. The authority should serve a notice on the contributor specifying the weekly sum he/she should contribute and the arrangements for payment. In determining the sum payable, regard must be had to the ability of the contributor to pay. If the authority and the contributor agree in writing on a sum to be paid, any sum due may be recovered as a civil debt if it is overdue or unpaid. Where they fail to agree, or the contributor withdraws in writing his/her agreement, the authority may apply to the magistrates' court for a contribution order. A contribution order may not specify a sum greater than that in the original notice, and the court must have regard to the person's ability to pay. An order may be discharged if the authority and the contributor subsequently agree on a sum to be paid; the court must be notified of any such agreement. Contribution orders may be varied or revoked on the application of either party. (See Sch 2 Part III paras 22 and 23 CA 1989.)

*(d) Supervision orders*

As seen at page 46, a court has the power to make a supervision order in respect of a child subject to proceedings under s 31 CA 1989. A supervision order is a recognition that a child needs some form of assistance, and that this is best provided within the community in a structured manner. Supervision orders are regulated by Sch 3 CA 1989. A supervision order may require a child to comply with directions given from time to time by the supervisor. Such directions may require the child to do all or any of the following:

(i) to live at a place specified for a period or periods so specified;
(ii) to present himself/herself to a person or persons specified in the directions at a specified place and time;
(iii) to participate in activities in the directions on a day or days so specified.

(Sch 3 Part I para 2(1) CA 1989.)

It is for the supervisor to decide whether, and to what extent, he/she should exercise the power to give directions (Sch 3 Part I para 2(2) CA 1989). A person having parental responsibility or with whom the child is living may be required to agree to take all reasonable steps to ensure that the child complies with any directions. Furthermore he/she may be required to comply with directions given by the supervisor which oblige him/her to attend a place for the purpose of taking part in specified activities. He/She may be required by the direction to accompany the child

*Community care*

or to attend on his/her own. (See Sch 3 Part I para 3 CA 1989.)

The supervisor cannot direct that the child undergoes medical treatment or examination. However, a supervision order may require that the child submits to a medical or psychiatric examination. The order may specify a time for the examination, or it may be left to the supervisor to do so. An examination must be conducted by, or under the direction of, a registered medical practitioner specified in the order.

It may be carried out at a place specified in the order at which the child is to attend as a non-resident patient. Alternatively, it may take place at a health service hospital or, in the case of a psychiatric examination, a hospital or mental nursing hospital at which the child is to attend as a resident patient. A requirement that the examination is conducted at a place where the child is to attend as a resident patient may not be included unless the court is satisfied on the evidence of a registered medical practitioner that:

(i) the child may be suffering from a physical or mental condition that requires, and may be susceptible to, treatment; and

(ii) a period as a resident patient is necessary if the examination is to be carried out properly.

No court shall include a medical or psychiatric examination requirement unless satisfied that where the child has sufficient understanding he/she has consented to its inclusion. Furthermore the court must be satisfied that arrangements have been, or can be, made for the examination. (See Sch 3 Part I para 4(3) and (4) CA 1989.)

Where a court which proposes to make or to vary a supervision order is satisfied that the mental condition of the child is such as requires, and may be susceptible to, treatment but is not such as to warrant a hospital order under Part III MHA 1983, it may include a requirement that he/she submits to treatment. The order must specify the period of the treatment and its nature. Before deciding whether to include such a requirement, the court must be so satisfied on the basis of evidence from a registered medical practitioner approved under s 12 MHA 1983. Treatment must be by, or under the direction of, a specified registered medical practitioner. The child may receive it as a non-resident patient at a place specified in the order. Alternatively, he/she may receive it as a resident patient in a hospital or mental nursing home. (See Sch 3 Part I para 5(1) and (2) CA 1989.)

If the medical practitioner responsible for the treatment of the child is unwilling to continue, he/she must inform the supervisor in writing. He/She must also inform the supervisor in writing if he/she forms the opinion that:

(i) the treatment should be continued beyond the period specified in the order;
(ii) the child needs different treatment;
(iii) he/she is not susceptible to treatment; or
(iv) he/she does not require further treatment.

When he/she receives a written report from the practitioner, the supervisor must refer it to the court. Upon such a reference the court may make an order cancelling or varying the requirement. (See Sch 3 Part I paras 5(2),(3),(6) and (7) CA 1989.)

*(e) Children with special educational needs*

Under the Education Act 1981 ("EA 1981"), a local education authority must have regard to the need for securing special educational provision for pupils who have special educational needs (s 8(2)(c) Education Act 1944). A child has special educational needs if he/she has a learning difficulty which calls for special educational provision to be made for him/her. He/She has "learning difficulty" if:

(i) he/she has a significantly greater difficulty in learning than the majority of children of his/her age; or
(ii) he/she has a disability which either prevents or hinders him/her from making use of educational facilities of a kind generally provided in schools, within the area of the local authority concerned, for children of his/her age; or
(iii) he/she is under the age of five years and is, or would be if special educational provision is not made, likely to fall within (i) or (ii) when over that age.

(s 1(2)(a)–(c) EA 1981.)

A child with a mental handicap or a child with a mental disorder may fall within this definition. "Special educational provision" in relation to a child who has attained the age of two years means that which is additional to, or different from, that made generally for children of his/her age in local educational authority maintained schools. In relation to a child under two years it means education provision of any kind. (See s 1(3)(a) and (b) EA 1981.)

Every local education authority is under a duty to identify

children for whom it is responsible who have special educational needs and are in need of special educational provision (s 4(1) EA 1981). If the authority is of the opinion that a child falls into this category, or probably falls into it, an assessment of his/her special educational needs must be made. Where it proposes to make an assessment, it must serve notice on the parents informing them of the proposal, the name of the officer from whom further information may be obtained, and of their right to make written representations (within a period of not less than twenty-nine days). Details of the procedure to be followed must also be included in the notice. Copies of the notice must be sent to the local social services authority and the district health authority (r 3 Education (Special Educational Needs) Regulations 1983 – "E(SEN)R 1983").

Once the period within which representations may be made has expired, the local education authority may decide to assess the educational needs of the child. If appropriate, it should take into account any representations made or evidence presented in response to the notice. The child's parents must be notified in writing of the decision to assess; reasons for the decision must be given. If, after making an assessment, the authority decides that it is not required to determine what special educational provision should be made for the child, the local authority must inform the parents of their right to appeal in writing to the Secretary of State. The Secretary of State may, if he/she thinks fit, direct the authority to reconsider its decision. Where the authority decides not to assess, the parents must be informed in writing. (See s 5(1)–(10) EA 1981.) In the case of such a child who is under two years of age, the authority *may* make an assessment and must do so if requested by the parent (s 6 EA 1981). An authority may be requested by a parent for an assessment to be made of a child where no statement is maintained in respect of him/her. The authority must comply with such a request unless it is, in its opinion, unreasonable to do so. (See s 9(1) EA 1981.)

When making an assessment, an authority must seek educational, medical and psychological advice about the child as well as any other advice which it considers desirable for the purpose of arriving at a satisfactory assessment. This advice must be presented in writing. The person giving the advice may consult other people if he/she considers it expedient to do so and he/she must consult a particular person if required by the authority. Under r 4(2) E(SEN)R 1983, the advice sought must relate to:

    (i) the educational, medical, psychological or other features

of the case which appear to be relevant to his/her educational needs (including future needs);
(ii) how those features affect the child's educational needs; and
(iii) the special education or other provision rendered necessary by those features if the child is to benefit properly from his/her education.

(r 4(2) E(SEN)R 1983.)

Educational advice should normally be obtained from the head-teacher of a school which the child has attended at some time in the preceding eighteen months. If the head-teacher has not himself/herself taught the child, he/she should consult a teacher who has. In cases where such advice cannot be obtained (either because the child has not attended a school, or otherwise), a person with experience of teaching children with special educational needs should be consulted. (See r 5(1) and (2) E(SEN)R 1983.)

Medical advice must be obtained from a fully registered medical practitioner who is either designated for the purpose of the E(SEN)R 1983 or nominated for the child in question. Psychological advice should be sought from a person either regularly employed or engaged by the education authority as an educational psychologist. He/She should consult any other psychologist he/she has reason to believe has some knowledge of the child. When it makes the assessment of the child, the education authority must take into consideration the r 4(3) advice. It must also take into consideration representations made by the child's parents, evidence submitted by or on behalf of the parent, and any information relating to the health or welfare of the child provided by any district health authority or any social services authority (r 8 E(SEN)R 1983).

After making an assessment, if the local education authority is of the opinion that it should determine the special educational provision for the child, it must make and maintain a statement of his/her special educational needs. A statement must specify the following:

(i) the special educational provision which the authority considers appropriate to meet the needs identified;
(ii) *either* the type of school which the authority considers appropriate for the child (including the name of a particular school if possible) *or* if it is considered appropriate that the child should be provided with

education other than at school, particulars of the provision considered to be appropriate;
(iii) any additional non-educational provision:
- which (unless proposed to be made by the education authority) it is satisfied will be made available by the district health authority, a social services authority or some other body; and
- of which advantage should be taken if the child is to benefit from the special educational provision specified above;
(iv) the representations, evidence, advice and information taken into consideration under r 8 E(SEN)R 1983 must be set out.

(r 10(1) E(SEN)R 1983.)

Statements are confidential and should not be disclosed without the parent's consent except where the authority considers disclosure to be in the educational interests of the child. Disclosure is also permissible for the purposes of s 8 EA 1981 appeal (see above), for bona fide educational research, on the order of any court or for the purposes of criminal proceedings or for a maladministration investigation under Part III Local Government Act 1974. (See r 11(1) E(SEN)R 1983.)

The authority is under an obligation to arrange the special educational provision specified in a statement unless his/her parents have made suitable arrangements. The authority may arrange that any non-educational provision should be made for him/her in such a manner as it considers appropriate (see s 7(2)(a) and (b) EA 1981). Before making a statement, the authority must serve on the parent a copy of the proposed statement. If the parent disagrees with any part of it, he/she may make representations to the authority and request a meeting in order to discuss the statement. Any meeting must take place within fifteen days of the service of the notice of the proposed statement. Should the parent, after attending a meeting with the authority, still disagree, one or more further meetings must be arranged within the following fifteen days if requested. Any further meetings are designed to enable the parents to discuss any advice given in connection with the contentious part of the statement; the person who gave that advice should be present. After considering any representations made by a parent, the authority may make a statement in the form originally proposed, or make a modified statement, or decide to make no statement. The parent must be notified in writing of the authority's decision. When making the statement, the authority must serve on the parent a copy of it, notice in writing of his/her right of appeal (see below), and notice in writing of the person whom he/she may contact about information and advice on the child's special educational needs. (See s 7(1)–(10) EA 1981.)

Every local education authority must make arrangements for enabling a parent of a child to appeal against a first or subsequent assessment of the child's special educational needs, made under the above provision. Appeal against an amendment of the special educational needs in the statement is also possible. An appeal committee was established under para 1 of Part I of Sch 2 to the Education Act 1980. This committee may confirm the statement or remit back to the authority for reconsideration in the light of any comments which it may make. Where the committee remit the statement, the authority must reconsider it and take account of the committee's comments. The parents must then be informed of the authority's decision. An appeal to the Secretary of State may be made from the committee's decision to confirm the statement, and the authority's decision after a remit to it from the committee. Upon appeal the Secretary of State may confirm or amend the statement, or direct the authority to cease to maintain the statement. (See s 8(1)–(7) EA 1981.)

A mandatory re-assessment of a child who is the subject of a statement must be made if his/her educational needs have not been assessed since before he/she reached the age of twelve years and six months. This re-assessment must take place during the period of twelve months beginning with the day that he/she attains the age of thirteen years and six months. (See r 9 E(SEN)R 1983.)

If the parent of a child for whom a statement is being maintained asks for an assessment of the child's educational needs, and such an assessment has not been carried out within the last six months, the authority must comply with the request unless satisfied that it would be inappropriate. Once made, a statement must be reviewed by the education authority at least once every twelve months beginning with the date of the making of the statement (Sch 1 Part II para 5 EA 1981). Unlike a re-assessment, a review does not require the authority to follow the procedure outlined above.

Where an authority proposes to amend or to cease to maintain a statement, it must serve on the parent of the child notice in writing of the proposal and of the right of appeal. Upon receipt of this notice the parent may, within fifteen days of service, make representations to the authority. Consideration must be given to

*Community care*

any representations and the authority must then inform the parent in writing of the decision. This provision does not apply where the authority ceases to maintain a statement in respect of a child who has ceased to be its responsibility (for example, he/she ceases to be registered as a pupil at a school). (See Sch 1 Part I paras 6 and 9 EA 1981.)

Provision is made to ease the transition from school to adulthood of a child who is subject to a statement under the EA 1981. The DP(SCR)A 1986 seeks to ensure that there is proper co-operation between the local education authority and the local social services authority as the child approaches school-leaving age. Section 5 DP(SCR)A 1986 requires the local education authority to seek an opinion from the local social services authority on whether a statemented child is a disabled person. "Disabled person" has the same meaning as it has in s 29 NAA 1948 in respect of persons aged eighteen years or over (see page 146), and in the case of persons under that age as in Part III CA 1989 (see page 150). Where there is a statement in respect of a child under the age of fourteen years and it is still maintained at the time of the first annual review or the mandatory re-assessment after the fourteenth birthday, whichever is the earlier, the education authority shall require the appropriate officer to determine whether the child is a disabled person. If it is determined that the child is not disabled, but after his/her fourteenth birthday the education authority observes a significant change in his/her mental or physical condition which gives it reason to believe that he/she may now be disabled, the appropriate officer must give another opinion on the child. An opinion must also be sought from the appropriate officer if the child is first statemented after reaching the age of fourteen years. An appropriate officer is a person appointed by the local authority for the purposes of the DP(SCR)A 1986. (See s 5(1) and (2) DP(SCR)A 1986.)

If the appropriate officer determines that the child is disabled, the education authority must give the officer notice that the child is ceasing education. Where it appears to the education authority that a child under the age of nineteen years on the "relevant date" will be leaving full-time schooling and not going on to further education, or that he/she is leaving further education, it must give the appropriate officer written notice. "Relevant date" means eight months before the date upon which he/she is to leave school or further education. The notice must be given not earlier than twelve and not later than eight months before the date of leaving. (See s 5(3) DP(SCR)A 1986.) In cases where notice would be required to be given under s 5(3), but the child leaves school or further education unexpectedly and the giving of requisite notice is not possible, the education authority must provide the appropriate officer with written notice as soon as is reasonably practicable. (See s 5(4) DP(SCR)A 1986.)

When the appropriate officer receives notice under s 5(3) or (4) DP(SCR)A 1986, he/she must make arrangements for the local authority to carry out an assessment of needs of the child with respect to the provision by it of statutory services under the "welfare enactments". The "welfare enactments" are Part III NAA 1948, s 2 CSDPA 1970, Sch 8 NHSA 1977 and Part III CA 1989. In the case of a notice given under s 5(3) DP(SCR)A 1986, the assessment must be carried out within five months of its receipt; if under s 5(4) DP(SCR)A 1986, the assessment must take place before the date of leaving education if it is reasonably practicable, and in any event not later than five months after receipt of the notice. (See s 5(5) DP(SCR)A 1986.) However, the appropriate officer will not be required to make arrangements for an assessment if the child has attained the age of sixteen years and has requested that the assessment should not take place. Similarly, if the child is under the age of sixteen years and the parent or person having parental responsibility requests that arrangements should not be made, the appropriate officer is not required to make them. (See s 5(7) DP(SCR)A 1986.) Where it transpires that the child will be continuing school or further education after the date specified in the notice, the education authority must give notice to the appropriate officer. The officer must then cease to make arrangements for the child's assessment. (See s 5(6) DP(SCR)A 1986.)

In order to meet the requirements of s 5 DP(SCR)A 1986, a local education authority must keep under review the dates when certain children are expected to cease full-time education at school or in further education (s 6(1) DP(SCR)A 1986). The children to whom s 6(1) DP(SCR)A 1986 applies are:

(i) any child for whom the authority is responsible under the EA 1981 and in respect of whom an opinion has been given (whether to that authority or to some other) that he/she is disabled; or

(ii) any child at a further education establishment for whom the authority was responsible immediately before he/she ceased to receive full-time education at school and in respect of whom there has been an opinion that he/she is disabled.

(s 6(2) DP(SCR)A 1986.)

## 8. The Social Fund

### (a) Introduction

The Social Security Act 1986 introduced the Social Fund which replaced single payments, maternity grants and death grants (ss 32–35 Social Security Act 1986). According to the DHSS publication *A Guide to The Social Fund* (DHSS SB16), the Social Fund is "intended for people on a low income who cannot meet exceptional expenses from their regular income". Under the Social Fund, assistance is available by way of payment, loan or grant. Payments cover maternity payments and funeral payments, are non-discretionary and paid if the applicant comes within stated criteria (see Social Fund Maternity and Funeral Expenses (General) Regulations 1987 SI No. 481 and The Social Fund Maternity and Funeral Expenses (General) Amendment Regulations 1988 SI No. 36). The Discretionary Social Fund covers loans and grants. A budgeting loan may be available to meet expenses a person is having difficulty in meeting if he/she or his/her partner is in receipt of income support. It may cover items such as furniture and fuel meter installation (high priority applications), hire purchase debts and non-essential items of furniture (medium priority applications), and rent in advance and leisure items (low priority applications). Domestic assistance and respite care are not covered by budgeting loans. A crisis loan may be available to a person who needs financial help after an emergency or unexpected payment. The person need not be in receipt of income support. Among the examples given of the potential use of crisis loans is that of emergency travel expenses for somebody who is stranded away from home. Domestic assistance, respite care and mobility needs do not come within the crisis loans scheme. Both budgeting loans and crisis loans must be repaid at an agreed rate; they are interest free. They are discretionary payments and the social fund officers will be working within cash limits.

Of particular interest to the mentally ill and the mentally handicapped are the community care grants ("CCGs") which are designed to give assistance to people to live in the community rather than in institutional care.

### (b) Community care grants

Grants may be made under the Social Fund in respect of persons or people caring for them by way of a CCG. Persons getting income support may be eligible for a CCG. Such grants are not repayable. The purpose of a CCG is "to help people live as independent a life as possible in the community". Local authorities have statutory duties to make provision for mentally ill and mentally handicapped persons (see pages 140–164), and a CCG cannot be used to meet any expenses which the local authority has such a duty to meet. However, the social fund officer may make a CCG to complement the authorities' role in the provision of community care. Social fund officers are also expected to liaise closely with local social services authorities and discuss, amongst other matters, proposed priorities, responsibilities, consultation, co-operation and referral (paras 6001–6006 Social Fund Manual – "SFM").

Section 33(9) Social Security Act 1986 requires the social fund officer to have regard to the following matters when determining whether or not a CCG should be made:

(i) the nature, extent and urgency of the need;
(ii) the existence of resources which the applicant may have which may be used to meet the need;
(iii) the possibility that the need may be met, in whole or in part, by some other person or body (for example a local authority);
(iv) the relevant budget limit within which the officer is required to work.

(paras 6008–6009 SFM.)

The officer may exercise his/her discretion within these guidelines, but subject to any directions which the Secretary of State may make. He/She must also take account of any guidance which the Secretary of State may issue. (See s 33(10) Social Security Act 1986.)

A number of directions have been made by the Secretary of State which affect the working of CCGs. Direction 30 deals with the making of applications for a CCG. The direction requires applications to be in writing by the applicant or by somebody acting on his/her behalf. The date of the application is the date upon which it is received by the DSS office. Wherever practicable, a decision on an application should be made within twenty-eight days of its receipt. A person is eligible for a CCG:

"4 ............. to promote community care:

(a) by assisting an eligible person with expenses (except those included by the directions) where such assistance will:

## Community care

(i) help that person, or a member of his family, to re-establish himself in the community following a stay in institutional or residential care; or

(ii) help that person, or a member of his family, to remain in the community rather than enter institutional or residential care; or

(iii) ease exceptional pressures on that person and his family; or

(b) by assisting an eligible person, or a member of his family, with expenses of travel within the United Kingdom in order to:

(i) visit someone who is ill; or

(ii) attend a relative's funeral; or

(iii) ease a domestic crisis; or ...

(iv) move to suitable accommodation."

(direction 4(a) and (b).)

If the conditions set out in direction 4(a)(i) are satisfied and it is intended that the applicant will be discharged into the community within six weeks of a written application, a CCG may be made if the officer is of the opinion that he/she is likely to receive income support upon discharge. If in these circumstances it subsequently transpires that the applicant is not entitled to income support, and he/she has indicated in writing a willingness to repay the grant, the officer must determine that the CCG is repayable (direction 6). The SFM states that where there is an application before the determination of income support, payment of the CCG must be deferred until two weeks before discharge. A CCG cannot be awarded if there is a repeat application within twenty-six weeks of a previous application for a grant towards the same item of service for which payment has already been made. This prohibition does not, however, apply if it can be shown that there has been a change of circumstances since the last application (direction 7).

Mentally ill and mentally handicapped people are within the category of "priority cases". This is not a guarantee that a CCG will be made for CCGs are discretionary, but it does mean that together with others in the priority category their applications will be more likely to succeed than those outside it. The social fund officer must, under the guidance issued, consider the priority of the application in the light of the budget for grants and any locally established priorities. If the applicant or his/her partner hold capital of less than £500 it will be ignored for the purpose of a CCG. For savings over £500, the size of any CCG will be reduced on a pound for pound basis (direction 27). The decision must be reasonable in all the circumstances and it must, along with the reasons for it, be recorded.

So far as the mentally ill or mentally handicapped are concerned, a CCG may be awarded in the following circumstances:

### Leaving institutional or residential care

A CCG is intended to assist people who are leaving institutional or residential care to adjust to living in the community. The particular types of institutional or residential care are outlined below. Generally, the person must have been in such care for a period of at least three months, but a person will still be eligible if there is a pattern of regular and frequent admission which is linked to the disability (para 6201 SFM). Although it will not normally be appropriate to make more than one CCG under this heading, the SFM does draw to the attention of the social fund officers the difficulty which might be experienced before a person is successfully settled in the community. A social fund officer should confirm with the applicant that he/she intends to live in the proposed accommodation permanently. This is important as it may mean that a CCG is unavailable for a move to a "half-way house" which is being used as part of a longer resettlement programme. The SFM recommends that the applicant should be told that a CCG may be awarded when he/she actually moves to more permanent accommodation. The SFM further advises officers that the intention must be to live in the applicant's own home rather than board and lodging establishments, guest houses, hostels, lodgings or staffed group homes. Nor should a CCG be paid to people entering residential homes or nursing homes. If the applicant is sharing and paying rent for the accommodation, a CCG may be paid; the example given in the SFM is where he/she is resident in an unstaffed home for former psychiatric patients. A CCG may be available for persons who are going to live permanently with family or close friends. (See para 6204 SFM.)

The following CCGs may be available to persons leaving institutional or residential care (see below for the circumstances in which each grant is available):

(i) "start-up" grants : this CCG is designed to enable the recipient to provide furniture, bedding, household equipment etc which will be necessary to start up his/her home. The grant may be paid on the basis of what items the applicant actually requires, or it may be by way of a lump sum up to a maximum of £500 for a single person and £750 for a couple. A start-up grant may be reduced if the home is partly furnished, if several people are moving out of institutional care and into the same accommodation or if the applicant already has the item. Where the applicant has only requested one item, the officer may consider whether he/she requires further items to help in setting up home;

(ii) clothing: a person should have at least one change of clothing and also protective clothing. It is assumed that applicants leaving Part III accommodation will already have sufficient clothing and footwear. A lump sum of up to £150 can be made;

(iii) removal expenses: this may be made as an alternative to all or part of the start-up grant where the applicant already has his/her own furniture. A CCG may be applied to storage charges if it is decided that the furniture is needed in the new home. The officer should accept the lower of two estimates provided;

(iv) fares when moving home: the CCG should normally cover:
   – standard rate public transport (excluding air fares); or
   – the cost of petrol either up to the cost of public transport if available, or in full if not available; or
   – a taxi fare if no public transport is available or the applicant or his/her partner cannot use public transport because of physical disability;

(v) reasonable connection charges: the cost of connecting domestic appliances may be met if the charge is reasonable.

The above CCGs are available to the mentally ill and mentally handicapped in the following circumstances:

(i) discharge from hospital or other NHS establishment or a nursing home;

(ii) leaving a home or a hostel (ie group home, residential care home, resettlement unit, hostel, supported lodging and staff-intensive housing providing a major level of personal care);

(iii) discharge from prison or youth centre (ie prison, youth custody or detention centre, youth treatment centre and any other centre where custodial sentences may be served).

Start-up grants, fares and connection charges may also be awarded to young people over the age of sixteen years who are leaving local authority care or foster care and who have decided to set up home on their own. The SFM advises social fund officers to contact the social services to check whether the person can cope independently after leaving care.

*Moving house to look after somebody who is moving from institutional or residential care*

Applicants will normally be relatives of the person moving into the community although the SFM states that social fund officers may make awards to close friends or neighbours of that person. They must be in receipt of income support. The person leaving care must be mentally ill or mentally handicapped (ie in the priority group). The person moving must be doing so because the new property is more suitable for caring for the mentally ill or mentally handicapped person. The following needs may be met:

(i) removal expenses;
(ii) fares when moving home;
(iii) connection charges;
(iv) furniture and furnishings.

A CCG under (iv) will only be available in exceptional circumstances such as where the applicant is leaving furnished or partly furnished accommodation. The applicant will not be entitled to a furniture grant if the person needing care has already received a start-up grant.

*Moving to more suitable accommodation*

A CCG may be available where the mentally ill or mentally handicapped applicant is living in the community and wishes to move to more suitable accommodation. There must be good reasons for the move which relate to the person's disability. It must also be shown that the move will help the applicant and his/her partner to remain in the community rather than enter institutional or residential care. The move must be to a home of his/her own and he/she must be responsible for payment of rent and/or providing his/her own furniture. Before a CCG can be made under this heading, the officer must be satisfied that the present accommodation is unsuitable for the applicant's or his/

## Community care

her partner's needs. Matters of health and mobility should be taken into account. Specific account should be taken of steep stairways, difficulty in reaching bathrooms, inadequate toilet/washing facilities, insanitary conditions, structural defects and the size of the accommodation (either too big or too small). Where there is any doubt, the officer should discuss with other parties such as the social services and the environmental health department.

A CCG under this heading may cover the following:

(i) removal expenses (removal expenses should not be awarded where the local authority is responsible for the move under the Housing Act 1985, for example where there is a compulsory exchange of local authority tenancies, or the applicant is being rehoused after a compulsory purchase, closing or redevelopment order);

(ii) fares when moving home;

(iii) connection charges;

(iv) furniture and furnishings (available only in exceptional circumstances – for example, household items have been damaged because of dampness, or where the applicant moves from furnished or partly furnished to unfurnished accommodation.)

(paras 6339–6345.)

### Moving nearer to supportive relatives or friends who will provide "permanent" support

The social fund officer should try to ensure that the support will be permanent. This may involve talking to the carer and/or social services and others. Normally, support will be limited to removal expenses, fares, connection charges and furniture and furnishings (where the applicant is living in furnished/partly furnished accommodation and the new home is sparsely furnished). (See para 6353 SFM.)

### Moving house to be nearer, or to live with, a mentally ill or mentally handicapped person

The mentally ill or mentally handicapped person may or may not be getting income support, but the applicant must be receiving it. The applicant must be providing attention or supervision on a daily basis and should be a relative or close friend of the person in need of care. Needs which may be met should normally be confined to:

(i) removal expenses;

(ii) fares;
(iii) connection charges;
(iv) furniture and furnishings.
(para 6358 SFM.)

*Living in the community but moving in order to set up an independent home for the first time*

This covers a mentally ill or mentally handicapped person currently living with relatives or friends and who is now considering moving to independent living. He/She must have been attending a day centre and be ready for independent living. The CCG will generally be confined to:

(i) a start-up grant;
(ii) removal expenses and storage charges;
(iii) fares when moving home;
(iv) connection charges.
(para 6361 SFM.)

*Staying in the community, rather than entering institutions or residential care, and improving living conditions*

A CCG may be available to assist the applicant to stay in the community rather than enter residential or institutional care. The prospect of care does not have to be immediate. The CCG may cover:

(i) Minor repairs and maintenance (where, unless the repairs or maintenance are carried out, the applicant or partner is likely to be taken into residential care). Grants up to £400 are available. A grant will only be awarded if the applicant is responsible for the repairs, and the home does not belong to a local authority or similar organisation. If the local authority has a duty to carry out the work under the Chronically Sick and Disabled Persons Act 1970, a CCG will not be payable. Similarly, no CCG will be payable if a housing department, charity, friend or relative is available to meet the cost. Help towards paying interest on a loan or mortgage for major repairs may be included in income support; CCGs may help towards survey fees but not legal fees for arranging such a loan.

(ii) Internal redecoration and refurbishment (where the applicant or his/her partner is responsible for

## Community care

redecoration and spends a good deal of time in the home). Decorating, furnishing and floor covering may be covered by the grant; the officer must decide whether the standard of decoration is adequate, and should accept that furniture which has some life left in it may soon need replacing. A CCG may also be available to cover damage to the home or its contents caused by the applicant or his/her partner as a consequence of the applicant's particular condition (see para 6378 SFM). A reasonable sum should be awarded by way of CCG; it will generally only cover costs of materials, but labour costs may be included if relatives, friends, neighbours, charities or a community programme project are not available to do the work (paras 6380–6381 SFM).

(iii) Bedding or extra warmth. Grants for bedding are available where the applicant or partner has an exceptional need for bedding: he/she must be bedridden and incontinent, with the result that the bedding needs to be changed regularly. Grants for extra warmth are payable where he/she is confined to bed for long periods, or is housebound, and needs extra warmth. Exceptionally, CCGs may be made for heaters. Schemes to improve home insulation should also be considered by the social fund officer.

(iv) Fuel costs. A CCG cannot be made available to cover fuel bills incurred by an applicant. Rather, it should be awarded to cover reconnection charges, and to pay for the re-siting of meters to allow easier access, or the installation of pre-payment meters.

(v) Laundry. A CCG may meet heavy laundry needs if the applicant or the partner is incontinent. Where there is no washing machine, a CCG may be awarded for a new machine unless help can be obtained from another agency. Connection charges may be covered by a CCG, as, too, may repairs to an old washing machine. If there are no suitable drying facilities, a CCG may be awarded to cover the cost of a tumble dryer, or, if appropriate, a dual-function washing machine and dryer. Connection charges may be met by the CCG.

(vi) Furniture. When considering the provision of furniture, regard must be had to the responsibilities of local authorities to provide for the sick and disabled (see page 140). If a local authority does not have a responsibility to provide a particular type of furniture (for example upright, firm armchairs for elderly persons) a CCG may be awarded. An award may also be made in respect of furniture which has been seriously damaged as a result of the applicant's or his/her partner's behaviour. A CCG may be granted for a bed for the chronically sick where their health is such that the partners must sleep in separate beds. Other forms of payment for furniture should be dealt with by a budgeting loan (para 6388 SFM).

(vii) Clothing and footwear. These are to be treated as low priority. A CCG may be awarded if, through illness or disability, excessive wear and tear is caused to clothing or there is rapid weight gain or loss.

*Travelling expenses*

Travelling expenses may be payable by way of a CCG if a person incurs them while visiting a mentally ill or mentally handicapped person who is a close relative, or a relative not visited by any other person, or a member of the household who is a patient in a hospital, a nursing home, or a registered care home (or one which is too small to register), or who is in Part III accommodation or staff-intensive housing which provides a major level of personal care. (See direction 4 and paras 6551–6554 SFM.) A CCG may also be awarded to enable a member of a family to visit somebody who is not in hospital but who is critically ill (para 6561 SFM).

## Chapter 6

# Mental capacity and the criminal law

## 1. The defence of insanity

### (a) Introduction

Despite the development in the identification and treatment of mental disorder, insanity as a defence in criminal law has its origins in the nineteenth century. As a defence, it is unpopular because it results in the person found not guilty by reason of insanity being admitted to a hospital with a restriction order without limitation of time, regardless of the nature of the alleged offence for which he/she has been acquitted. Criminal law normally requires an *actus reus* and a *mens rea*. Everybody is presumed to be sane and therefore capable of forming the necessary *mens rea* of a crime unless the contrary is proved. Proof of insanity is one way in which this presumption can be rebutted. However, insanity in the criminal law is quite different from what is generally recognised as insanity in other areas of the law and in medicine. For the definition of insanity it is necessary to refer to *R* v *M'Naughten* (1843).

### (b) The M'Naughten Rules

The M'Naughten Rules provide the basic statement of law relating to the defence of insanity. It is important to emphasise that the Rules provide a legal and not a medical definition of insanity (see Goddard CJ in *R* v *Rivett* (1950)). In their advice to the House of Lords, the judges formulated the first two limbs of the Rules as follows:

> "... the jury ought to be told in all cases that every man is presumed to be sane, and to possess a sufficient degree of reason to be responsible for his crimes, until the

contrary be proved to their satisfaction; and that, to establish a defence on the ground of insanity, it must be clearly proved that, at the time of the committing of the act, the party accused was labouring under such a defect of reason, from disease of the mind, as not to know the nature and quality of the act he was doing, or, if he did know it, that he did not know he was doing what was wrong."

In the case of a person suffering from a partial delusion, the judges advised that he/she "must be considered in the same situation as to responsibility as if the facts with respect to which the delusion exists were real". This third limb is generally regarded as being subsumed in the first two.

The first two limbs require proof of a defect of reason arising from a disease of the mind. It must then be shown that as a consequence the accused did not know the nature and quality of his/her acts, or, if he/she did, that he/she did not know it was wrong. Each of these elements will now be considered.

*Defect of reason arising from a disease of the mind:* This requirement is essential when distinguishing insanity from diminished responsibility (see page 182). The expression "disease of the mind" has caused the judiciary much trouble and it is difficult to discern any consistent reasoning in the cases other than a wish to respond to the perceived danger posed by the actual accused before the court. Whether or not a person is suffering from a disease of the mind is to be determined by the trial judge and does not have to be left to the jury. In *R* v *Kemp* (1956), Devlin J stressed that the words were included in the Rules to avoid the defence being available to a person whose defect of reason was caused by "brutish stupidity without rational power". Thus a person with a healthy mind who has never learned to exercise his/her reason should not fall within the M'Naughten Rules. Furthermore, the words "disease of the mind" should not be used to introduce a distinction between diseases of the mind and the body. In *Kemp* the accused was suffering from arteriosclerosis. He argued that this was not a disease of the mind but a physical disease; consequently he sought to avail himself of the absolute defence of non-insane automatism. Devlin J rejected this argument saying that whatever the medical categorization of arteriosclerosis, for the purposes of the criminal law it was a disease capable of affecting the mind by causing a defect of reason and therefore fell within the Rules.

Barry J in *R* v *Charlson* (1955) adopted a more restrictive approach. He assumed that diseases such as epilepsy or cerebral tumours were not diseases of the mind even though they manifest themselves in violence which is likely to recur. In *Bratty* v *Attorney-General for Northern Ireland* (1961), Lord Denning favoured the approach of Devlin J. He advocated a wide test which stated that any mental disorder manifesting itself in violence and which is prone to recur is a disease of the mind or is "the sort of disease for which a person should be detained in hospital rather than given an unqualified acquittal".

Further support for Devlin J was given by the House of Lords in *R* v *Sullivan* (1983). During a psychomotor epilepsy seizure, the accused violently attacked a friend. On appeal he argued that psychomotor epilepsy was not a disease of the mind. In support of this argument it was claimed that a "disease of the mind" or a "mental illness" (the appellant wrongly regarded these terms as interchangeable) must be prolonged for a period of time. Lord Diplock referred with approval to Devlin J's refusal to distinguish between mental and physical disorders. He said:

> "If the effect of a disease is to impair (the mental faculties of reason, memory and understanding) so severely as to have either of the consequences referred to in the latter part of the Rules, it matters not whether the aetiology of the impairment is organic, as in epilepsy, or functional, or whether the impairment itself is permanent or is transient and intermittent, provided that it subsisted at the time of commission of the act."

The purpose of the defence is to protect society against recurrence of dangerous behaviour. Its intermittent nature is relevant only to the Secretary of State as regards subsequent treatment, and not to the applicability of the defence.

The House of Lords in *DPP* v *Beard* (1920) considered the relationship between insanity and drunkenness. Lord Birkenhead LC stated that insanity caused by drunkenness is a defence and rejected a line of authorities which limited the defence to cases of a continuing and lasting state of insanity. The law takes no cognizance of the cause of the insanity, so the fact that it is a result of self-induced drunkenness is not relevant if the accused comes within the M'Naughten Rules. It should be emphasised that the drunkenness must bring on a disease of the mind (for example, *delirium tremens*) causing a defect of reason. Furthermore, one of the first two limbs of M'Naughten must be satisfied (see *Attorney-General for Northern Ireland* v *Gallagher* (1961) and *R* v *Davis* (1881)).

*Not knowing the nature and quality of the act:* This refers to the physical nature of the act rather than to its moral character (see Reading CJ in *R* v *Codere* (1916)). So, for example, if the accused imagines he/she is chopping wood when in fact he/she is attacking another person with an axe, the conduct will fall within this category. The lack of awareness of the nature and quality of the act must be a consequence of a defect of reason arising from a disease of the mind.

*He/She did not know that the act was wrong:* If the accused knows that the act is wrong according to the law, then he/she does not come within this limb of the Rules even though he/she may believe it to be morally right (see *R* v *Codere* and *R* v *Windle* (1952)). Problems arise where the accused does not know that the act is wrong according to the law, but is aware that it is morally wrong. According to Goddard CJ in *Windle,* such a person would come within this limb as " 'wrong' means contrary to law and not 'wrong' according to the opinion of one man or of a number of people". Strictly speaking, this part of Goddard CJ's judgment is *obiter dicta,* although it is generally accepted as a correct statement of the law.

*Irresistible impulses:* The accused may not come within the M'Naughten Rules but be unable to control his/her actions. As such, an irresistible impulse does not provide a defence in law. The courts have adopted the view that the law should seek to "assist" people suffering from such influences and by "rendering the crime dispunishable, you at once withdraw a most powerful legal restraint – that forbidding and punishing its perpetration". (See *R* v *Haynes* (1859).)

It should not be assumed that, as a matter of law, a person acting under an irresistible impulse is automatically within the M'Naughten Rules, and any direction to a jury to that effect will be incorrect (see *Attorney-General for South Australia* v *Brown* (1960)). The courts have steadfastly refused to extend the Rules to include cases of irresistible impulse where the accused does not fall within their original formulation (see *Sodeman* v *The King* (1936)). Of course, the presence of such an impulse may be relevant evidence in proving insanity in which case it will be admissible. However, medical evidence will be necessary to support this argument. The relevance of irresistible impulse in cases of diminished responsibility will be considered below (see pages 182–185).

## (c) Proof of insanity

Before the defence of insanity can be considered, the court must be satisfied beyond all reasonable doubt that the defendant committed the act which is the substance of the alleged offence. If it is not satisfied that this is the case, the defendant is entitled to an acquittal. Under the M'Naughten Rules every person is assumed to be sane; therefore the burden of proof is on the defendant to show that he/she was insane at the time that the alleged offence took place. It is not sufficient for him/her merely to raise the issue and then expect the prosecution to rebut the assertion beyond all reasonable doubt. Instead, the defence has to prove that on a balance of probabilities the accused was insane at the time of the alleged offence (see *R* v *Burns* (1973), and the House of Lords in *Bratty*).

It is the jury and not the medical profession which decides the issue of insanity (see *R* v *Rivett* (1950)). Where there is disagreement between the medical experts, or doubt is cast upon their opinions, the jury is responsible for determining the issue. However, if the medical evidence is clear and is not contradicted by other evidence, an appeal will lie against a conviction which is contrary to those opinions (see *R* v *Matheson* (1958)). Proof of insanity will generally depend upon medical evidence, but this does not mean that it cannot be proved other than by such evidence. In *Attorney-General for South Australia* v *Brown,* the Privy Council stated that the previous and contemporaneous acts of the accused "may often be preferred" to medical theory. The use of the word "often" overstates the value of alternative evidence; it is sufficient to note that the evidence need not be exclusively, or even mainly, medical, although in practice it usually will be.

Subject to the one exception noted below, the prosecution has no right to raise the issue of insanity (see *R* v *Dickie* (1984)). Where the accused raises insanity, the prosecution may adduce its own evidence to rebut the defence. This applies not only where the defence presents its own evidence of insanity, but also where it is relying solely on the cross-examination of prosecution witnesses (see *R* v *Abramovitch* (1912)). If the prosecution has in its possession evidence of the accused's insanity, it has a duty to make it available to the defence (*R* v *Dickie*).

The exception to this rule arises where the accused in a murder trial raises the defence of diminished responsibility (see page 182). Under s 6 Criminal Procedure (Insanity) Act 1964, if the accused raises the defence of diminished responsibility the prosecution may introduce evidence of insanity. Similarly, where the accused contends that he/she was insane, the prosecution may adduce evidence to show diminished responsibility.

In exceptional circumstances, a judge can raise the issue of insanity and let the jury decide whether or not the accused comes within the M'Naughten Rules (*R* v *Dickie*). There must be prima facie evidence before the court that the accused is within the Rules. Before leaving the matter to the jury the judge must afford the defence and the prosecution the opportunity of calling any evidence they consider necessary to respond to his/her decision. In such cases an adjournment may be appropriate.

*(d) "The special verdict"*

If the accused is found to be within the M'Naughten Rules, s 2 Trial of Lunatics Act 1833 requires the court to return a special verdict of "not guilty by reason of insanity". The court must make an order that the accused be admitted to such hospital as may be specified by the Secretary of State (see s 5(1) Criminal Procedure (Insanity) Act 1964). This order is sufficient authority for a person acting under or for the Secretary of State to convey the person, within a period of two months from the date of the making of the order, to the specified hospital. The court may give directions relating to the conveyance to, and detention in, a place of safety of the person pending his/her admission to the hospital. By virtue of the order, the hospital managers have authority to detain the person as if a hospital order had been made under s 37 MHA 1983 together with a restriction order made under s 41 MHA 1983 without limitation of time. (See Sch 1 Criminal Procedure (Insanity) Act 1964, and pages 56 and 62.)

*(e) Appeals against a finding of not guilty by reason of insanity*

It is ironic that an accused person may appeal against a finding of not guilty by reason of insanity. However, this is likely if he/she put forward the defence of diminished responsibility and the prosecution then successfully raised the issue of insanity. A conviction of manslaughter may be more acceptable than a special verdict in view of the potentially wide powers of detention which the latter attracts. Therefore, s 12 Criminal Appeal Act 1968 ("CAA 1968") enables such a person to appeal to the Court of Appeal against the verdict. An appeal may be made on any ground which involves a question of law and, provided the court is satisfied that a bona fide question of law is involved, such an appeal is as of right (s 12(a) CAA 1968). An appeal on a question of fact, or mixed fact and law, is only possible where the court of trial grants a certificate that the case is fit for appeal or with the leave of the Court of Appeal (s 12(b) CAA 1968).

The Court of Appeal's powers of disposal of s 12 CAA 1968 appeals follow closely its powers to determine appeals under s 2 CAA 1968. Subject to the proviso noted below, the Court of Appeal must allow the appeal if:

(i) the verdict should be set aside on the ground that under all the circumstances of the case it is unsafe or unsatisfactory; or

(ii) the order of the court giving effect to the verdict should be set aside on the ground of a wrong decision of any question of law; or

(iii) there was a material irregularity in the course of the trial.

(s 13(1)(a) – (c) CAA 1968.)

However, the Court of Appeal does have a discretion to dismiss the appeal, despite the fact that the point raised is decided in favour of the appellant, where it is satisfied that no miscarriage of justice has actually occurred (see s 13(2) CAA 1968). The case law applicable to s 2 CAA 1968 applies where appropriate and with the necessary modifications to appeals under s 12 of the Act.

If the Court of Appeal decides that the jury's finding of insanity should not stand, and finds that the appellant is guilty of an offence (either the one alleged or some other offence for which the jury could have found him/her guilty), it may substitute for the finding of insanity a verdict of guilty of that offence. In these circumstances the Court of Appeal has all the powers of sentencing that would have been available to the court of trial (s 13(4)(a)(i) and (ii) CAA 1968). However, in those rare cases where the death penalty still applies, the court cannot sentence the appellant to death; it must instead pass a sentence of life imprisonment (s 13(5) CAA 1968).

In all other cases where the appeal is allowed, the Court of Appeal must substitute for the jury's verdict a verdict of acquittal (s 13(4)(b) CAA 1968). However, the Court of Appeal does have the power in such cases to make an order that the appellant be admitted for assessment to a hospital specified by the Secretary of State (s 14(2) CAA 1968). The Court of Appeal must be of the opinion that:

(i) the appellant is suffering from a mental disorder of a nature or degree which warrants his/her detention in a hospital for assessment (or for assessment followed by medical treatment) for at least a limited period; and

(ii) he/she ought to be so detained in the interests of his/her own safety or with a view to the protection of other persons.

(s14(2)(a) and (b) CAA 1968.)

A person must be conveyed within seven days of the order to the specified hospital. He/She shall be treated for the purposes of Part II MHA 1983 as if he/she were admitted in pursuance of an application for admission for assessment made under s 2 of that Act (see Sch 1 para 3 CAA 1968). Detention in hospital for assessment is dealt with in Chapter 1.

The Court of Appeal may find that there should not have been a verdict of not guilty by reason of insanity but instead a finding that the accused was under a disability (see pages 186–189). In this type of case, the Court of Appeal must order that the appellant be admitted to a hospital specified by the Secretary of State (s 14(1) CAA 1968). An order is sufficient authority to take the person to the specified hospital within two months of the order being made. A person admitted under this subsection is to be treated as though he/she were admitted under s 37 MHA 1983 together with a restriction order made under s 41 without limitation of time (Sch 1 para 4 CAA 1968; for ss 37 and 41 MHA 1983 see pages 56 and 62).

The Secretary of State may refer the whole or part of a case where there has been a finding of not guilty by reason of insanity to the Court of Appeal under s 17 CAA 1968. The provisions are the same as in cases of finding of disability.

*(f) Appeals against conviction*

When hearing appeals against conviction under the CAA 1968 the Court of Appeal may, if it considers that not guilty by reason of insanity would have been the proper verdict, make an order that the appellant be admitted to a hospital specified by the Secretary of State (s 6(1)(a) CAA 1968). The provisions of Sch 1 CAA 1968 apply to such orders in the same way that they apply to orders under s 14(1) CAA 1968 (see above).

## 2. Diminished responsibility

*(a) Section 2 Homicide Act 1957*

The partial defence of diminished responsibility was introduced by s 2 Homicide Act 1957. Unlike insanity, it only applies as a defence to a charge of murder and it has the effect of reducing the conviction to one of manslaughter. Section 2 states:

> "(1) Where a person kills or is a party to the killing of another, he shall not be convicted of murder if he was suffering from such abnormality of mind (whether arising from a condition of arrested or retarded development of mind or any inherent causes or induced by disease or injury) as substantially impaired his mental responsibility for his acts and omissions in doing or being a party to the killing.
>
> (2) On a charge of murder, it shall be for the defence to prove that the person charged is by virtue of this section not liable to be convicted of murder.
>
> (3) A person who but for this section would be liable ... to be convicted of murder shall be liable to be convicted of manslaughter."
>
> (s 2(1)–(3) Homicide Act 1957.)

A conviction of manslaughter under this section does not affect the question whether any other party to the killing can be convicted of murder (s 2(4) Homicide Act 1957).

*(b) The elements of the defence*

*Abnormality of mind:* Abnormality of mind must be clearly distinguished from disease of the mind as used in the M'Naughten Rules. In *R* v *Byrne* (1960), the Court of Appeal said that abnormality of mind means "a state of mind so different from that of ordinary human beings that a reasonable man would term it abnormal". In making this determination, the jury must have regard not only to the medical evidence but to all the facts and circumstances of the case. Abnormality covers all aspects of the mind's activities including not only the perception of physical acts and matters and the ability to form a rational judgement whether an act is right or wrong, but also the ability to exercise will-power to control physical acts in accordance with that rational judgement. The person does not have to be born with the abnormality (see *R* v *Gomez* (1964)).

This definition is wide enough to include irresistible impulse which is excluded from the M'Naughten Rules (see page 178). Complete inability to exercise control will be diminished responsibility; where the accused has difficulty in controlling physical acts, the jury's decision will be made by reference to the standard of the reasonable person. However, a clear distinction must be made between "he did not resist his impulse" and "he could not resist his impulse". Parker CJ in *Byrne* conceded that measuring degrees of difficulty in controlling impulses is incapable of scientific proof and has to be approached by the jury in a broad common-sense way.

*Cause and consequences of the abnormality:* The abnormality of mind must arise from a condition of arrested or retarded development; or from an inherent cause; or it must be induced by disease or injury. These words distinguish diminished responsibility from those cases involving emotions such as greed, jealousy or the desire for revenge which arise in other ways. They limit the defence to pathological disorders rather than other factors which may affect the functioning of the mind. There is disagreement as to the way in which the same conditions are classified by the medical profession. For example, one report discovered that although depression was usually classified as a disease, it was also quite often attributed to inherent causes. Where the depression was caused by a major emotional upset, it was attributed to "psychological injury" (see *Murder Into Manslaughter* (Oxford University Press, 1984) by Dell). Whereas the jury determine the existence of the abnormality, its cause is determined by expert evidence (see *Byrne*).

The effects of alcohol have been considered in a number of cases. In *R* v *Fenton* (1975), the court recognised that there would be cases where a craving for drink or drugs produces in itself an abnormality of mind. However, on the facts of that case the court could not see "how self-induced intoxication can of itself produce an abnormality of mind due to inherent causes" which is what the statute demands. This approach was approved by the Court of Appeal in *R* v *Gittens* (1984). The Court said that the judge should direct the jury to disregard the effect of alcohol or drugs on the defendant since abnormality of mind induced by drink or drugs was not (generally speaking) due to inherent causes. Once it had done this, the jury should then consider whether the combined effect of the other evidence amounted to an abnormality of mind within s 2(1) of the 1957 Act (see also *R* v *Atkinson* (1985)). In *R* v *Tandy* (1988), the appellant, who was an alcoholic, was convicted of murdering her eleven year old daughter. At the time of the killing, she had consumed nine tenths of a bottle of vodka; normally she drank Cinzano or barleywine. Watkins LJ said in the Court of Appeal that she had to show (1) that she was suffering from abnormality of mind at the time of the killing, (2) that the abnormality of mind was induced by the disease of alcoholism, and (3) that this substantially impaired her mental responsibility for the act of killing her daughter. The principles involved in answering these questions are:

> "The appellant would not establish the second element of the defence unless the evidence showed that the abnormality of mind at the time of the killing was due to the fact that she was a chronic alcoholic ... (I)f the appellant were able to establish that alcoholism had reached the level where although the brain had not been (injured), the appellant's drinking had become involuntary, that is to say she was no longer able to resist the temptation, to resist the impulse to drink, then the defence of diminished responsibility would be available to her, subject to her establishing the first and third elements, because if her drinking was involuntary, then her abnormality of mind at the time of the act of strangulation was induced by her condition of alcoholism."

However, if the appellant had simply not resisted the impulse to take the first drink on the day of the killing and it was the drink that had brought about the impairment of judgement and emotional response, the diminished responsibility defence was not available. The trial judge was correct in telling the jury that if the taking of the first drink was not involuntary, then the whole of the drinking was not involuntary.

Whether or not the transient effect of drink, even if it produces a toxic effect, could ever amount to an injury within s 2(1) Homicide Act 1957 was doubted by the Court of Appeal in *R* v *Di Duca* (1959). The point was touched upon *obiter dicta* in *Tandy*. Watkins LJ said:

> "If the alcoholism had reached the level at which her brain had been injured by the repeated insult from intoxicants so that there was gross impairment of her judgement and emotional responses, then the defence of diminished responsibility was available to her, provided that she satisfied the jury that the third element of the defence existed."

## 3. Fitness to plead

*(a) Introduction*

An accused person may be suffering from a disability which should prevent him/her being tried for the alleged offence. Section 4(1) Criminal Procedure (Insanity) Act 1964 ("CP(I)A 1964") covers cases where the person accused is "under any disability such that apart from this Act it would constitute a bar to his being tried". The disability referred to in s 4(1) CP(I)A 1964 is one which was originally dealt with in the Criminal Lunatics Act 1800. This Act referred to a person being insane so that he/she could not be tried upon indictment. However, the fact that the accused is suffering from a severe abnormality of mind does not mean that he/she is incapable of following the trial, giving evidence or instructing counsel. As an alternative to using s 4 CP(I)A 1964, a remand to hospital for treatment may, if appropriate, be considered (see s 36 MHA 1983 — page 54 above). Section 4 CP(I) A 1964 is not available in the magistrates' court.

The cases suggest that a person is unfit to plead under s 4 if he/she is unable to understand the charges that are being brought and unable to appreciate the difference between a plea of guilty and not guilty. A jury must base its findings on the accused's ability to challenge jurors, instruct counsel, understand the evidence and give evidence (see *R* v *Pritchard* (1836)). However, the fact that he/she is not capable of doing things which are in his/her best interest is not sufficient for a finding of disability. The issue for the jury is not whether he/she is capable of conducting his/her defence to his/her best advantage, but rather whether he/she can conduct it at all (see *R* v *Robertson* (1968)).

Section 4 CP(I)A 1964 deals with the state of mind of the accused at the time of the trial. Thus he/she will not be under a disability if he/she suffered a genuine loss of memory of events before and during the alleged offence but is perfectly able to understand the proceedings at the trial (see *R* v *Podola* (1959)). It was argued on behalf of the appellant in *Podola* that the partial obliteration of memory prevented him from making a proper defence as he could not comprehend the evidence against him. Lord Parker CJ held that it was neither in accordance with reason nor common sense to include within the definition of disability "persons who are mentally normal at the time of the hearing of the proceedings against them and are perfectly capable of instructing their solicitors as to what submission their counsel is to put forward ..."

## (b) Proof of disability

Section 4(1) states that the question of disability may be raised "at the instance of the defence or otherwise". Despite the inquisitorial nature of the proceeding, the courts have emphasised the importance of the onus of proof. If the defence raise the issue, they have the burden of proving disability on a balance of probabilities (see *R* v *Podola*). If the prosecution raise the issue, they have to satisfy the court beyond all reasonable doubt (*R* v *Podola*). The judge may also raise the issue of disability. If he/she has doubts about the accused person's fitness and neither party has raised the issue he/she should do so (see *R* v *McCarthy* (1966)). Whereas the judge may look at medical reports in an attempt to resolve his/her doubts, it is undesirable for him/her to hear medical evidence. If the judge raises the issue, the standard of proof will be the same as if it had been raised by the prosecution.

Normally the issue of disability is determined if either the defence, prosecution or judge raise it before the arraignment (s 4(3) CP(I)A 1964). However, an early finding of disability may be disadvantageous to an accused person where the prosecution case against him/her is weak. For example, the accused may have an alibi for the time of commission of the alleged crime. It would mean that he/she is subject to one of the orders considered below when, if the trial had proceeded to the end of the prosecution case, he/she might have had an absolute acquittal. To meet such cases, s 4(2) gives the court a discretion to postpone consideration of the question of disability where it is expedient to do so and it is in the interests of the accused. The matter may be postponed up until the opening of the defence case.

This discretion requires the judge to assess the strength of the prosecution case. He/She must decide whether the defence will be able to demolish the prosecution case through cross-examination or on a point of law, and if he/she decides there is such a chance the unfitness point should be postponed (see *R* v *Webb* (1969)). It is necessary for him/her to assess the strength of the prosecution case by looking at the committal papers, and then to consider any medical reports that may have been made on the accused. Whether or not he/she decides to postpone the issue will depend upon the likelihood of an acquittal if the prosecution case proceeds (see *R* v *Burles* (1970)). The question of disability cannot be determined at any time after the jury has returned a verdict of acquittal.

Whether or not the accused is under a disability is to be

determined by a jury. If the question falls to be determined upon the arraignment of the accused and the trial proceeds, he/she must be tried by a new jury. Where the question is postponed to some later stage, the court may direct that it be determined either by the jury by whom the accused is being tried or by a separate jury. (See s 4(4)(a) and (b) CP(I)A 1964.)

*(c) The order of the court*

Upon a finding of disability, the court must make an order that the accused be admitted to such hospital as is specified by the Secretary of State (s 5(1)(c) CP(I)A 1964). A person admitted to hospital under this section is treated as though he/she had been admitted in pursuance of a hospital order made under s 37 MHA 1983 together with a restriction order made under s 41 MHA 1983 without limitation of time (Sch 1 para 2(1) CP(I)A 1964; see pages 56 and 62). The provisions relating to conveyance to hospital and the authority of the hospital managers are the same as in findings of not guilty by reason of insanity (see page 180). While the person is detained in pursuance of an order under s 5(1) CP(I)A 1964, the Secretary of State may in consultation with the responsible medical officer conclude that he/she can properly be tried. In such a case, the Secretary of State may remit the person to a remand centre pending trial. The order under s 5(1)(c) CP(I)A 1964 will then cease to have effect upon the person's arrival at prison or remand centre. (See s 5(4) and Sch 1 CP(I)A 1964.) No remit may be made if the Secretary of State has directed that the person cease to be subject to the restrictions imposed under s 41 MHA 1983 (Sch 1 para 2(2) CP(I)A 1964; for restrictions under MHA 1983, see page 64).

Appeals against a finding of disability may be made to the Court of Appeal under s 15 CAA 1968. The grounds of appeal may involve a question of law alone, a question of fact or a mixed question of law and fact (s 15(2)(a) and (b) CAA 1968). An appeal solely on a question of law is as of right; appeals on questions of fact or mixed fact and law must be with the leave of the Court of Appeal or under a certificate issued by the trial judge. The powers of disposal of appeal follow those applicable in appeals against a finding of not guilty by reason of insanity, including the right to dismiss the appeal if no miscarriage of justice has actually occurred (see page 180). An appeal may also be allowed where the question of disability was determined later than on arraignment, if the Court of Appeal considers that he/she should, on the evidence, have been acquitted before the fitness to plead issue was considered (s 16(2) CAA 1968). The Court of Appeal must quash the finding of disability and also direct a verdict of acquittal. It may not substitute a verdict of not guilty by reason of insanity. If the appellant is successful in appealing against a finding of disability (other than under s 16(2) CAA 1968), he/she may be tried for the offence with which he/she was originally charged. The Court of Appeal may make such orders for his/her custody as it considers necessary or expedient pending the trial. Alternatively it may release the person on bail or require continued detention under Part III MHA 1983. (See s 16(3) and Sch 3 paras 1 and 2 CAA 1968; for Part III MHA 1983 see pages 52–71.)

The general rule is that no appeal can be made against a finding of fitness to plead. However, in *Podola* the appellant had been convicted of killing a police officer. At the trial, the preliminary issue of fitness to plead had been decided against him so the trial proceeded. An appeal was made by the Home Secretary on the basis that an important point of law (the onus of proof in cases of disability) was involved. The Court of Criminal Appeal held that if a convicted person appeals on the ground that the hearing of the preliminary issue was open to objection for error in law so that he/she should never have been tried on the substantive charge, the Court of Appeal had jurisdiction to hear an appeal. Thus where the trial judge misdirects a jury on the question of disability, and the jury finds the accused fit to plead, an appeal may be made based upon that misdirection. It must be stressed that this is only a limited exception to the general rule that no appeal against a finding of fitness to plead is possible.

Where a person has been found to be under a disability, the Secretary of State may, if he/she thinks fit, refer the whole of the case to the Court of Appeal. The case will then be treated for all purposes as if it were an appeal by that person. He/She will be entitled to raise any matter which could have been raised if he/she had appealed under s 15 CAA 1968 (s 17(1)(a) CAA 1968). Alternatively, the Secretary of State may refer to the Court of Appeal a particular point arising in the case if he/she desires its assistance. The Court of Appeal must then provide the Secretary of State with its opinion on that point (s 17(1)(b) CAA 1968).

## Chapter 7

# Protecting the property and financial affairs of patients

## 1. The Court of Protection

### (a) Introduction

The Court of Protection exists as an office of the Supreme Court of Judicature; it is not a court in the usual sense of the word. Much of its work is done by senior court officials rather than judges, and it is invariably carried out by correspondence rather than formal judicial hearing. Under s 93(2) MHA 1983, it exists for the "protection and management, as provided by (Part VII MHA 1983), of the property and affairs of a person under disability". Important changes in organisation were made in 1987 by the Public Trustee and Administration of Funds Act 1986 which created the Public Trust Office. Although this office is separate from the court, it carries out the administrative functions. The head of this new division has the title of Accountant General of the Supreme Court and Public Trustee; in his/her capacity as Public Trustee, this person may act as a receiver for a patient if nobody else is able to act (see below). A branch of the Public Trust Office is the Protection Division which is responsible for much of the work done by the court.

The Lord Chancellor must nominate one or more judges of the Supreme Court to act as "nominated judges" for the purpose of Part VII MHA 1983. All the judges of the Chancery Division are nominated judges except those who are judges of the Patents Court. A master of the Court of Protection must also be appointed by the Lord Chancellor, and he/she will be required to take the oath of allegiance and judicial oath. Other officers of the court are nominated to act under Part VII MHA 1983 — these are known as "nominated officers" and are the assistant masters of the court. (See s 93(1)–(4) MHA 1983.) Much of the court's work is done by the nominated officers who enjoy wide jurisdiction under the MHA 1983.

The functions of the court are normally exercisable when, after considering medical evidence, it is satisfied that the person is by reason of mental disorder incapable of managing and administering his/her property and affairs (s 94(2) MHA 1983). Such a person is then known as "the patient". It is important to note that proof of mental disorder (see page 1 for the definition) is not in itself sufficient as it is also necessary to prove that the person is incapable of managing and administering his/ her property and affairs in consequence of the disorder. Thus not all patients subject to compulsory admission or guardianship will come within the jurisdiction of the court. No specific requirements are laid down as to the nature of the medical evidence required or the qualifications of the doctor required to provide it. Under r 49 Court of Protection Rules 1984 – SI No 2035 ("COPR 1984") a judge or the master may make an order for the patient's attendance at a specified time and place for examination by the master, a visitor (see page 205) or any medical practitioner. In emergencies, the court may perform the functions under s 95 MHA 1983 (see below) even though not completely satisfied that the person is suffering from a mental disorder. The court must have reason to believe that the person may be incapable as a result of a mental disorder of administering his/her property and affairs, and also be of the opinion that it is necessary to make immediate provision under s 95 MHA 1983. At this stage, medical evidence need not have been presented to the judge, but any that is available should be presented in order that he/she may act on the best available evidence. The court may direct that the patient be visited by a medical visitor who will report to it on the capacity of the patient to manage and administer his/her property and affairs (r 66(1)(b) COPR 1984). Until it is determined whether or not the person is under such an incapacity, the judge can exercise the powers conferred by Part VII MHA 1983. It must be stressed that this is an emergency procedure and is limited to situations where immediate action is necessary. (See s 98 MHA 1983 and page 202 for receiver *ad interim* and interim certificates.)

The jurisdiction of the court covers the "property and affairs" of a person under disability. Although it appears to be wide, in practice the jurisdiction is limited. In *Re W* (1970), Ungoed-Thomas J said that the court's jurisdiction is not limited to "dealing with the patient's property or financial affairs, nor limited to dealing with such other matters as may be within its jurisdiction in their property or financial aspects ... it has exclusive jurisdiction over all the property and affairs of the patient in all their aspects; but not the management or care of the patient's person".

This point was re-emphasised in *T* v *T* (1988) where it was made clear that the Court of Protection's jurisdiction did not include deciding whether a mentally handicapped person should be sterilised.

*(b) Functions and powers of a judge in respect of a patient's property and affairs*

By virtue of s 95(1) MHA 1983, the Court of Protection may do such things as are necessary or expedient:

(i) for the maintenance or other benefit of the patient (s 95(1)(a) MHA 1983);

(ii) for the maintenance or other benefit of the patient's family (s 95(1)(b) MHA 1983);

(iii) for making provision for other persons or purposes for whom or which the patient may be expected to provide if he/she were not mentally disordered (s 95(1)(c) MHA 1983);

(iv) otherwise for administering the patient's affairs (s 95(1)(d) MHA 1983).

In performing these functions, the court is required to act in the way in which a "sane man – properly advised and with a glimmer of decency" would act in the circumstances (*Re T B* (1967)).

"Benefit" is given a wide meaning and is not restricted to matters which are financially or materially beneficial to the patient. The court must base its decisions on what is necessary or expedient for the benefit of the patient (*Re E (Mental Health Patient)* (1985)). Regard must be had firstly to all the requirements of the patient. His/Her creditors will only be considered when it is certain that the estate is sufficient to maintain him/her (*Re Winkle* (1894)). In those circumstances, the court may, in administering the patient's affairs, have regard to the interests of the creditors. It should then also have regard to meeting any obligations of the patient which are not legally enforceable. If the estate is insufficient to meet the claims of creditors without threatening

## Protecting the property and financial affairs of patients

the welfare of the patient, the creditors should consider an application for a charging order (see page 194).

Without prejudice to s 95 MHA 1983, the Court of Protection may give such orders, directions and authorities as it considers fit for the carrying out of those functions. In particular, it may give orders, directions or authorities for:

(i) the control and management of any property of any patient (the court has exclusive control over such property) (s 96(1)(a) MHA 1983);

(ii) the sale, exchange, charging or other disposition of or dealing with any property of the patient (s 96(1)(b) MHA 1983);

(iii) the acquisition of any property in the name of or on behalf of the patient (s 96(1)(c) MHA 1983);

(iv) the settlement of any property of the patient, or the gift of any of his/her property to members of his/her family, or making provision for other persons or purposes which he/she might otherwise be expected to provide (s 96(1)(d) MHA 1983);

(v) the execution for the patient of a will making any provision which could have been included in a will executed by him/her if not mentally disordered (s 96(1)(e) MHA 1983);

(vi) the carrying on by a suitable person of any trade, profession or business of the patient (s 96(1)(f) MHA 1983);

(vii) the dissolution of any partnership of which the patient is a member (s 96(1)(g) MHA 1983);

(viii) the performance of any contract entered into by the patient (s 96(1)(h) MHA 1983);

(ix) the conduct of legal proceedings in the name of or on behalf of the patient (s 96(1)(i) MHA 1983);

(x) the reimbursement out of the property of the patient, with or without interest, of money used by any person in the payment of the patient's debts (legally enforceable or otherwise), for the maintenance or other benefit of the patient or members of his/her family, or in making provision for other persons or purposes which the patient might otherwise have made (s 96(1)(j) MHA 1983);

(xi) the exercise of any power (including the power of

consent) vested in the patient, or held as guardian, trustee, or otherwise (s 96(1)(k) MHA 1983).

This is not an exhaustive list of the powers that are available to the court in administering the patient's property. A number of these powers require more detailed consideration.

*Maintaining the patient:* Section 95(1)(a) MHA 1983 empowers the court to do all such things as appear necessary or expedient for the maintenance or other benefit of the patient. In exercising the powers under s 96 MHA 1983, especially those in ss (a)–(c) and (f)–(i), maintenance and support must be a primary consideration. Thus it is important that provision is made *inter alia* for food, clothing, accommodation and holidays. In determining what amount to make available for such items, the court will have regard to the income generated by the patient's capital and normally should seek to ensure that capital is not dissipated. However, there may be circumstances where the court will require capital to be spent on the charges for the patient's accommodation in a residential care home or a nursing or mental nursing home (see Chapter 3). Where the patient is accommodated in Part III NAA 1948 accommodation, capital held by the patient will be taken into account in determining the amount which he/she is required to pay (see page 143). Capital will also be relevant in determining whether a patient will be entitled to a community care grant upon leaving institutional care. If the patient has insufficient resources to meet the demands of his/her creditors, after proper allowance is made for his/her maintenance, it is open to the creditors to apply for a charging order. The effect of such an order is to delay enforcement of the creditors' claim until after the death of the patient. During the intervening period, the property will still be within the control of the court which can make such allowances as are proper for the maintenance of the patient, even though the effect may be to reduce the available capital to an amount below that which is subject to any charging orders. Before the court makes such allowances, notice must be given to any chargee.

*Settlements and gifts:* The power to make a settlement or gift is restricted to the purposes specified in s 95(1)(b) and (c) MHA 1983 (see above). So far as the maintenance or other benefit of the patient's family is concerned, the courts have adopted a narrow view of the people covered. It covers spouses and dependent children but does not include collateral relatives such as nephews or nieces who will have to come within subsection (c) rather than (b) (See *Re D.M.L.* (1965)).

It must be emphasised that the mere fact that a person is the patient's next of kin who would be entitled to the estate upon intestacy does not automatically mean that he/she should be entitled to benefit. Before such a person becomes so entitled, it must be shown that the patient would have so provided if not suffering from a mental disorder.

Under s 95(1)(c) MHA 1983, a gift or settlement can also be made for "purposes" for which the patient might be expected to provide if not mentally disordered. These purposes will include charities in which the patient has shown an interest. However, the court will be cautious in making provision for a mental nursing home in which the patient is, or has recently been, accommodated. In such circumstances undue influence will be presumed.

When a settlement is made under s 96(1)(d) MHA 1983, the court may also direct that any consequential vesting or other orders are made (s 96(2) MHA 1983). If, after making a settlement, the Lord Chancellor or a nominated judge is satisfied, at any time before the death of the patient, that any material fact was not disclosed, an appropriate variation in the settlement may be ordered (s 96(3) MHA 1983).

*Making a will:* The validity of a will may be challenged because the testator lacks testamentary capacity at the time of its execution (see page 231). To avoid such problems arising, a judge may under s 96(1)(e) MHA 1983 execute a will making any provision which could have been executed by the patient if he/she was not suffering from mental disorder ("statutory will"). This also includes the power to make a codicil which amends an already existing will (s 112 MHA 1983). Before exercising this power, the judge must have "reason to believe" that the patient lacks "testamentary capacity", that is he/she has an inability to make and understand a will. It should be noted that having "reason to believe" is not synonymous with being "satisfied" as to lack of capacity. The power is not exercisable when the patient is a minor (ie under the age of eighteen years). (See s 96(4) MHA 1983.)

Megarry VC in *Re D(J)* (1982) identified five principles or factors which the judge should take into account in making a statutory will:

(i) it must be assumed that the patient is having a brief lucid moment at the time that the will is made;
(ii) during the lucid interval, it must be assumed that the patient has a full knowledge of the past, a full realisation that as soon as the will is executed he/she will relapse into

the actual mental state that previously existed, with the prognosis as it actually is (see *Re L(WJG)* (1965));

(iii) the *actual* patient has to be considered, and not a hypothetical patient — it is a subjective and not an objective test;

(iv) during the lucid moment, it must be assumed that the patient is being advised by a competent solicitor;

(v) in all normal cases the patient is to be envisaged as "taking a broad brush" to the claims on his/her bounty rather than an "accountant's pen" — thus the judge should take account of any moral obligations the patient may be assumed to feel in deciding on disposition.

If a judge gives an order, direction or authority under s 96(1)(e) MHA 1983 to execute a statutory will, he/she must authorise a person to execute a will for the patient — this person is known as the "authorised person". Usually the authorised person will be the receiver (see page 200). The will must be signed by the authorised person in the presence of two or more witnesses, and attested and subscribed by those witnesses in the presence of the authorised person. The name of the patient and the authorised person must be on the will. The will is regarded as being signed by the patient acting through the authorised person. Finally, the will must be sealed with the seal of the Court of Protection. (See s 97(1)(a)–(c) MHA 1983.)

With minor modification, the Wills Act 1837 applies to statutory wills, and consequently they have largely the same effect as those made by a person with testamentary capacity. The provisions of s 9 Wills Act 1837, which relate to the signing of a will, do not apply to statutory wills, but for the purposes of execution and effect the two types of will are treated in the same manner. For example, a statutory will has the effect of revoking earlier wills in the same manner as an ordinary one. There is, however, a difference between the two types of will when considering immovable property situated outside England and Wales; a statutory will can have no effect in relation to such property (s 97(4)(a) MHA 1983). Special provisions also apply to statutory wills where the patient is domiciled in Scotland or Northern Ireland, or in some other country or territory outside the United Kingdom. In these circumstances, a statutory will will be ineffective to transfer movable property of the patient unless the law of his/her domicile, determined in accordance with the rules of private international law, directs that testamentary capacity is to be determined under the law of England and Wales (s 97(4)(b) MHA 1983). For the procedure upon the death of the patient, see page 203.

*Carrying on of the patient's trade, profession or business:* If, on the basis of evidence presented to the judge, it is considered appropriate that the patient's business should be continued despite his/her mental disability, the judge may make provision for it to be carried on by a suitable person. In some cases this person may be the receiver, or some other person possessing the necessary expertise. It is important that the judge should be provided with up-to-date information on the affairs of the business — this includes accounts and any future estimates. The following directions to the receiver (see below) are usually contained in any order that the judge may make for the continuation of the business:

(i) to procure a valuation of stock in trade, fixtures, fittings etc and to file it with the court. Within three months of the date of filing a report should be made to the court on the position and prospects of the business;

(ii) to open a new bank account for the business and to use that account exclusively for that purpose;

(iii) to open a second new bank account earmarked for the receivership generally and to use that account for all receipts and payments not relating to the business;

(iv) no overdraft, or increase in existing overdrafts, is to be incurred in respect of either bank account except with authority bearing the seal of the court;

(v) the business account is not to be used other than for business purposes and the receivership account (but see (vi) below) is not to be drawn upon for the purposes of the business;

(vi) drawings on account of profits from the business must be made from the business account in favour of the receivership account;

(vii) proper accounts must be kept;

(viii) if the court authorises the carrying on of the business beyond the three month period, annual accounts, together with a report on the business, must be prepared and presented to the court within one month after the close of account along with the annual receivership account.

(See para 2870 *The Supreme Court Practice 1988*.)

A partnership of which the patient is a member may be dissolved by the Court of Protection (s 96(1)(g) MHA 1983). However, the limited powers of the court over partnership matters mean that it will only exercise this power when there are no disputes between the partners, and a receiver (see below) has been appointed. Thus, if the partners do not agree as to the contributions each made to the partnership, the matter should be referred to the Chancery Division of the High Court rather than the Court of Protection. The Partnership Act 1890 also provides for dissolution wherever circumstances have arisen which, in the opinion of the High Court (or a county court in certain circumstances), render it just and equitable that the partnership be dissolved (s 35(f) Partnership Act 1890). Thus, if one of the partners is suffering from a form of mental disorder, this may be a basis for dissolution. Originally the power to dissolve a partnership directly on grounds of mental disorder was found in s 35(a) Partnership Act 1890; this provision was repealed by the Mental Health Act 1959. However, this repeal has resulted in some confusion in the interpretation of s 35(b) (of the 1890 Act) which is still in force. Under this subsection a partner may apply for dissolution if another partner "becomes *in any other way* incapable of performing his part of the partnership contract". Until the repeal of s 35(a), this provision was intended to apply to cases other than mental disorder; since the repeal, the words *in any other way* have become redundant. The effect is that Parliament may have unintentionally created a second alternative to dissolution by the Court of Protection. However, if proceeding under s 35(b) Partnership Act 1890, the High Court (or county court) must be satisfied that the incapacity is permanent and not just temporary.

If the patient holds shares in a public company, it is unusual for the court to order that the voting rights should be exercised on his/her behalf. However, in the case of a private company, the court will take account of the importance of the patient's shareholding in the future performance of the company and will be more prepared to ensure that somebody is appointed to vote on his/her behalf. If, as is most often the case, the patient is required to relinquish any directorship of such a company, the court may order that sufficient shares are transferred to the receiver to enable him/her to be eligible for appointment as director. Any dividends from the shares transferred will be payable into the receivership account. So far as the remaining shares are concerned, the court may order that the receiver should exercise the right to vote on behalf of the patient. If this is done certain matters, such as borrowing and fixing the fees of the directors, will require the express prior approval of the court. (See also s 96(1)(k) MHA 1983.)

*Legal proceedings on behalf of the patient:* A receiver contemplating legal proceedings on behalf of, or in the name of, the patient must obtain authorisation from the court. Unless there is some conflict of interests between the receiver and the patient, the receiver will act as the next friend or guardian *ad litem* of the patient. Where there is a potential conflict of interests, another person may be appointed to act in that capacity, or alternatively the Official Solicitor may act.

*Preserving interests in the patient's property:* The power of the court over the property and affairs of the patient is extensive. In exercising this power, there is considerable potential for interfering with contingent interests of third parties in the property of the patient, for example rights of succession. Section 101 MHA 1983 provides some protection for such interests. Where property is disposed of under Part VII MHA 1983 and some other person would (by virtue of a will, intestacy, gift perfected, or nomination *taking effect upon death*) have otherwise taken an interest in it, he/she takes the same interest in property of the deceased patient's estate which represents it (s 101(1)(a) MHA 1983). If real property was disposed of, any property, including personal, which represents it is treated as realty so long as it remains part of the estate (s 101(1)(b) MHA 1983). However, where an interest in personal property is represented by real property, the court has a discretion to direct that it is to be treated as personal for so long as it remains part of the estate (s 101(2) MHA 1983). For the purposes of the section, disposal of property is defined as:

(i) sale, exchange, charging or other dealing with property other than money;

(ii) the removal of property from one place to another;

(iii) the application of money in acquiring property; or

(iv) the transfer of money from one account to another.

(s 101(3)(a) – (c) MHA 1983.)

When making an order disposing of property, the court may make any directions which are necessary to give effect to s 101 MHA 1983 (s 101(4) MHA 1983).

## (c) The appointment of a receiver

This section deals with patients whose estates exceed £5,000 in value; the specal provisions for estates below that value are considered in *(e)* below. In order to assist in the administration and management of the patient's affairs, a receiver may be appointed by the court. A receiver may be a named person (for example, a close relative), or he/she may for the time being be the holder of an office (for example, the director of the local social services authority). If an application for receivership is made by an officer of a local authority with that authority's permission, any expenses incurred by him/her in making the application or exercising his/her duties under the office may be defrayed by the authority insofar as they are not recoverable from some other source (s 49 NAA 1948). Although the receiver will invariably be a near relative or a close friend of the patient, the court may appoint a solicitor to act. If no other suitable person is available to act as receiver, the court may appoint the Public Trustee. Where a receiver is appointed, the court may during the receivership allow him/her to receive remuneration for his/her services. The remuneration will be at a rate which the court considers reasonable and proper and it will be a debt due to the receiver out of the patient's estate (r 42(1) COPR 1984). (See s 99(1) MHA 1983.)

Under s 99(2) MHA 1983, a receiver appointed by the court must perform such duties as the court, exercising its functions and powers under ss 95 and 96, orders or directs him/her to do. He/She *may* do any thing in relation to the property and affairs of the patient as the court authorises him to do. (See s 99(2) MHA 1983.) The order appointing a receiver will identify the person appointed and specify powers which he/she is to have in respect of the patient's property and affairs, such as the receipt of social security benefit and the sale of the patient's property (see Court of Protection Form 8).

A first application to the court for appointment must be made on Form A. It may be made by a relative, friend, solicitor, creditor or concerned person or body such as a local authority. The applicant must specify whether or not he/she is applying for his/her own appointment as receiver, and whether he/she is a relation of the patient and if so, the nature of the relationship. The applicant may apply for the appointment of some other person to act as receiver; the form must identify that person and state whether he/she is a relative and if so, the nature of the relationship. Alternatively, the application may be for the appointment of "some other suitable person", for example the

Public Trustee. A medical certificate in support of the first application must also be included (Form CP3). This requires a doctor to certify, *inter alia,* that the patient is incapable by reason of mental disorder as defined in the MHA 1983 of managing and administering his/her property and affairs. In addition, a Certificate of Family and Property (Form CP5) must be included giving details of family, property, income, marital status, whether subject to guardianship, maintenance, wills, powers of attorney and whether the patient holds a current driving licence.

Where an application is made for the appointment of a receiver, notification must be given to the patient. Notification is given on Form CP6; it informs the patient that because of his/her present incapacity it might be in his/her best interests to appoint a named person as receiver. It will also inform the patient of the date and the time at which the court will consider the application. If the patient wishes to make any observations or to object to the making of an order appointing a receiver, or to the person named to act as such, he/she may write to, or telephone the Court of Protection (see r 23(1) COPR 1984). Not less than ten clear days' notice of the hearing must be given (r 18(5)(a) COPR 1984). Notice may be dispensed with if the court is satisfied that the patient is incapable of understanding it, or it would be injurious to the patient's health (supporting medical evidence must be provided) or for some other appropriate reason (r 23(2) COPR 1984). Where notification is dispensed with, the court may request a visitor to visit the patient and report as to his/her condition and welfare (r 23(3) COPR 1984; see page 205 for visitors). In cases where the patient is a minor, notice must be given to his/her parent or guardian, or if he/she has none the person with whom he/she resides or in whose care he/she is, regardless of whether notice to the patient has been dispensed with (r 23(4) COPR 1984). Notice of the hearing must also be given to such other persons who appear to the court to be interested in the proceedings; ten days' notice must be given (r 18(4) COPR 1984). Unless the court directs otherwise, a certificate of service showing where, when, how and by whom service was effected shall be filed as soon as practicable after the patient has been served with notice. If it thinks fit, the court may instead order that an affidavit of service should be filed. (See r 24(1) and (2) COPR 1984.)

The appointing order will specify the person to be appointed as receiver. In addition, it will give authorisations and directions relating to the maintenance of the patient and the management of his/her property and affairs. It will also require the receiver to prepare accounts for the court as and when required, the first accounts to be submitted for the period of twelve months from the date of the order. These will all be subject to any subsequent direction or authority from the court. One important matter that will be dealt with by the order is that of the security to be given by the receiver. The court may direct that security is to be provided by the receiver, other than the Official Receiver, to cover the possibility of him/her misappropriating the funds or being negligent in performing his/her duties. In fixing the level of security, regard will be had to the amount of money which passes through the patient's estate; this may be varied if that amount increases or decreases. Under the COPR 1984, security may be given in any of the following ways:

(i) by a fidelity guarantee bond – the premium is payable out of the patient's estate;
(ii) by lodging in court a sufficient sum of money or stock; or
(iii) in such other manner as the court may approve.
(r 56(1) COPR 1984.)

An order cannot normally be issued until the security has been arranged. Once the process is complete, the order will be impressed with the seal of the court. Sealed office copies of the order are proof of the receiver's appointment, and can be produced for banks, the Department of Social Security and other organisations to prove that he/she is acting in that capacity. These bodies may wish to mark the copy of the order as having been registered with them.

It may be necessary to make immediate provision for a patient where the delay involved in the appointment of a receiver is unacceptable. The COPR 1984 allow for interim provision to be made. Firstly, the court can by certificate direct or authorise any person to do any specified act or carry out any specified transaction in relation to the matters referred to in s 95(1) MHA 1983 (r 41(1)(a) COPR 1984). There must be an immediate need for a certificate such as the urgent necessity of providing money to find accommodation for the patient.

Secondly, the court may appoint a receiver *ad interim* (r 41(1)(b) COPR 1984). If a receiver *ad interim* is appointed, and unless the court directs otherwise, the order must be served on the patient within such time as it specifies. The patient may then, within the time limit specified in the order, apply for reconsideration under r 54 COPR 1984 of the order by the court or if the order was made by a judge, apply to have it set aside (r 41(2) COPR 1984). A certificate of service of the order should be filed. As with interim

## Protecting the property and financial affairs of patients

certificates, receivers *ad interim* can only be appointed if immediate provision is necessary; such appointments are made pending the determination of what further steps should be taken. The receiver is to act at once without the need to give security, although the order will specify the security that is to be provided by him/her within a reasonable time (for security see page 202). Normally the order will give specific directions regarding the preservation of the patient's estate or the management of his/her affairs. Questions of the maintenance of the patient are usually left until the appointment of the substantive receiver. (See also page 191 for emergency applications.)

### (d) Discharge of a receiver

The office of receiver will come to an end upon the death or illness of the receiver, his/her retirement, or by discharge for some other reason (for example, he/she is unsuitable, or there is a conflict of interests between receiver and patient). In these circumstances it will be necessary, if the patient continues under the disability, to appoint a new receiver. Where the receiver is retiring, he/she should make an application for the appointment of a replacement. In other cases, applications may be made by the persons who might normally make a first application. Where no other suitable person is able and willing to make the application, or where the court thinks fit, it may direct an officer of the court or, if he/she consents, the Official Solicitor to do so (r 10 COPR 1984). Rule 10 COPR 1984 also provides for such a person to apply for the discharge of a receiver. Procedure for discharge applications is similar to that for the first application. The order of the court will discharge the old receiver, identify the new receiver and stipulate any security which he/she may be required to provide. It will also give directions concerning the passing of or dispensing with the final accounts of the old receiver.

The death of the patient brings the office of receiver to an end; he/she is automatically discharged (s 99(3) MHA 1983). Notification of the patient's death must be given to the court as soon as possible. When a patient dies, special provisions require the court to give final directions formally discharging the receiver and dealing with final accounts. Where the value of the deceased's estate is £5,000 or more, a grant of representation by his/her personal representatives must be obtained from the Probate Division before these final directions can be given by the Court of Protection. If the patient has left a will, the persons named as executors or trustees will make the application for the grant; in the case of there being no will, the application will be made by the closest relatives of the patient who will be entitled to a share of the estate upon intestacy. The grant of representation must be produced to the court and an application for final directions made. Normally this application is made informally by the personal representatives in a letter to the court. However, a formal application will be necessary if an enforceable order for the payment of costs in the proceedings is required (see generally r 84(1) and (3) COPR 1984). When making the application, the personal representatives may ask the court either to pass or to dispense with a final account, together with a request for the discharge of any security; make payments of any funds held by the court to the personal representatives or the beneficiaries; release documents such as deeds and certificates held under the direction of the court at a bank unless they were only to be held during the patient's lifetime; remove restrictions on any of the patient's assets, and pay any costs arising out of the exercise of the court's jurisdiction. In some cases, it may be desirable to meet taxation demands arising from the patient's death before the grant of representation is made. Payments out of funds in court may be made in these circumstances upon the application of the person who is entitled to apply for grant of representation (see above). Details of the duty payable and the means by which the money may be raised from the patient's estate should be included. Normally applications are formal unless the court directs otherwise.

A receiver must be discharged if the patient has become capable of managing and administering his/her property and affairs (s 99(3) MHA 1983). As with the decision to initiate the jurisdiction of the court, this matter must be distinguished from the question whether the patient is suffering from mental disorder. It is possible that the patient may still be suffering from such a disorder and yet has become capable of taking care of his/her own affairs. In these circumstances, the receiver should be discharged. A receiver should also be discharged if the patient recovers from his/her mental disorder even though he/she may, for some other reason, be incapable of conducting his/her own affairs; this is because the jurisdiction of the court depends upon the incapability arising from the disorder. A formal application for discharge must be made by the patient to the court. In it the patient must provide a medical certificate stating that, in the opinion of the deponent doctor, he/she is now capable of managing and administering his/her property and affairs. If satisfied that the patient is so capable, the court will order that

## Protecting the property and financial affairs of patients

any funds in court are transferred to the patient subject to any costs or fees due to be paid in respect of the court's administration of the fund. Under s 99(3) MHA 1983, the court can also discharge the receiver if it considers it "expedient to do so"; this has been interpreted as meaning expedient for the patient rather than the relatives or the receiver (*Re N, decd.*, (1977)).

### (e) Estates not exceeding £5,000

If it appears to the court that the patient's property does not exceed £5,000 in value and that it is not necessary to appoint a receiver, the court may make an order under r 7(2) COPR 1984. The order directs an officer of the court or some other named suitable person to deal with the patient's property and affairs in a specified manner. An order under r 7 may be made whether or not an application has been made for the appointment of a receiver. This procedure is known as the "short procedure".

Special provisions also apply to estates not exceeding £5,000 upon the death of the patient. The court may, if it thinks fit, make final directions without a grant of representation being obtained (r 73(2) COPR 1984). It may provide for the payment of funeral expenses out of any funds in court. Furthermore, it may order that any property or funds under its control or direction be released to the personal representative or the person who appears to be entitled to apply for a grant of representation. An application to the court may be made by the person who is entitled to apply for the grant of representation.

### (f) The Lord Chancellor's visitors

Three panels of Lord Chancellor's visitors exist, namely the panels of medical visitors, legal visitors and general visitors (s 102(1)(a)–(c) MHA 1983). The members of these panels are appointed by the Lord Chancellor for such terms and conditions as he/she may determine. Only registered medical practitioners having special knowledge and experience of mental disorder can be medical visitors, and only solicitors or barristers of at least ten years' standing can be legal visitors (s 102(3)(a) and (b) MHA 1983). General visitors are not required to possess either legal or medical qualifications. Visitors are independent of the court; however they work subject to directions which the court may give them.

As the name suggests, the function of the visitor is to visit the patient "in such circumstances, and in such manner, as may be prescribed by directions of a standing nature given by the Master of the Court of Protection with the concurrence of the Lord Chancellor". (See s 103(1) MHA 1983.) The court may order that a visitor must visit a patient where it is necessary either to investigate questions of the patient's capacity to manage and administer his/her property and affairs, or for the purpose of exercising the functions of the judge under the MHA 1983. For example, a visitor may be used where it is not yet determined whether the person falls within the jurisdiction of the Court of Protection (see page 190). Section 103(10) MHA 1983 makes it clear that a visitor may visit persons who are *alleged* to be incapable by reason of mental disorder from managing their own affairs. By virtue of s 10(1)(a) Enduring Powers of Attorney Act 1985, s 103 MHA 1983 is extended to cover a donor of an enduring power of attorney (see below).

Visits will usually be made by a general visitor; however, the court may direct that a legal or medical visitor should go to the patient, because their specialist expertise is required. When visiting a patient, a visitor may interview him/her in private. Medical visitors may carry out in private a medical examination of the patient and may insist upon the production of medical records. At the end of the visit, the visitor will make a report on the patient's circumstances and any other matter which the court has specified. This report is confidential and will only be disclosed to the court; any further disclosure will be subject to the court's express authorisation. It is an offence to disclose without authorisation the contents of a report. (See s 103(3)–(9) MHA 1983). It is also an offence under s 129 MHA 1983 to obstruct a Lord Chancellor's visitor in the performance of his/her duties (see page 13).

## 2. Enduring powers of attorney

Use of the Court of Protection as outlined above allows intervention in order to protect the property and financial interests of a person with a mental disorder and incapable of administering his/her own affairs. It may, however, be desirable to resolve such matters before the person actually becomes incapable of administering his/her affairs. Such an approach enables the person himself/herself to determine who it is that they would like to see administer their affairs if they subsequently become incapable of doing so. The Enduring Powers of Attorney Act 1985 ("EPA 1985") provides a procedure whereby such arrangements can be made. The EPA 1985 is based upon a report by the Law Commission which provides a useful background to the legislation (see *The Incapacitated Principal* (Law Commission, No 122)). Normally a power of attorney will be revoked upon the donor's mental incapacity. However, if the power is created under the EPA 1985, it will "endure" that incapacity. The EPA 1985 extends to the donor of an enduring power of attorney some of the provisions of the MHA 1983 even though he/she may not be suffering from a mental disorder within that Act. Sections 103, 104, 105(1) and 106 (but not 106(4)) MHA 1983 apply to persons within, and proceedings under the EPA 1985 (s 10 EPA 1985).

It is essential that the instrument creating an enduring power of attorney follows the prescribed form, although immaterial differences in form or mode of expression will not be fatal (s 2(6) EPA 1985). The prescribed form must incorporate information explaining the general effect of creating or accepting the enduring power (s 2(2)(a) EPA 1985). Section 2(1) EPA 1985 states that a power of attorney will be an enduring one if the instrument creating the power:

(i) is in the prescribed form;
(ii) was executed in the prescribed manner by the donor and the attorney (see below); and
(iii) incorporated, at the time of execution by the donor, the prescribed explanatory information.

(s 2(1) (a)–(c) EPA 1985.)

The prescribed form for powers executed on or after 1 July 1988 is found in the Enduring Powers of Attorney (Prescribed Form) Regulations 1987 (SI No 1612). Both the donor (the person appointing the attorney) and the attorney (the person appointed) must execute the power using the prescribed form, making the necessary insertions and deletions. An important part of the prescribed form is the statement that the donor intends the power to continue after he/she becomes mentally incapable. He/She must also declare that he/she has read the relevant notes attached to the form or has had them read to him/her. The attorney must also make a statement that he/she understands the duty of registration as imposed by the EPA 1985. (See s 2(2)(b) EPA 1985.)

An enduring power of attorney must be executed by both the donor and the attorney, although not necessarily at the same time. It must be done in the presence of a witness, although not necessarily the same person. Witnesses must provide their full names and addresses. The moment at which the enduring power commences depends upon any restrictions or conditions which may be included. A restriction on the attorney acting until he/she has reason to believe that the donor is becoming incapable means that the donor will retain control until that date. If no such restriction is imposed, the enduring power arises as soon as the donor and the attorney have signed the prescribed form. Other conditions or restrictions may be included, for example a restriction on the sale of the donor's house. The form also allows the donor to grant a general power or a specific power, each of which may be subject to the conditions or restrictions mentioned above. A general power gives the attorney authority, subject to s 3(5) EPA 1985 (see below), to do on behalf of the donor anything which the donor can lawfully do (s 3(2) EPA 1985). A specific power allows the attorney to do only those things specified in the form.

An attorney, whether subject to a general or specific power, may dispose of the donor's property without consent by way of gift only to the following extent:

(i) gifts of a seasonal nature, for anniversaries or for births and marriages, to persons (including himself/herself) who are related to or connected with the donor; and

(ii) gifts to any charity to whom the donor made, or might be expected to make, gifts.

(s 3(5)(a) and (b) EPA 1985.)

No other form of gift may be made. The value of such gifts must not be unreasonable having regard to all the circumstances, and in particular the size of the donor's estate.

In addition to the power to make gifts, the attorney may, subject to contrary conditions or restrictions, and without obtaining consent, act so as to benefit himself/herself or persons other than the donor to the following extent:

(i) he/she may so act in respect of himself/herself or some other person if the donor might be expected to make such provision for that person's need; and

(ii) he/she may do whatever the donor might be expected to do to meet those needs.

(s 3(4)(a) and (b) EPA 1985.)

No other such provision may be made. If the donor is a trustee of a trust, the attorney may exercise or execute all or any of the trusts, powers or discretions vested in the donor; he/she may also give a valid receipt for capital or other moneys received (s 3(3) EPA 1985).

A donor must have attained eighteen years and be mentally capable. An attorney must have attained eighteen years and not have been adjudged bankrupt; the attorney's duties may be performed by a trust corporation (for example a bank). Where the attorney is a trust corporation, the form may be adapted to provide for sealing with its common seal. (See s 2(7)(a) and (b) EPA 1985, and r 2(3) Enduring Powers of Attorney (Prescribed Form) Regulations 1987.)

More than one attorney may be appointed; however, an enduring power cannot be created unless the attorneys are appointed to act either jointly, or jointly and severally (s 11(1) EPA 1985). Where they are appointed to act jointly, incapacity on the part of any one of them will prevent execution of the instrument (s 2(7) and Sch 3 Part 1 para 1 EPA 1985). In the case of an appointment to act jointly and severally, a failure on the part of any attorney to comply with the requirements as to capacity will not prevent the enduring power from being created in respect of the other or others (s 11(4) EPA 1985). As far as the incapacitated attorney is concerned, a power of attorney which is not enduring will be created.

A power of attorney under s 25 Trustee Act 1925 cannot be an enduring power. Section 25 of the 1925 Act enables a trustee to delegate all or any of his/her powers (that is, to grant a "power of attorney") to some other person for a period of up to twelve months. It was felt that there would be little value in setting up an enduring power for such a short period of time; consequently, such delegations are excluded from the EPA 1985. Although an enduring power of attorney has limited power to delegate functions which the donor would not have expected him/her to perform, a power of attorney which gives him/her the right to appoint his/her successor cannot be an enduring power (s 2(9) EPA 1985). In the case of joint attorneys, the subsection must be read as a reference to any one of them.

An enduring power is revoked by the bankruptcy of the attorney, whatever the circumstances of that bankruptcy (s 2(10) EPA 1985). If there are attorneys acting jointly, the bankruptcy of any one of them will revoke the power (Sch 3 Part 1 para 2 EPA 1985). Where they act jointly and severally the power is only revoked upon the bankruptcy of the last remaining attorney; however, the bankruptcy of one or more of the other attorneys before that time will mean that he/she ceases to act as such (Sch 3 Part 1 para 7 EPA 1985).

Enduring powers may also be revoked by direction of the Court of Protection when exercising its powers under Part VII MHA

1983. Thus, if the court appoints a receiver under s 99 MHA 1983, it may direct that any enduring power of attorney be revoked. (See s 2(11) EPA 1985; for Part VII MHA 1983 see page 190.)

An attorney wishing to disclaim his/her enduring power must give written notice to a donor who is still mentally capable. However, if the donor is or is becoming mentally incapable, written notice must be given to the court. Similarly, where an instrument has been registered, notice must be given to the court. (See ss 2(12), 4(6), 7(1) and 13(1) EPA 1985.)

At common law, a power of attorney is invariably revoked upon the donor becoming mentally incapable. An enduring power is not revoked by such incapacity (s 1(1)(a) EPA 1985). For the purposes of the EPA 1985, a person is mentally incapable if he/she is incapable by reason of mental disorder of managing and administering his/her property and affairs (s 13(10) EPA 1985). Upon the donor's incapacity the attorney, if he/she wishes to exercise the full powers, must comply with the registration procedure in the EPA 1985. Between the time of the incapacity arising and the time of registration, the powers of the attorney are limited. From the time of incapacity until the time of the application for registration, the attorney may not do anything under the authority of the power unless there is a court order under s 5 EPA 1985 (see below). Some protection is given to an attorney or a third person during this period in situations where they did not know of the incapacity. Section 5 Powers of Attorney Act 1971, which protects innocent attorneys and third persons, applies during the period of suspension as if the enduring power had actually been revoked by the incapacity. This suspension of powers is designed to encourage the attorney to make a speedy application for registration. Once the application is made, and until registration is determined, the attorney may take action under his/her power:

(i) to maintain the donor or prevent loss to his/her estate; or

(ii) to maintain himself or other persons so far as s 3(4) EPA 1985 (see above) permits him/her to do so.

(s 1(2)(a) and (b) EPA 1985.)

These powers are very limited. In maintaining the donor or preventing loss, the attorney could, for example, pay accommodation bills or sell investments if that was necessary to prevent loss. If an application is made by one or more, but not both or all, joint and several attorneys, the s 1(2) powers may be exercised by all of them regardless of whether they are party to the application or not (s 11(5)(a) EPA 1985).

## Protecting the property and financial affairs of patients

During the period between incapacity arising and registration, the Court of Protection has certain powers under s 5 EPA 1985. Section 11(5)(a) also applies to s 5 EPA 1985. If the court has reason to believe that the donor of an enduring power may be, or may be becoming, mentally incapable it may, if necessary, exercise any of the powers which would normally only be available to it after registration under s 8(2) EPA 1985 (see below). This power may be exercised even though no application for registration has been made. The Law Commission, in recommending this provision, stressed that it should only be rarely used and confined to urgent cases. For example, the attorney may be in doubt as to whether he/she has power to sell an investment which needs to be disposed of urgently, or a relative of the donor may feel that the donor had become incapacitated but the attorney is not willing to commence the registration process (see Law Commission No 122 para 4.82).

If an attorney under an enduring power has reason to believe that the donor is becoming mentally incapable, he/she must, as soon as is practicable, apply to the court for registration of the instrument creating the power (s 4(1) and (2) EPA 1985). Note that the attorney is not required to be completely sure of the donor's mental state; it is sufficient if he/she has "reason to believe". Any person who knowingly makes a false statement in an application for registration is guilty of a criminal offence (s 11(7) EPA 1985). If, at the time of application, the attorney wishes to give up his/her office he/she must give written notice of his/her intention to the court. The duty to give notice applies only to those attorneys who are aware of the donor's impending or actual mental incapacity where there are joint and several attorneys. This requirement of notice enables the court to make appropriate arrangements for the donor at this critical time. (See s 4(6) and Sch 3 para 8 EPA 1985.)

Before making an application, the attorney must give notice of his/her intention to the following persons:

- (i) the donor's spouse;
- (ii) the donor's children;
- (iii) the donor's parents;
- (iv) the donor's brothers or sisters (both whole and half blood);
- (v) the widow or widower of a child of the donor;
- (vi) the donor's grandchildren;
- (vii) the children of the donor's brothers and sisters of the whole blood;

- (viii) the children of the donor's brothers and sisters of the half blood;
- (ix) the donor's uncles and aunts of the whole blood;
- (x) the children of the donor's uncles and aunts of the whole blood.

(s 4 (3) and Sch 1 Part I para 2(1)(a)–(j) EPA 1985.)

Notice need not be given to a person whose name or address is unknown to the attorney and cannot be reasonably ascertained by him/her. Similarly, no notice is required to be given to a person whom the attorney has reason to believe is under eighteen years or mentally incapable. Normally, not more than three persons in the above list are entitled to receive notice. Persons higher up the list are preferred to those lower down. However, where there is at least one person within a class who would be entitled to receive notice, all persons within that class will then be so entitled. (See Sch 1 Part I para 2(4) EPA 1985.)

Notice need not be given to an attorney who is making the application, or joining in making the application, notwithstanding the fact that he/she would be entitled to receive notice under the above provisions. Subject to this exception, all joint and several attorneys must be given notice whether or not they are joining in making the application (s 11(5)(b) EPA 1985). Before making the application, the attorney must also give notice to the donor (Sch 1 Part I para 4(1) EPA 1985).

The attorney may, before applying for registration, make an application to the court that he/she be dispensed from giving notice to any of the persons entitled under the above provisions. Such an application shall be granted by the court if it is satisfied that:

- (i) it would be undesirable or impracticable for the attorney to give that person notice; or
- (ii) no useful purpose would be served by giving him/her notice.

(Sch 1 Part I para 3(1) EPA 1985.)

It is also open to the attorney, before making an application, to refer to the court for its determination any question relating to the validity of the enduring power (s 4(5) EPA 1985). This provision may be used where the attorney is uncertain as to the validity of the enduring power created by the instrument. The attorney is bound to comply with any directions given by the court.

Upon receipt of an application for registration under s 4 EPA

1985, the court shall register the instrument to which it relates unless there is a receivership order under the MHA 1983 in operation or the case falls within s 6(4) EPA 1985. Where there is an order appointing a receiver for the donor under the MHA 1983 (see page 200) which has not been revoked, then, unless it directs otherwise, the court should not exercise its powers under the EPA 1985 and should reject the application (s 6(2) EPA 1985). Thus the powers under Part VII MHA 1983 will prevail (see page 190).

Section 6(4) EPA 1985 identifies those situations in which the court, upon receipt of an application, must neither register nor refuse to register the instrument until further enquiries have been made. The first situation is where a valid notice of objection to registration is received by the court within five weeks of the date on which notice was given under Sch 1 EPA 1985. A valid notice of objection must be in writing; it must set out the name and address of the objector and the donor (if some other person), the relationship with the donor (if relevant), the name and address of the attorney and the grounds for objecting to registration. A notice to a relative under the EPA 1985 must inform the recipient that he/she may object to the proposed registration by notice in writing to the court. A notice of objection is valid if it is made on one or more of the following grounds:

(i) that the power purported to have been created by the instrument was not valid as an enduring power of attorney (eg not properly witnessed);

(ii) that the power created by the instrument no longer subsists (eg because of the donor's valid revocation – see page 215);

(iii) that the application is premature because the donor is not yet mentally incapable;

(iv) that fraud or undue pressure was used to induce the donor to create the power;

(v) that having regard to all the circumstances of the case and in particular the attorney's relationship to or connection with the donor, the attorney is unsuitable to act as such.

(s 6(5) EPA 1985.)

In its report, the Law Commission stressed that ground (v) should not be available simply because one of the relatives objected to the donor's choice of attorney. What is important is that the particular attorney is suitable to act as such for the particular donor; the court, before reaching any decision, should examine carefully all the circumstances of the case, particularly the relationship between the donor and attorney (Law Commission No 122 para 4.49). If the court is satisfied that one of these grounds exists, it must refuse the application. However, registration must not be refused because a ground of objection is established in respect of one or some of joint and several attorneys. Registration is effective for the other attorney or attorneys (s 11(6) EPA 1985). If the court is not satisfied as to the existence of one of these grounds, it must register the instrument to which the application relates. (See s 6(6) EPA 1985.) Where the court has reason to believe that appropriate enquiries might reveal evidence that there is a valid ground of objection under s 6(5) EPA 1985, it must neither register nor refuse to register (s 6(4)(c) EPA 1985).

The other situation in which the court must neither register nor refuse to register is where it appears from the application that there is nobody to whom notice has been given under Sch 1 (s 6(4)(b) EPA 1985). In these circumstances, the court should make appropriate enquiries to see whether any such relatives do exist. If it appears from the application that notice has not been given to a person entitled to receive it, and there is no order dispensing with such notice, the court can direct that it is in accordance with s 4(3) EPA 1985 if satisfied, as regards that individual, that:

- (i) it was undesirable or impracticable for the attorney to give notice; or
- (ii) no useful purpose is likely to be served by giving notice.

(s 6(3) EPA 1985.)

The legal effects of registration are as follows:

- (i) no revocation of the instrument by the donor shall be valid unless and until the court confirms it under s 8(3) EPA 1985 (see below);
- (ii) no disclaimer of the power by an attorney is valid unless and until the attorney gives notice to the court;
- (iii) the donor cannot extend or restrict the scope of the authority conferred by the instrument;
- (iv) instructions or consents given by the donor will not have legal effect.

(s 7(1)(a)–(c) EPA 1985.)

In order to create certainty, s 7(1) EPA 1985 applies for the duration of registration regardless of whether the donor is for the time being mentally incapable (s 7(2) EPA 1985). Upon an application by the donor, or on his/her behalf, for confirmation of revocation, the court must confirm if it is satisfied that the donor has done what is necessary and was, at the time of doing it, mentally capable (s 8(3) EPA 1985). Revocation will not be effective until it is confirmed by the court. Upon confirmation, the registration will be cancelled. Registration will also be cancelled upon receipt of notice of disclaimer. (See s 8(4)(a) EPA 1985.)

Registration gives the court certain functions with respect to the enduring power and the roles of the donor and the attorney. The court may:

(i) determine any question as to the meaning or effect of the instrument;
(ii) give directions with respect to:
 - the management or disposal by the attorney of the property and affairs of the donor;
 - the rendering of accounts by the attorney and the production of the records kept by him/her for the purpose;
 - the remuneration of expenses of the attorney, whether or not in default of or in accordance with any provisions made by the instrument, including directions for the repayment of excessive, or the payment of additional, remuneration;
(iii) require the attorney to furnish information or produce documents or things in his/her possession as attorney;
(iv) give any consent or authorisation to act which the attorney would have to obtain from a mentally capable donor (eg where a conflict of interest might arise between the donor and attorney);
(v) authorise the attorney to act so as to benefit himself/herself or some person other than the donor, other than in accordance with s 3(4) and (5) EPA 1985 (see page 208);
(vi) relieve the attorney wholly or partly from any liability which he/she has or may have incurred on account of his/her duties as attorney.

(s 8(2) EPA 1985.)

The court also has the power to cancel registration of an instrument. In addition to the power to confirm a revocation under s 8(3) or to receive notice of disclaimer under s 7(1)(b), it may also cancel in any of the following circumstances:

(i) on giving a direction revoking the power when exercising any of its powers under Part VII MHA 1983;

(ii) on being satisfied that the donor is and is likely to remain mentally capable;

(iii) on being satisfied that the power has expired or been revoked by the death or bankruptcy of the donor or the death, mental incapacity or bankruptcy of the attorney, or if the attorney is a body corporate, its winding up or dissolution;

(iv) on being satisfied that the power was not a valid and subsisting enduring power when the registration was effected;

(v) on being satisfied that fraud or undue pressure was used to induce the donor to create the power; or

(vi) on being satisfied that, having regard to all the circumstances and particularly the attorney's relationship to or connection with the donor he/she is unsuitable to be the donor's attorney.

(s 8(4)(a)–(g) EPA 1985.)

Where the court is satisfied that one of these conditions applies, it must cancel the registration and send a notice to the attorney requiring him/her to deliver to the court the original instrument (r 24 Enduring Powers of Attorney Rules 1986 (SI 1986 No 127). If the registration is cancelled on ground (ii) above, the instrument will become an unregistered enduring power of attorney which may subsequently be re-registered if the donor becomes mentally incapable (s 8(6) EPA 1985 and r 24(4) Enduring Powers of Attorney Rules 1986). Cancellation on grounds (v) or (vi) requires the court to revoke by order the power created by the instrument (s 8(5) EPA 1985 and r 24(3) Enduring Powers of Attorney Rules 1986). In all other cases the instrument must be delivered to the court to be cancelled unless the court directs otherwise (s 8(6) EPA 1985). However, registration will not be cancelled if one of the above grounds is satisfied in respect of only one or some of joint and several attorneys. In this situation, the registration will only be vitiated in respect of that or those attorney(s) and will be qualified to that extent (s 11(7) EPA 1985).

Ordinary powers of attorney provide some protection for "innocent" attorneys or third parties where they acted in

## Protecting the property and financial affairs of patients

ignorance of the fact that the power had been revoked. The EPA 1985 goes further and provides protection for such people where an instrument which did not create a valid power has been registered under s 6 EPA 1985. An attorney who acts under such a power does not incur liability against the donor or any other person unless at the time of acting he/she knew that:

(i) the instrument did not create a valid enduring power; or

(ii) an event had occurred which, had the instrument created a valid power, would have had the effect of revoking that power (for example the donor ceases to be under a mental disability); or

(iii) if the instrument had created a valid enduring power, it would have expired before that time.

(s 9(2)(a)−(c) EPA 1985.)

As far as a party to a transaction with the attorney is concerned, any transaction in his/her favour is valid unless he/she had knowledge of any of the matters mentioned in s 9(2)(a)−(c) (s 9(3) EPA 1985). Both these subsections apply whether or not the registration has been cancelled at the time of the act or transaction in question.

Where the interest of a purchaser depends upon whether a transaction is valid under s 9(3), it shall be conclusively presumed in favour of him/her that it is valid if:

(i) the transaction between the attorney and the other person was completed within twelve months of the date on which the instrument was registered; or

(ii) the other person makes a statutory declaration either before or within three months after completion of the purchase, that he/she had no reason at the time of the transaction with the attorney to doubt that there was authority to dispose of the property.

(s 9(4) EPA 1985.)

This added protection for attorneys and third persons emphasises the importance attached to the process of registration.

Schedule 2 EPA 1985 makes provision for the protection of attorneys and third persons when an instrument in a form prescribed by s 2(2) creates a power which is not a valid enduring power and that power has been revoked by the donor's mental incapacity. This type of situation might arise if there has been a drafting error. The attorney will not by reason of the revocation incur any liability unless at the time of acting he/she knew that the instrument did not create a valid enduring power *and* that the donor has become mentally incapable (Sch 2 para 2 EPA 1985). A transaction between an attorney and another person will be valid in favour of that person unless at the time of acting he/she knew that the instrument did not create a valid enduring power *and* that the donor had become mentally incapable (Sch 2 para 3 EPA 1985). Where the interest of a purchaser depends upon the validity under Sch 2 para 3 of a transaction between an attorney and another person, s 9(4) EPA 1985 applies in the same way as it applies to s 9(3) EPA 1985 (see page 217).

## 3. Miscellaneous methods of protecting property and income

In addition to the methods outlined above, there are other miscellaneous ways of protecting the property and income of persons suffering from some form of mental disability. Under the NAA 1948, a local authority has a duty to take reasonable steps to prevent or mitigate loss or damage to the movable property of a person admitted as a patient to any hospital, or who is admitted to Part III accommodation or removed to suitable premises under s 47 NAA 1948 (s 48(1) NAA 1948 — see pages 44 and 143). In order to carry out this duty, the authority has power to enter the patient's home at a reasonable time and deal with the property as is necessary (s 48(2) NAA 1948). Reasonable expenses incurred may be recovered from the patient or any person liable to maintain him/her (s 48(3) NAA 1948).

Where pay, pensions or other periodical payments payable directly out of money provided by Parliament or the government are due to a person who, by reason of mental disorder, is unable to manage and administer his/her property and affairs, s 142 MHA 1983 allows alternative arrangements for payment to be made. If so satisfied, after hearing medical evidence, the authority responsible for payment may pay the sum due or part of it to the institution or person having care of the patient, to be applied for his/her benefit. Where a part payment is made, the remainder may be paid to the benefit of the patient's family or other persons for whom he/she might have been expected to provide if not mentally disordered. The remainder may also be used to reimburse any person who has paid any of the patient's debts, whether legally enforceable or not, or who has used money to support the patient's family or other dependants (s 142(2)(a) and (b) MHA 1983).

## Protecting the property and financial affairs of patients

The Department of Social Security may appoint a person to receive benefits on behalf of a person suffering from a mental disorder. Normally the appointee will be the nearest relative. An appointment comes to an end upon the appointment of a receiver.

# Chapter 8

# Mental health and legal capacity

## 1. Family law

*(a) The marriage ceremony*

A patient compulsorily detained in hospital may find it difficult to arrange a ceremony of marriage due to restrictions on his/her freedom of movement outside the hospital. Important changes in the law were made by s 1 Marriage Act 1983 (see DHSS LAC (84)9). This section does not affect the capacity to marry which is dealt with in *(b)* below. It does, however, enable a marriage ceremony to take place within the hospital. Only persons detained under s 3 MHA 1983 may benefit from this provision; those subject to short term detention must arrange for their marriage to take place at an authorised place outside the hospital. The detained person must give the usual notice of marriage under s 27 Marriage Act 1949, but it must be accompanied by a statement in the prescribed form by the hospital managers (see Annex B DHSS LAC (84)10). The form must identify the hospital where the person is detained and state that the hospital managers have no objection to it being used for the solemnisation of the marriage. Such a statement must have been made within the twenty-one days before the s 27 notice is given. Under s 1 Marriage Act 1983, the marriage may be solemnised on the authority of a registrar's certificate issued under Part III Marriage Act 1949 at the hospital.

*(b) The nullity of marriage*

The presence of certain impediments may render a marriage void or voidable. Sections 11 and 12 Matrimonial Causes Act 1973 ("MCA 1973") specify the grounds upon which a decree of nullity may be obtained in respect of marriages celebrated after

## Mental health and legal capacity

31 July 1971. Unlike the previous law, mental capacity only features as a ground upon which a marriage is voidable. A voidable marriage is regarded as valid and subsisting up until the time that the decree is granted (s 16 MCA 1973). Unlike void marriages, a decree is required to bring the marriage to an end. Only the parties to the marriage may present a petition. Thus relatives of a person of unsound mind may not present a petition, for example, if they wish to challenge a will made in contemplation of the marriage. It is not possible to petition after the death of one of the parties. The mental capacity of one of the spouses is relevant under two of the grounds upon which a marriage may be voidable; these are ss 12(c) and (d) MCA 1973.

Section 12(c) MCA 1973 states that a marriage will be voidable if "either party to the marriage did not validly consent to it ... in consequence of ... unsoundness of mind ...". Since consent is the basis of marriage, its absence renders the marriage voidable. The test to be applied in determining whether there was valid consent at the time of the ceremony is that laid down by Singleton LJ in *In the Estate of Park* (1953). He said that the court must determine whether the person was at the time of the marriage ceremony "capable of understanding the nature of the contract into which he was entering, or was his mental condition such that he was incapable of understanding it?" He/She must be mentally capable of appreciating that it involves the responsibilities normally attaching to marriage. The burden of proving lack of consent is on the person asserting it (*Harrod* v *Harrod* (1854)).

Under s 12(d) MCA 1973, a marriage will be voidable if "at the time of the marriage either party, though capable of giving a valid consent, was suffering (whether continuously or intermittently) from a mental disorder within the meaning of the Mental Health Act 1983 of such a kind or to such an extent as to be unfitted for marriage". This differs from s 12(c) MCA 1973 in that it assumes that the party is capable of giving consent. Ormrod J in *Bennett* v *Bennett* (1969) said the court should ask whether the person was "capable of living in a married state, and of carrying out the ordinary duties and obligations of marriage". Note that it is the person's state of mind at the time of the marriage ceremony that is relevant — was the person at that moment suffering from a mental disorder? If not, a recurrence of an earlier disorder or the emergence of a disorder after the ceremony may be a basis for divorce rather than nullity (see page 222).

It should be noted that the petition under either subsection can be presented either by the spouse suffering from the unsoundness of mind or the other spouse. A petition based on s 12 (c) or (d) MCA 1973 should be presented within three years of the date of the ceremony (s 13(3) MCA 1973). However, the court may grant leave to petition outside that period if satisfied that *the petitioner* (not necessarily the person against whom allegations of unsoundness of mind will be made) has suffered from a mental disorder within the MHA 1983 at some time during the period, and is also satisfied that it would be just to grant leave (s 13(4) MCA 1973).

*(c) Divorce*

Under s 1 MCA 1973, there is only one ground of divorce, namely the irretrievable breakdown of marriage (s 1(1) MCA 1973 – this Act consolidates the Divorce Reform Act 1969 and other related legislation). This is, however, a little misleading as irretrievable breakdown can only be proved by showing that one of the "five facts" in s 1(2) MCA 1973 has been satisfied. The five facts are:

(i) that the respondent has committed adultery and the petitioner finds it intolerable to live with him/her (s 1(2)(a) MCA 1973);

(ii) that the respondent has behaved in such a way that the petitioner cannot reasonably be expected to live with him/her ("unreasonable behaviour") (s 1(2)(b) MCA 1973);

(iii) that the respondent has deserted the petitioner for a continuous period of at least two years immediately preceding the presentation of the petition (s 1(2)(c) MCA 1973);

(iv) that the parties to the marriage have lived apart for a continuous period of at least two years immediately preceding the presentation of the petition and the respondent consents to a decree being granted (s 1(2)(d) MCA 1973);

(v) that the parties to the marriage have lived apart for a continuous period of five years immediately preceding the presentation of the petition (s 1(2)(e) MCA 1973).

The states of mind of the petitioner and respondent feature in each of the five facts; they will now be considered in turn. A more detailed study of the law of divorce is outside the scope of this book.

*Adultery:* Adultery involves consensual sexual intercourse between a married person and a person of the opposite sex who is not his/her spouse, during the subsistence of the marriage. The question arises whether a person's ability to consent to intercourse for the purpose of MCA 1973 is affected by his/her state of mind. For example, can insanity negate consent to intercourse? The point was discussed in *S* v *S* (1961). In this case it was held that as the co-respondent came within the second limb of the M'Naughten Rules (see page 175) she could not be found guilty of adultery. Two comments need to be made on this case. Firstly, it was decided at a time when it was necessary to have a finding of guilt on the part of the co-respondent. Under present law this is unnecessary; what matters now is the state of mind of the respondent (that is, the "guilty" husband or wife). Only if he/she is incapable of consenting to intercourse through mental incapacity can the defence be available. The state of mind of the co-respondent is irrelevant. Secondly, the reference to the criminal law test of insanity found in the M'Naughten Rules is inappropriate for family matters. A more appropriate test should be a variation of the test applied in *In the Estate of Park*: does the respondent understand the nature of the act of intercourse with a non-spouse during the validity of his/her marriage?

*Unreasonable behaviour:* The cases require the courts to look at the effect of the conduct of the respondent on the petitioner. Despite the use of the word "reasonable", a subjective element is present. Bagnall J in *Ash* v *Ash* (1972) put it like this:

> "Can this petitioner, with his or her character and personality, with his or her faults and other attributes, good and bad, and having regard to his or her behaviour during the marriage, reasonably be expected to live with this respondent?"

This subjective element is important in determining whether mental illness is a sufficient basis for a divorce based on unreasonable behaviour. Under the old law of cruelty, the House of Lords held in *Williams* v *Williams* (1963) that the courts should look to the consequences of conduct and not the intention of the respondent. Thus a respondent who was certifiably insane and who did not know that his conduct was wrong could still be guilty of cruelty. Lord Reid in *Williams* said that "the facts are such that after making all allowances for his disabilities and for the temperament of both parties, it must be held that the character and gravity of his conduct was such as to amount to cruelty".

How relevant is *Williams* under the reformed law? In *Katz* v *Katz* (1972), Sir George Baker P agreed with the test as laid down by Lord Reid but substituted the words "unreasonable behaviour" for cruelty. In *Katz* the respondent suffered from a manic-depressive illness. He wrongly accused his wife of having an affair – she attempted suicide. Baker P stressed that the court must consider the *effect* of the behaviour on Mrs Katz and ask whether it was so grave that she could not reasonably be expected to live with him. A decree of divorce was granted. A different approach was adopted by Judge Pickering in *Smith* v *Smith* (1973). The wife suffered from pre-senile dementia and at the time of the petition her life was described as vegetable-like. Judge Pickering said that it was impossible to say that her involuntary actions constituted behaviour. A different approach was adopted by Rees J in *Thurlow* v *Thurlow* (1975). Mrs Thurlow suffered from epilepsy and a neurological disorder. She was on occasions violent towards Mr Thurlow's mother; she was also unable to cope with housework and she spent a lot of time in hospital. Mr Thurlow petitioned on the basis of unreasonable behaviour. Rees J dismissed the *Smith* approach. He said:

> "... behaviour which may found a decree under s 1(2)(b) of the 1973 Act may be either positive or negative in character, or both, and may include cases where the behaviour is caused by mental or physical illness or injury, and may be involuntary. It will be for the judge to decide subject to review on appeal whether behaviour is sufficiently grave to make it unreasonable to expect the petitioner to endure it."

In reaching a conclusion, the judge should have regard to all the circumstances of the case. These include the disabilities and temperaments of both parties; the causes of the behaviour and whether they were known to the petitioner; the presence or absence of intention; the impact on the petitioner and the family unit; the duration of the behaviour and the prospect of cure or improvement in the future. Taking all these matters into consideration, Rees J granted a decree of divorce.

The approach in *Thurlow* is generally considered to be the correct one and in line with the policy of the legislation, although some find it objectionable that the mentally ill are placed in the same category as violent spouses. An alternative approach would be to use the five year separation fact. As will be seen below, there are certain advantages in using five years' separation, particularly as regards financial security for the mentally ill respondent.

*Desertion:* For desertion it is necessary to prove factual separation for a two year period, an intention to desert for the duration of that period, an absence of consent on the part of the deserted spouse and an absence of just cause for leaving. All four criteria must be satisfied. Mere factual separation does not constitute desertion. For example, if a husband is detained in hospital under the MHA 1983 it does not mean that he has deserted his wife. However, if he forms an intention to desert at the inception or during the period of separation, desertion will commence if the other two requirements are met. This raises the question of the capacity to form an intention to desert. In *Perry* v *Perry* (1963), the court held that a man who suffered from paranoid psychosis did not have the mental capacity to form an intention to desert. Thus it is essential that the respondent has the necessary mental capacity to *form* an intention to desert. Whether or not that mental capacity must exist for the duration of the two year period depends upon the operation of s 2(4) MCA 1973. Under this subsection:

> "... the court may treat a period of desertion *as having continued* at a time when the deserting party was incapable of continuing the necessary intention if the evidence before the court is such that, had that party not been so incapable, the court would have inferred that his desertion continued at that time."

Statements made by the respondent during lucid moments and his/her response to visits from the other spouse will be relevant in deciding his/her intention for the purposes of s 2(4) MCA 1973 (see *Kaczmarz* v *Kaczmarz* (1967)).

In certain circumstances a spouse may have a just cause for leaving. For example, if the other spouse is violent towards him/her, it would be unreasonable to find him/her in desertion simply because he/she moved out for reasons of safety. This raises the question whether the acts or omissions of a mentally ill spouse will provide a just cause for the other spouse leaving. The logic of the *Thurlow* decision is that in certain circumstances they will. In deciding whether there is a just cause, the court must take account of all the circumstances of the case, including the personalities of both spouses and the nature of the behaviour.

A patient detained in a hospital may petition on the basis of the desertion of his/her spouse if, in addition to the factual separation, that spouse has formed the intention to desert and the other two conditions are satisfied. Evidence of an intention to desert may be deduced from a statement to that effect, or an absence of visits, letters or gifts.

*Living apart for two years and consent to decree being granted:*
It should be noted that under this fact it is consent to the decree that is required and not consent to the living apart. The respondent must be mentally capable of giving consent. In *Mason* v *Mason* (1972), the husband and wife had lived apart for two

years during which time the husband was a patient in a mental hospital. He signed a consent form and a psychiatrist gave evidence that he was able to understand the implications of divorce proceedings. Sir George Baker said that the test of capacity is the same as that for consent to marriage, ie the test put forward in *In the Estate of Park* (see above). If the validity of the consent is in issue, the burden of proving it will be on the petitioner.

*Living apart for five years:* Judge Pickering in *Smith* v *Smith* (see above) favoured the use of this fact when divorcing mentally ill people. Two advantages arise from the use of this fact rather than unreasonable behaviour. Firstly, the mentally ill person is not put in the same category of respondents who clearly intend disruptive and cruel conduct. Secondly, under s 5 MCA 1973, if granting a decree based on five years' separation (and no other fact) would cause grave financial or other hardship to the respondent and it would, in all the circumstances, be wrong to dissolve the marriage, the court may dismiss the petition. It must be stressed that the courts have been very reluctant to use their powers under s 5 MCA 1973 for fear that it would defeat the purpose behind the legislation. The hardship, financial or other, must arise from the *dissolution* rather than the breakdown of the marriage (*Talbot* v *Talbot* (1971)). The cases have stressed that this issue must be addressed subjectively; matters such as financial and emotional dependence can be taken into account (*Dorrell* v *Dorrell* (1972)). Financial hardship will invariably arise from the loss of a pension right. In most cases this potential loss can be mitigated by the purchase of an annuity in favour of the respondent (*Parker* v *Parker* (1972)). "Other hardship" may include the loss of support given by the petitioner, although the courts are even more reluctant to find this type of hardship than financial hardship. Very few cases under s 5 MCA 1973 have been successful (see, for example *Julian* v *Julian* (1972) and *Lee* v *Lee* (1973)). However, the main advantage of the availability of the procedure is that it places the respondent in a strong bargaining position, particularly in relation to financial provision.

*(d) Financial provision and property adjustment after a decree of divorce or nullity*

Under the MCA 1973, the court may make an order for ancillary relief in connection with divorce and nullity proceedings. Such orders may be made in favour of a respondent or a petitioner, a wife or a husband. The types of order that can be made include periodical payments, lump sum awards, property adjustment orders, settlement of property and orders for the sale of property (see ss 23–24A MCA 1973). Where the court makes an order and is satisfied that the beneficiary is incapable by reason of a mental disorder under MHA 1983 of managing and administering his/her property or affairs, it may direct that the payment be made, or property transferred, to a person having charge of him/her. This is subject to any order, direction or authority given by the Court of Protection (s 40 MCA 1973 – for Court of Protection see page 190). Most of the orders may also be made in favour of a child of the family in addition to the spouses.

In deciding how to exercise these powers, the court must have regard to the matters in s 25 MCA 1973. Of particular interest to the mentally ill or those with a mental handicap who are involved in divorce proceedings are those which refer to income and earning capacity, financial needs and the physical and mental disability of either of the parties. Section 25(2)(a) MCA 1973 requires the court to have regard to the "income, earning capacity, property and other financial resources" which the parties have or are likely to have in the foreseeable future. It must also consider any increase which it would be reasonable to expect him/her to take steps to acquire after the granting of the decree. Insofar as a mentally ill person or a person with mental handicap is concerned, this may be relevant both where he/she is the intended beneficiary or the intended provider. For example, the income etc of a person detained in hospital under MHA 1983 will often be low or non-existent, unless there is investment income. This will affect his/her ability to provide for the other spouse and his/her own needs. Financial needs etc are referred to in s 25(2)(b) MCA 1973: a person in hospital or residential care, or who is confined to home, may have special needs which should be catered for under the provisions for ancillary relief if a decree is granted. Under s 25(2)(e) MCA 1973, the court must have regard to "any physical or mental disability" of either party. In most cases this will be considered under other headings such as income and needs.

The matters to be taken into account in deciding whether to make an order in favour of a child of the family include income, needs and physical or mental disability (s 25(3) MCA 1973). Normally an order in favour of a child will cease in the first instance when he/she attains the upper limit of compulsory school leaving age (that is, the child's sixteenth birthday). It may be extended to the date of the child's eighteenth birthday. However, it may only continue beyond that age if either the child is undergoing some form of education or training, or "there are special circumstances which justify the making of an order without complying ..." with the above limitations (see s 29(2) and (3) MCA 1973). The court may, therefore, extend the duration of the order beyond eighteen if the child has special needs resulting from a mental disability. Such an order may be varied to take account of any State benefits which may be available to a person of the age of majority.

*(e) Procedural matters*

A person who, by reason of suffering from a mental disorder under the MHA 1983, is incapable of managing and administering his/her property and affairs ("the patient") may commence matrimonial proceedings by his/her next friend, and defend them by a guardian *ad litem*. The Matrimonial Causes Rules 1977 ("MCR 1977") impose the following requirements:

(i) no person's name can be used as a next friend unless he/she is the Official Solicitor or the documents mentioned in r 112(8) MCR 1977 have been filed (r 112(3) MCR 1977);

(ii) if a person has been authorised by the Court of Protection to conduct such matrimonial proceedings on behalf of a patient, that person is entitled to be a next friend or guardian *ad litem* provided the r 112(8) MCR 1977 documents have been filed (r 112(4) MCR 1977);

(iii) where no person is authorised under (ii) to defend proceedings in the patient's name, the Official Solicitor, if he/she consents, shall be the guardian *ad litem* but an application (on giving not less than four days' notice to the Official Solicitor) may be made for some other person to act in that capacity; in any other case, an application may be made on behalf of the patient for the appointment of a guardian *ad litem* (in either case, r 112(8) MCR 1977 documents must be filed) (r 112(5) MCR 1977);

(iv) where proceedings have been initiated against a person who there are reasonable grounds for believing is under a disability, and no notice of intention to defend has been given, the party who initiated the proceedings must, before going any further, apply to the registrar for directions as to whether a guardian *ad litem* should be appointed — the registrar may, if he/she considers it necessary to protect the interests of that person, order that a guardian *ad litem* be appointed (r 112(6) MCR 1977);

(v) no notice of intention to defend shall be given, or answer or affidavit be filed, by or on behalf of a patient unless the person doing so is the Official Solicitor or the person appointed guardian *ad litem* under (iii) above, or in any other case has filed the r 112(8) MCR 1977 documents (r 112(7) MCR 1977).

The r 112(8) MCR 1977 documents are:

(i) a written consent to act as next friend or guardian *ad litem*;

(ii) if the next friend or guardian *ad litem* is authorised by the Court of Protection to act in such matrimonial proceedings, an office copy of the authorisation sealed with the seal of the Court of Protection must be provided;

(iii) in all other cases the solicitor acting for the patient must certify:
   − that he/she knows or believes that the person to whom the certificate relates is a patient (grounds for this knowledge or belief must be stated) and that nobody has been appointed to act under (ii);
   − that the person named in the certificate as next friend has no interest in the cause or matter adverse to that of the patient, and that he/she is a proper person to act as next friend.

Documents which are required to be served on a patient shall be served:

(i) on any person authorised under Part VII MHA 1983 to conduct legal proceedings, or

(ii) if no such person is authorised, on the Official Solicitor if he/she has consented under r 112(5) MCR 1977 to be guardian *ad litem,* or

(iii) in any other case, on a person with whom the patient resides or in whose care he/she is.

(r 113(1)(b) MCR 1977.)

Where a petition for nullity is presented under s 12(d) MCA1973 alleging that the respondent is suffering from a mental disorder under the MHA 1983, leave of the registrar is necessary before the petitioner can proceed with the cause. The registrar may make it a condition of granting leave that a proper person is appointed to act as guardian *ad litem* for the respondent. (See r 114(1) and (2) MCR 1977.)

## 2. Contract

At common law, a contract entered into by a person "who was so insane at the time (of entering it) that he did not know what he was doing" will be valid unless it can be shown that the other party was aware of the incapacity (*Imperial Loan Company* v *Stone* (1892)). Where the other party is so aware, the contract is voidable at the option of the person suffering from the incapacity. It is open to him/her to ratify the contract at some subsequent lucid moment, in which case the contract becomes fully enforceable (*Birkin* v *Wing* (1890) and *Matthews* v *Baxter* (1873)). The incapacity must exist at the time that the contract is made. If it arises subsequently, the contract will be valid. The incapacity must be of a type that prevents the person from understanding the nature and effect of the contract under consideration. This is a question of fact, and the court will have to take into consideration the nature of the contract and its complexity; it will not be required to make a finding as to the person's capacity to enter contracts in general. The mere fact that a person is suffering from a form of mental illness does not mean that all his/her contracts will be voidable under the above rule. Furthermore, it must be shown that the other party was aware of the incapacity. This requires proof of a personal knowledge by that person; it is insufficient to show that it was generally known in the community that the other party was suffering from incapacity (*Greenslade* v *Dare* (1855)).

There are exceptions to this general rule which relate to the supply of necessaries to a person lacking capacity to contract. Where necessaries suitable for his/her position in life are supplied to such a person he/she will be liable to pay for them, *quasi ex contractu,* even though the other party was aware of the incapacity (*Re Rhodes* (1890)). This includes, for example, expenditure on professional services necessary to preserve his/her property or capital. The other party must have intended that he/she should be paid as opposed to making a gift. In the case of necessaries which are sold and delivered to a person under an incapacity, s 3 Sale of Goods Act 1979 requires that he/she must pay a reasonable price for them (s 3(2) Sale of Goods Act 1979). "Necessaries" under the Act are defined as "goods suitable to the condition in life (of the person) ... and to his actual requirements at the time of sale and delivery".

If the person is subject to the jurisdiction of the Court of Protection, valid contracts can be made under the direct authority of the court or indirectly through the receiver. Whilst subject to the jurisdiction, the patient cannot enter a valid contract even during a lucid moment as this would defeat the purpose behind the court's powers (*Re Walker* (1905)). However, the court may order the carrying out of any contract entered into by the patient prior to the proceedings (s 96(1)(h) MHA 1983 – see page 193).

## 3. Wills

Statutory wills and the jurisdiction of the Court of Protection in respect of wills are considered at page 195. In order to make a valid will, the testator must have testamentary capacity. As in other areas of capacity, the fact that the person may be suffering from a mental disorder under the MHA 1983 does not in itself mean that he/she lacks testamentary capacity. It must be shown that the testator has a "sound and disposing mind and memory" (*Banks* v *Goodfellow* (1870) per Cockburn CJ). Cockburn CJ said that the testator must be capable of understanding the nature of the business in which he/she is engaged; have a recollection of the property he/she means to dispose of; be aware of any relatives to whom he/she has responsibilities, and be aware of the manner in which he/she wishes to distribute his/her estate. When deciding whether a person has capacity, it must be borne in mind that there is considerable freedom to dispose of property by will in whatever manner the testator desires. Subject to possible proceedings under the Inheritance (Provision for Family and Dependants) Act 1975, a testator can leave his/her worldly goods for the benefit of whatever lawful cause he/she desires. Thus, the mere fact that the will is not what the testator's nearest and dearest would have expected of him/her does not prove testamentary incapacity. As Wigram VC said in *Bird* v *Luckie* (1850) "No man is bound to make a will in such a manner as to deserve approbation from the prudent, the wise, or the good". However, the irrational nature of the disposition may be used in support when there is other evidence of incapacity such as, for example, mental illness under the MHA 1983. The testamentary incapacity must exist at the time of the making of the will. If, at that time, the testator is going through a lucid period the will is valid. Incapacity subsequent to the making of the will does not revoke it. However, in this situation it is difficult, if not impossible, for the person to revoke, as revocation also requires testamentary capacity (*Re Sabatini* (1969)). In this situation, recourse to the Court of Protection may be necessary unless revocation is effected during a subsequent lucid period.

The person propounding (proving) the will must show that the testator had the requisite testamentary capacity – he/she has the *legal* burden of proof. This does not mean that he/she must in all cases produce medical evidence as to the testator's state of mind, although such evidence may make his/her task easier. A presumption of testamentary capacity arises where a rational will which has been properly executed is produced. To rebut this presumption, it is necessary for the contesting party to produce prima facie evidence of testamentary incapacity. It is, however, important to stress that the legal burden of proof has not been transferred to that other party, only the evidential burden (that is, the obligation to "raise the issue"). The legal burden of proof remains with the party propounding the will who should now adduce evidence to rebut that of incapacity. A will which appears to be irrational in that it makes unusual or unexpected dispositions does not raise the presumption of testamentary capacity. Of course, as noted above, there is an initial difficulty in deciding whether a will is irrational, given the freedom that testators have to dispose of their property. In these circumstances the person propounding the will must produce evidence of testamentary capacity sufficient to satisfy the legal burden of proof.

## 4. Tort

There is very little case law on the extent to which mental disorder can effect liability in tort. Winfield and Jolowicz argue that the "true question in each case is whether the defendant was possessed of the requisite state of mind for the particular tort with which he was charged". This pragmatic approach appears to be the most sensible and the one favoured by the judiciary. Thus, in an action for malicious prosecution, the defendant must have sufficient mental capacity to form the necessary specific intent. However, in torts of strict liability the mental capacity of the defendant will be irrelevant. Only if the defendant's acts were involuntary will he/she successfully defend such an action (see Stable J in *Morriss* v *Marsden* (1952)).

Negligence poses something of a problem. As a basis for liability it eliminates the personal characteristics of the defendant. For example, the same standard of care is expected of a learner driver

## Mental health and legal capacity

as of an experienced driver. It should follow that mental incapacity does not provide a defence to an action based on negligence, although clear authority on the point is lacking.

Stable J in *Morriss* v *Marsden* had to consider whether mental illness could constitute a defence to the tort of assault and battery. The defendant knew what he was doing, but did not know that it was wrong. It was argued that criminal law's M'Naughten Rules should apply (see page 175). This was rejected by the judge who said that "where there is capacity to know the nature and quality of the act, that is sufficient although the mind directing the hand that did the wrong was diseased".

### 5. The electoral process

There is a lack of clarity in the law relating to the right of people with a mental disorder to vote in Parliamentary, local government and European elections. At common law, it appears that an "idiot" does not have capacity to vote (*Burgess Case* (1785)). An idiot is a person who is born without reason. On the other hand, a "lunatic" may vote, but only during a lucid moment (*Robins Case* (1791)). The terminology indicates the unsatisfactory state of the common law. Such a person living at home will be registered (although a number are left off the register because it is assumed that they cannot vote) as the registration form and accompanying guidance does not address the matter of mental capacity. All that can be done is for the person to be challenged at the time he/she requests a ballot paper at the polling booth. At this stage, if the presiding officer suspects that the person lacks mental capacity at common law, he/she may ask certain questions under r 35(1) Parliamentary Election Rules (see Sch 1 Representation of the People Act 1983 ("RPA 1983")). A candidate, or his/her election or polling agent, may require the presiding officer to put the r 35(1) questions. The questions in r 35(1) are the only means by which the presiding officer can challenge the right of a registered person to vote; no further enquiry is permitted (r 35(4)). However, the questions are inappropriate for the purpose of determining a person's mental capacity as they include enquiries such as "Are you the person registered in the register of Parliamentary electors for this election as follows?" and "Have you already voted, here or elsewhere, at this election . . . ?" A ballot paper must not be given to a person unless he/she has answered the questions satisfactorily (r 35(3)).

The position of a detained mental patient is clearer. Section 7(1) RPA 1983 states that:

> "A person who is detained at any place by virtue of any enactment relating to persons suffering from mental disorder shall not by reason thereof be treated for the purposes of sections 1 and 2 above as resident there."

Sections 1 and 2 RPA 1983 require a person to be on the electoral register before he/she can vote. To be on the electoral register it is necessary to be resident in the constituency. The effect of s 7(1) RPA 1983 is to disenfranchise the detained mental patient. He/She cannot register at the address of his/her home before detention as his/her constructive residence at that address is interrupted because he/she is unable to return there without breaching a legal obligation to remain in the place of detention (see *Powell* v *Guest* (1864)).

A voluntary mental patient in a mental hospital is entitled to register but only if he/she makes a declaration under s 7(4) RPA 1983. Mental hospital is defined as "any establishment maintained wholly or mainly for the reception and treatment of persons suffering from any form of mental disorder". This includes mental nursing homes and hospitals (see s 7(2) and (3) RPA 1983). The patient must be able to make the declaration without assistance other than that necessitated by blindness or other physical incapacity. A declaration must be made every twelve months and include the following:

(i) the date of the declaration;

(ii) a declaration that the patient is a voluntary mental patient on that date;

(iii) the address of the mental hospital in which the declarant is a voluntary patient;

(iv) the address where he/she would be resident if not a voluntary patient; if he/she cannot give such an address, then an address (other than a mental hospital) at which he/she has resided in the United Kingdom;

(v) a statement that on the date of the declaration he/she is a Commonwealth citizen or a citizen of the United Kingdom; and

(vi) a statement as to whether the declarant attained the age of eighteen years on the date of the declaration and, if not, the date of his/her birth.

(s 7(4)(d) RPA 1983.)

## Mental health and legal capacity

A declaration must be attested by a person who is a member of the staff of the mental hospital in which the declarant is a patient. That person must be authorised for the purpose by the managers of the hospital (see page 73). He/She must be satisfied either on the production of such evidence that he/she may require, or on the basis of his/her own knowledge, that the particulars recorded on the declaration are true.

Once completed, the declaration must be sent to the registration officer for that part of the constituency in which the address stated in (iv) above is situated. This will be the address that is entered in the electoral register. (See s 7(7)(a) RPA 1983 and r 21 Representation of the People Regulations 1986 – SI 1986/1081). Where the registration officer is satisfied that the declaration is duly made he/she must notify the declarant. If he/she rejects an application for registration in pursuance of a declaration, he/she must return it to the patient setting out the reasons for doing so.

A person may be disqualified from being a candidate in a Parliamentary election on the same common law grounds of being an idiot or lunatic as outlined above in respect of the right to vote. Section 141 MHA 1983 deals with cases of Members of Parliament who are suffering from mental illness (the section does not refer to the other types of mental disorder). Where an MP is detained under the MHA 1983 (either through the civil or criminal process) on the ground that he/she is suffering from a mental illness, the following have a duty to notify the Speaker of the House of Commons:

(i) the court, authority or person making the order or application;

(ii) any registered medical practitioner upon whose recommendations the detention was authorised; and

(iii) the person in charge of the hospital or other place where the MP is authorised to be detained.

(s 141(1) MHA 1983.)

Upon receiving such notification, or if notified by two MPs that they have been credibly informed that authorisation has been given, the Speaker must arrange for the MP patient to be examined by two registered medical practitioners. Both practitioners must be appointed by the President of the Royal College of Psychiatrists and must have special experience in the diagnosis and treatment of mental disorders. The registered medical practitioners must report to the Speaker as to whether the MP is suffering from mental illness and is authorised to be detained. If the reports are affirmative, the Speaker must arrange for him/her to be re-examined in the same manner upon the expiry of six months. Where these second reports are also affirmative, the Speaker must arrange for them to be placed before the House and the MP's seat will become vacant. (See s 141 MHA 1983.)

## 6. Driving licences

The Road Traffic Act 1988 ("RTA 1988") makes it an offence to drive on a road a motor vehicle unless the driver holds a licence authorising him/her to drive a vehicle of the class being driven (s 87(1) RTA 1988). When applying for a driving licence the applicant must state whether he/she is suffering, or has at any time suffered, from a "relevant disability" or a "prospective disability" (s 91(1) RTA 1988). A relevant disability means a disability prescribed by the Secretary of State, or any other disability which is likely to cause the driving of a vehicle by a sufferer to be a source of danger to the public. One of the prescribed disabilities is severe mental handicap (r 24(1)(b) SI 1987 No 1378). A prospective disability is one which at the time of application for a licence is not a relevant disability, but may become one in the course of time by virtue of its intermittent or progressive nature. (See s 92(2) RTA 1988.) If it appears from the declaration, or from other satisfactory information, that the applicant is suffering from a relevant disability, the Secretary of State must refuse to grant a licence. Thus, in the case of a person with a severe mental handicap, his/her application for a licence will automatically be refused. Applicants with other forms of mental disability must come within the second limb of the provision before a licence can be refused. The Secretary of State has to determine whether the applicant, in consequence of the disability, will be a source of danger to the public. (See s 92 RTA 1988.)

The Secretary of State may, if satisfied on enquiry that a person holding a licence is suffering from a relevant disability which would justify refusing to grant a licence under s 92 RTA 1988, serve notice on the holder revoking the licence (s 93(1) RTA 1988). Revocation cannot be retroactive. If the Secretary of State is satisfied upon enquiry that a licence holder is suffering from a prospective disability, he/she may serve notice revoking the licence with effect from a date not earlier than the date of the notice (s 93(2)(a) RTA 1988). A person whose licence has been withdrawn under s 93(2)(a) RTA 1988 may apply to have a

*Mental health and legal capacity*

licence granted under s 99(1)(b) RTA 1988. This subsection allows the Secretary of State to grant a licence for a period of between one and three years' duration, allowing the case to be reviewed periodically.

A person whose licence is revoked under s 93(1) or (2) RTA 1988 must surrender his/her licence to the Secretary of State immediately upon revocation. However, if he/she does not have the licence because it is in the possession of the police as a consequence of a fixed penalty notice under the RTA 1988, he/she must deliver it to the Secretary of State immediately upon its return. (See s 93(3) and (4) RTA 1988.)

A licence holder is under a duty to inform the Secretary of State if he/she becomes aware that he/she is suffering from a relevant or prospective disability which has not previously been disclosed. The Secretary of State must also be informed if a relevant or prospective disability which has previously been disclosed has become more acute since the licence was granted (see s 94(1)(a) and (b) RTA 1988). It is an offence to fail without reasonable excuse to inform the Secretary of State under s 94(1) RTA 1988. However, a licence holder does not have to inform the Secretary of State if the disability is a new one and he/she has reasonable grounds for believing that it will not extend beyond three months from the date on which he/she first becomes aware of it (s 94(2) RTA 1988).

An applicant for, or a holder of a licence may be required by the Secretary of State to:

(i) authorise a registered medical practitioner who has given medical advice or attention to the applicant/holder to provide information on whether or not he/she may be suffering, or may have suffered, from a relevant or prospective disability;

(ii) submit himself/herself to examination by registered medical practitioner/s nominated by the Secretary of State, or a nominated officer in the case of a prescribed disability, for the purpose of determining whether or not he/she may be suffering, or may have suffered, from a relevant or prospective disability;

(iii) except in the case of a provisional licence, require the applicant/holder to undergo a test of competence to drive.

(s 94(5) and (6) RTA 1988.)

If the applicant/holder fails to comply with any of the above, the Secretary of State may exercise the powers under ss 92 and 93 RTA 1988 as if satisfied that the applicant/holder is suffering from a relevant or prospective disability (s 94(8) RTA 1988).

# Index

Abnormality of mind ................................. 183–185, 186
Absence:
    with leave ................................................. 40–41
    without leave ............................................. 41–43
Access to patient ............................................. 13–14
Accommodation, provision of by local authority ............. 143–146
    See also *Children*; *Social services authority, local*
Acting nearest relative – see *Nearest relative*
Admission:
    civil ......................................................... 1–51
    criminal ................................................... 52–71
    See also *Assessment*; *Hospital orders*; *In-patients*; *Remand to hospital*; *Treatment*
After-care ............................................ 74, 140–141
Alcoholism – see *Drunkenness*
Approved social worker:
    access to patient by ....................................... 13–14
    application for admission by ............... 5–7, 17–19, 21–23
    application for guardianship by ..................... 5, 30–32
    appointment and approval of ............................... 3–5
    emergency application for admission by ................. 24–26
    return of patient to hospital by ........................... 42, 65
Assessment, admission for ........................ 17–21, 181–182
    effect of application for ................................. 28–30
    emergency ............................................... 24–26
    mistakes in application for .............................. 27–28
    See also *Remand to hospital*
Attorney, enduring powers of .......................... 206–218

Business of patient ...................................... 197–199

Children:
    care orders ............................................... 46–50
    disabled .......................... 150–151, 152, 163–164
    local authority duties towards ......................... 149–152
    provision of accommodation for ...................... 152–156
    special educational needs, and ................. 109, 158–164
    supervision orders ................. 46–48, 50–51, 156–158

Community care ................................................ 138–174
  grants ................................................ 165–174, 194
Consent to treatment ............................................ 91–101
Contract, law of ................................................ 230–231
Correspondence of patient ........................................ 87–90
Court of Protection:
  jurisdiction ................................................ 100, 191–206
  membership ................................................ 190–191
Creditors ................................................ 192–193, 194
Criminal law ................................................ 52–71, 175–189

Death of patient ................................................ 108, 203–204, 205
Detention – see *Absence*; *Admission*; *Hospital orders*; *Interim order*; *Patient*; *Remand to hospital*; *Restriction order*
Diminished responsibility ................ 176, 178, 179–180, 182–185
Discharge of patient ................................................ 38–40
Disease of the mind ................................ 176–178, 183, 184
Divorce ................................................ 222–228
Driving licences ................................................ 236–238
Drunkenness ................................................ 177, 184–185

Education – see *Special educational needs*
Elections ................................................ 233–236
Emergency application for admission ........................ 24–26
Entry of premises ................................................ 13–17
Escape from detention ........................................ 17, 29

Fitness to plead ................................................ 186–189

Gifts ................................................ 194–195, 208
Guardian:
  duties of ................................................ 139–140
  powers of ................................................ 139
  See also *Guardianship*
Guardianship ................................ 30–33, 34, 36, 37, 38, 138–140
  applications for ................................................ 30–32
  court order for ................................................ 56–59
    effect of ................................................ 59–60
  transfer of ................................................ 32–33

Hospital
  definition of ................................................ 29, 53, 72–73
  managers, definition of ................................................ 73
  orders ................................................ 56–59, 180, 188
    effect of ................................................ 59–60
  return by patient to ................................................ 42, 61, 65
  special, definition of ................................................ 73
  See also *Absence*; *Assessment*; *Interim order*; *Restriction direction*; *Restriction order*; *Transfer direction*; *Treatment*

*Index*

Impulse, irresistible ............................ 178, 183, 184, 185
Informal patient ................................................ 73–74
Information, provision of to patient ......................... 86–87
In-patients, admission of ..................................... 26–27
    effect of application for ...................................... 29
Insanity:
    appeals against finding of ............................. 180–182
    defence of ....................................... 175–180, 186
    finding of ...................................... 180, 188, 189
    M'Naughten Rules, and .............. 175–180, 183, 184, 223, 233
Interim order ....................................................... 60–62
Interviews ...................................... 6, 13–14, 84–86

M'Naughten Rules – see *Insanity*
Maintenance of patience ......................... 192–194, 201, 202
Matrimonial proceedings .................................. 228–230
    See also *Patient, divorce and*; *Patient, marriage and*
Mental:
    disorder, definition of .......................................... 1
    illness, definition of ............................................ 2
    impairment, definition of ...................................... 2
    See also *Severe mental impairment*
Mental Health Act Commission ................. 84–85, 90, 93, 94, 95
Mental Health Review Tribunals ........................... 111–137
    applications to ............................ 112–114, 115–117
    membership of ...................................... 111–112
    powers of ........................................... 118–124
    procedure of ....................................... 125–137
        applications before ............................. 125–131
        assessment applications before ................ 131–133
        disclosure of documents by .................... 133–134
        hearings of ..................................... 135–137
        postponement of applications before ........... 129–131
        representation in ..................................... 134
    reclassification of disorders by ................................ 34
    references to ...................... 114–115, 117–118, 133
    restricted patients, power to discharge ................ 121–124
    unrestricted patients, power to discharge and reclassify ...... 118–121
Mental nursing home:
    cancellation of registration of .......................... 80–81
    definition of .................................................. 75
    discharge of patient from ................................ 39–40
        application for ........................................ 14
    registration of ........................................ 75–80
    regulation of ......................................... 81–84
    residential care home, and .................................. 102
    settlement in favour of ...................................... 195
Mistakes in application for admission ..................... 27–28

National Assistance Act 1948:
    arrangements under s 29 .............................. 146–149

    transfer under s 47 .................................................. 44–46
National Health Service Act 1977, arrangements under ........ 141–143
Nearest relative:
    acting ................................................................. 9–12
    application for admission by ..................... 6–7, 17–19, 21–23
        emergency ................................................... 24–26
    application for guardianship by ......................... 30–32
    definition of ......................................................... 8–9
    powers of discharge of ......................................... 38–39
Nursing home:
    cancellation of registration of .............................. 80–81
    definition of ....................................................... 74–75
    registration of .................................................... 75–80
    regulation of ...................................................... 81–84

Partnership, patient in ............................................... 198–199
Patient:
    access to ............................................................ 13–14
    business of ...................................................... 197–199
    contract, and .................................................... 230–231
    correspondence of ............................................... 87–90
    creditors, and ............................................. 192–193, 194
    death of ................................................ 108, 203–204, 205
    definition of ............................................................ 1
    discharge of ........................................................ 38–40
    divorce, and ..................................................... 222–228
    elections, and ................................................... 233–236
    examination of ............................... 14, 19, 23, 27, 29, 32
    gifts, and .................................................. 194–195, 208
    informal ............................................................. 73–74
    information, and ................................................. 86–87
    interviews of .................................... 6, 13–14, 84–86
    maintenance of ........................................ 192–194, 201, 202
    marriage, and ................................................... 220–222
        nullity of ...................................... 220–222, 226–228
    partnership, in .................................................. 198–199
    property of ............... 190–194, 199–203, 204, 205, 218–219
    protection of ...................................................... 84–86
    reclassification of ................................................ 33–34
    return to hospital of .................................... 42, 61, 65
    settlements, and ............................................. 194–195
    transfer of .......................................................... 34–38
    visits to ............................................................. 84–86
    wills, and .................... 195–197, 199, 203–204, 231–232
Place of safety .............................. 15, 16, 17, 54, 55, 57, 61
Police:
    entry of premises by ............................................ 15–17
    removal of person from public place by ........................ 16
    return of patient to hospital by ........................ 42, 61, 65

# Index

See also *Remand to hospital*
Psychiatric catchment areas .................................. 28–29
Psychopathic disorder, definition of ............................ 3

Receiver:
    appointment of ........................................ 200–203
    discharge of ........................................... 203–205
Reclassification of patient .................................... 33–34
Recommendations, medical ................. 19–20, 22–24, 25, 27–28
    guardianship applications, and ............................ 31–32
Remand to hospital:
    report, for ............................................... 52–54
    treatment, for ....................................... 54–55, 186
Removal of persons .............................. 15–16, 44–46
Residential care homes:
    conduct of ............................................. 107–110
    definition of .............................................. 101
    registration of ......................................... 102–107
Restriction direction ......................................... 70–71
Restriction order ................................ 62–63, 180, 188
    effect of ................................................ 63–65
    magistrates' power to commit for ......................... 65–66

Settlements ............................................... 194–195
Severe mental impairment, definition of .......................... 2
Social Fund, the ............................................... 165
    officer .......................................... 166–171, 173
Social services authority, local:
    acting nearest relative, as ................................ 10, 12
    after-care, and ......................................... 140–141
    approved social workers, and ................................. 3–7
    arrangements under National Health Service Act 1977 ....... 141–143
    discharge of patients, and ................................ 38–40
    guardianship, and ................................. 32–33, 34, 36
    psychiatric catchment areas, and ........................... 28–29
    responsible, definition of ................................... 31
    transfer of patients, and ................................. 36–38
    See also *Accommodation*; *Children*; *National Assistance Act*
Special educational needs ............................ 109, 158–164
Sterilisation ........................................... 91, 98–101

Tort ...................................................... 232–233
Transfer direction ............................................ 66–71
Transfer of patient ........................................... 34–38
Treatability test ....................................... 22, 24, 56
Treatment:
    admission for ....................................... 20, 21–24
    application for:
        effect of ............................................ 28–30
        mistakes in ......................................... 27–28

court order for ............................... 56–59, 188
      effect of ........................................ 59–60
   consent to ......................................... 91–101
   See also *Remand to hospital*

Visitors, Lord Chancellor's............................. 205–206
Visits to patients ...................................... 84–86

Wills ..................................... 199, 203–204, 231–232
   statutory ........................................... 195–197